IT WAS ALL

FOR THE LOVE

OF A HORSE

It Was All
for the Love
of a Horse

A Life Story

MARIO BELOTTI

Liber Apertus Press

SARATOGA, CALIFORNIA

Published by Liber Apertus Press
P.O. Box 261, Saratoga, CA 95071 USA

www.liberapertus.com
books@liberapertus.com

ISBN 978-0-9785881-9-9

Book design by Matt Kelsey
Printed in the United States of America

Postcard of Grumello del Monte circa 1920, p. 21, kindly provided by Studio Corini Fotografi, Grumello del Monte, Italy.

Permission is gratefully acknowledged for use of photos from Archives & Special Collections, Santa Clara University Library: p. 200, photo by Charles Barry, originally published in *Santa Clara Magazine*, 1994; p. 217, photo by Glenn Matsumura, 1985; p. 221, photo by Charles Barry, 1994; back cover, top image, photo by Charles Barry, 1994; back flap, photo by Charles Barry, 1990.

Contents

Preface

What follows is the story of my life. But it is more than my story. It also illustrates the places and way of life of the people living in the town where I was born, and the economic hardship they faced. Like almost every family in the town, my family worked the land on a sharecropping contract. We also raised silkworms, and we killed the family pig, rabbits, chickens, and geese in the courtyard. Our farmhouse, like all the others in town, did not have drinking water, nor electricity, nor a heating system.

The way I escaped the sharecropping trap was all due to a horse. The town where my mother brought me to light offered only a third-grade education. At that time, the government required children to finish the third grade or be eight years of age. After that it was almost impossible for children in the town to continue their education, and so they helped the family take care of the courtyard animals or found a job helping other families who needed an extra hand.

I was very lucky. While I was in the third grade, my grandfather sold our horse. My father really loved that horse, and so he moved us out of the farmhouse to another small town that had a fourth grade. A year later, my father found a job in a steel plant, and we moved to another town that had a fifth grade. We were now close to a big city where I could attend junior high and high school.

My father did not leave the town where I was born in order to give me a higher level of education; he himself had only a second-grade education. He moved because of his love for a horse. From then on, all my education was due to that horse.

In the chapters that follow, I recount all of my story. It includes growing up on a farm, living under Fascism, surviving through World War II, coming to the U.S., meeting my wife on the boat to New York, spending three days at Ellis Island, arriving in Texas, and working as a cowboy. There are the stories of summer work in Aspen, Colorado, visiting Taos, New Mexico, afternoon tea with Frieda Lawrence, and dinner with Mable Dodge and Taos artists including Georgia O'Keefe. My education at Midwestern University in Wichita Falls, Texas, enabled me to complete bachelor's and master's degrees in accounting. At the University of Texas in Austin, I earned a Ph.D. in economics, which helped me get a teaching job at Santa Clara University in California—where I am still teaching economics.

I wrote the story of my life for my children and grandchildren, because they are very far away from the life of their grandfather, with the hope that they will learn how it is possible to overcome many disappointments life can bring to us all.

I am taking this opportunity to thank my wife Rose for being so understanding while I was writing this book. I want particularly to thank Matt Kelsey for editing and helping publish it. I also want to thank Sharon Squyres and Marianne Farang of Santa Clara University for typing my story more than one time.

All Wrapped Up

I was born in 1926 into a family of sharecroppers in the town of Grumello del Monte in the province of Bergamo, in northern Italy. From my day of birth to about six or eight months, my body was wrapped all around, and from neck to toe, with a cloth ten inches wide and as much as eight feet long, the same way Egyptians wrapped the bodies of their dead. All the babies looked like little mummies. At two months my hands were freed, and at five or six months the feet were freed as well. I don't remember those months of my infancy directly, of course, but that is the way all children around me were swaddled. I also don't have any recollection of how good or how miserable I might have felt at the time, nor have I investigated how healthy or unhealthy the practice turned out to be. I suspect, however, that such immobilization permitted the mothers to carry out their chores without many interruptions. A mother could go to the fountain to get drinking water, feed the animals, and prepare dinner without worrying about her child falling down on the concrete floor, eating paper, or falling into the fireplace. Such practice today seems to have disappeared. Today it would probably be considered barbaric and the mother would be accused of child endangerment.

My family could not afford to buy clothes or shoes. What clothes we kids wore were never new, and we had no choice in selecting them. Up to the age of eight, I never wore a newly bought article or a new pair of shoes. That was the case for the other children in my family and for many of the children in town. Hand-me-downs and cutoffs were all our parents could provide. My mother knit socks and sweaters from the wool saved from discarded old sweaters, as did the other women. When finished, the new sweater showed a profusion of color, but not necessarily in a well-designed pattern.

At the age of eight, I neared the day of my Confirmation—an important ceremony in the Catholic Church. My mother worried because I did not have any good clothes to wear. A few weeks before the event, she obtained an old coat from her brother, Bernardo, who had just returned from his job in Switzerland, and had agreed to be my Confirmation sponsor.

My mother took me with the old coat to the only tailor in town. He and his family lived in a two-room apartment on the first floor of a building just across from the town church. His kitchen was his workplace. He looked at the old coat and he looked at me. He took the required measurements and sent us home. A week later, to the surprise of all of us, he had transformed that old coat into a suit, a jacket, and a pair of short pants. They fit me well. On the day of the ceremony, my uncle proudly accompanied me to church. The Bishop of Bergamo came, rubbed my forehead with oil, and pronounced, "At this moment you have become a Christian."

The Farmhouse
of the "Patam" Family

At the time of my birth, no more than three hundred people lived in Grumello del Monte. Half of the town was hilly and half flat. A castle, perched on a small hill on the north side of the town, dominated the landscape below. Much of the land, and many of the houses, belonged to descendants of the very rich and noble Gonzaga family of Mantova (*Mantua*). One of the descendants and his family lived in the castle, the Gonzaga Castle. The castle was built in the thirteenth century for defensive reasons and later was transformed into a patrician residence. Most town families worked the Gonzaga land under a sharecropping agreement. The owner provided the farmhouse and the land. The farming family supplied the labor and shared the crops the land produced fifty-fifty with the owner. This arrangement was referred to as *mezzadria*, from the Italian word *mezzo*, or half. The sharecroppers were called *mezzadri*. The major crops cultivated in the area were wheat and corn in the flat lands and wine grapes in the hills.

I was born into one of Grumello del Monte's sharecropping families. The farmhouse where the midwife delivered me into the world was almost in the shadow of the Gonzaga castle. My father, Lorenzo, and my mother, Rosa, lived there with my father's parents and his four brothers, two married with children and two single. It was a family of sixteen to feed, clothe, and shelter.

Our family was known in town as the "Patam" family. Even now, I do not know where that name came from, who gave it to us, or when. That was the name everyone in the town would use to identify us. Belotti was a common name in town as were other names. Many of the same last names also existed in the neighboring towns. To avoid confusion, each family had a kind of nickname. Ours was Patam.

Grandfather Antonio and Grandmother Luigia were the bosses of the family, the decision makers. They signed the sharecropping agreement. The farmhouse and the land were assigned to them. The contract required that a minimum of three adult men, members of the family, would stay home and work the land. The land assigned to the family was approximately fifty acres, all in the flat area. It was alluvial land, full of small rocks. One half of it could be irrigated and the other half could not. The rain would ultimately determine if the harvest would be good or poor. The land was on the other side of the railroad tracks, a ten- to fifteen-minute walk from the house. The owner also assigned us a small piece of land, next to the house, to be used as our family vegetable garden. An overseer (*fattore*), employed by the owner and living in a house next to the castle, instructed my grandfather and his sons, as well as the other sharecroppers, on the best agricultural practices of the time, and he enforced the contract.

The farmhouse was big enough to house two sharecropping families. We occupied the larger section of the building. We had a big kitchen, a bedroom plus two small rooms on the ground floor, and three bedrooms on the first floor. Each married couple, together with their children, occupied one of the bedrooms. The two unmarried brothers shared one of the small rooms on the ground floor, and the other served as a storage room. The family that occupied the other section of the farmhouse was named Sarzilla. They shared the courtyard with us, and used the same doors to enter and exit the building: a large wooden door, with a smaller door cut into one side. Our family had little contact with them; I don't know why. We children, however, did play in the courtyard with their children.

I was born at home, in my parents' bed. My grandmother, my aunt Nini, and the midwife helped my mother bring me to life. It could not have been a difficult birth because my mother had already given birth to three other sons. I was the fourth.

The bed I was born in was a very large bed, larger than king size. It was well built and had intricate woodwork, and was similar to the beds in many northern Italian peasant homes at the turn of the twentieth century. I slept in my parents' bed either in the middle between them or at their feet at the bottom of the bed until the age of seven. At that time it was very common for children to sleep in the same bed with their parents. I still have my parents' bed along with the dresser, armoire, and nightstands that went with it; the set is now at our Italian house in Lesa on Lago Maggiore.

The farmhouse we occupied, and where I spent most of my childhood, was located on Cardinal Ferrari Street, a very narrow cobblestone road. Like most farmhouses at the time, it did not have electricity, nor running water, and the only heating came from a large fireplace in the kitchen. The kitchen floor was dark grey concrete, and the wooden kitchen door was kept open most of the time. Except for the open door, a small window was our only source of light. Men, women, children, and courtyard animals went in and out of the kitchen many times a day, tracking dirt inside. The concrete floor made it easy to wash the dirt away.

The three younger women of the family, my mother and my aunts Nini and Carolina, took turns going to a communal fountain not far from the house, bringing home water with two buckets of about three gallons each per trip. The two buckets were carried at each end of a specially bent pole that they would lift across their shoulders.

The water from the fountain was used for drinking and for cooking. A bucket of drinking water with a ladle inside was always available in the kitchen for anyone who needed a drink. Everyone drank from the same ladle.

Water for other uses came from a creek at the end of the courtyard, on the near side of the vegetable garden. The water in the creek was a great gift to us. We filled many buckets for cleaning and washing, and many buckets to help our vegetables to grow. The women also used the creek and its water to wash or to rinse clothes previously washed in a wooden tub. A couple of large, flat stones installed on our side of the creek provided the place for the women to kneel and rinse the family clothes. (A beautiful painting by A. Ferraguti depicting a similar scene is found in the Museo del Paesaggio, in the city of Pallanza on Lago Maggiore in Italy; a detail is shown on the next page.) Drying was done by the sun. The ironing, if needed, was done on the kitchen table using an iron with small holes on the sides and hot coals inside.

No running water meant no bathroom in the house, no sink and no tub. Each bedroom had a free-standing cast iron frame supporting an enamel or porcelain wash basin on top and a *brocca* (water pitcher) below. A small mirror was mounted above the wash basin. Fancier ones had a rack for towels. The adults washed their faces, and the men shaved their beards, using the

Detail from La Lavandaie, *painting by Arnaldo Ferraguti*

water in the basin and the mirror above. The children washed up in a wooden tub on the porch outside the kitchen.

No one in the family ever brushed their teeth. I never saw a toothbrush or a tube of toothpaste anywhere in our house; I don't know if they were available at that time or if our family did not have the money to buy them. My grandparents, in their sixties, had already lost most of their teeth. My uncles, in their thirties and forties, had no teeth missing but their teeth were turning brown. There was no dentist in our town, nor in the nearby ones. When a tooth hurt, and my mother suffered from tooth infections more than other members of the family, the remedy was to grate a raw potato, wrap the pulp in a cloth, and wrap the cloth around the face so that the potato rested on the side of the aching tooth. One or two days later the swelling and toothache would disappear. A month or two later, the infection would return, either the same tooth or another. Another raw potato, another day or two with a bandage across the face, and everything would be back to normal again. When a tooth needed to come out, the extraction was done by the patient himself or by the family doctor at his office. The patient sat in a regular chair and the doctor pulled the tooth out with special pliers. No anesthetic was necessary; a few seconds and the operation was over. One lira or a few eggs was the fee.

At middle age, most men in the town had brown teeth. Most if not all smoked. My uncles all smoked, buying the cheapest cigarettes they could find. Often they would buy paper and tobacco and make their own cigarettes. My father smoked mainly cigars, the cheapest the Italian tobacco monopoly would sell. On many occasions, he would bite off a piece of cigar and chew it in his mouth for quite a long time, spitting out the dark brown saliva. He was not the only one chewing tobacco; most men in town smoking cigars did the same. The smoking and the chewing all contributed to the browning of their teeth.

None of the women in our family smoked. It was not proper for women to smoke. My grandmother, however, sniffed tobacco, like many of the older women in town. She kept the precious powder in a small, decorated box that my grandfather had given her as an anniversary gift, and she carried it with her all the time. When she wanted some, she carefully opened the little box, took a small amount of tobacco between two fingers, and slowly put the fingers under her nostrils and sniffed the powder in. At that time in her life, it was the only pleasure she would allow for herself, and one she could barely afford.

There were no bathrooms in the house. We kept a urinary vase under the bed, in case it was needed during the night. It was not of much use for me in my early childhood; I found it much easier to urinate in my parents' bed.

During the day we used an outhouse located in a very visible place to one side of the courtyard, next to the chicken coop. It was a small concrete building, with a concrete floor. A round hole, about eight inches in diameter, in the middle of the floor guided the waste into an underground holding tank. There was no water to flush, but once or twice a day someone from our family or from the Sarzilla family washed the floor with a bucket of water and a broom. An old broom that had served to wash the kitchen floor, reduced to half its regular length, was relegated to the outhouse.

Toilet paper was unknown to us. Pieces of paper that the grocer used to wrap our few groceries hung on a nail on one of the outhouse walls. It served the purpose reasonably well. Pieces of newspaper would also do the job except that they were very rare. If neither were available, the next best choice were the large leaves from trees. When nothing at all was available, the index finger was the substitute, albeit a poor one. What the index finger collected would end up on one of the white walls in a comma-like pattern. When the walls were dirty enough, someone would scrub them and a new coat of whitewash would cover whatever the scrubbing could not properly clean.

Once a year, in winter, when the snow had covered the tender leaves of the slowly growing wheat, two of the brothers, sometimes my father, hitched the horse to a special wagon which had a large wooden tank with an opening on top and a spigot at the bottom. At one time it had probably been a wine fermenting tub. The men used a bucket, reserved just for this work, to empty the underground septic tank into the wooden tub. Because of the horrible smell, this task was done in the middle of the night when the town was asleep.

The men took the loaded tank to the edge of one of our wheatfields. There the malodorous cargo was distributed bucket by bucket on top of the snow covering the wheat. In the morning, as daylight approached, the smell had mostly disappeared but the white snow of the field would have given way to a mosaic of white, brown, and yellow. As other farmers did the same work, in a week or two the town wheatfields turned from a beautiful rural scene into an ugly one. No one demonstrated or complained. Those ugly spots would bring home more food—organically grown. The cycle was complete.

Each room had a window providing light during the day. With no electricity, that was good enough for us kids to do our homework. As the evening darkened, most activities in the house ceased. We did have a kerosene lamp hanging from the ceiling of the kitchen, emanating a flickering, weak light. It would not have been easy to read with such light; however, reading was not something the family engaged in. I do not remember seeing any books in the house, except for a couple of religious books to be read on Sundays.

No newspapers were ever present in the house and no newspaper vendors existed in the village. Local news spread from mouth to mouth. More distant news came from the village bar, and the village priest transmitted important news to the community at the Sunday afternoon vespers service. As the evening darkened, and as the women finished cleaning up the supper pots, pans and dishes, my grandmother would lead all of us in reciting the rosary. Then everyone went to bed, with the light of a candle to help get there.

There was no heating in the house. The winters in northern Italy were cold, with frequent snow. We did have a large fireplace in the kitchen; my grandfather lit the fire early every morning. It stayed lit all day long, the flames changing color as the wood changed. The fireplace was also the only place the family had to cook meals. In the middle of the fireplace, a steel chain hung down from an iron bar inserted in the chimney sidewalls. The cooking pots were hung by their handles with the help of a peg on one of the chain rings at the proper height, depending on the size of the pot and the intensity of the fire. The morning milk, the polenta for lunch, and the soup for dinner were all cooked in different-sized pots. Other foods, such as chicken, beef or pork were cooked on a deep cast iron skillet resting on a heavy steel grate atop the burning coals.

The fireplace had built-in wooden benches on the right and left walls. The children, the sick, or anyone who felt cold and could find room, would keep warm in there. Chairs could also be brought in front of the fireplace if one needed to sit there. The chimney was cleaned once, sometimes twice a year. The chimney sweepers, a father and his young son, would tie a bundle of twigs in the middle of a long rope. The father went on the roof and dropped the rope and the bundle of twigs from the top of the chimney, keeping one end of the rope for himself. The son, standing underneath in the middle of the fireplace, grabbed the other end of the rope. Then they pulled the rope up and down so that the twigs scrubbed the walls of the chimney clear of the accumulated soot. We kids looked intently at the work the young boy was doing. We laughed as the hands, face, and legs of the young sweeper darkened with soot. He was not much older than us, certainly not more than ten or eleven. He could have easily come out of one of Dickens' books.

Besides the fireplace, during the cold winter months our stable provided a place where we could keep warm. It was located at the end of the courtyard on the left wing of the house. It had a small window and a wooden door, and housed our horse, cow, a young heifer, and pig. There were also one or two rabbit cages to provide shelter for female rabbits when they had their little ones. For most of the day, the door and window remained closed. The heat emanating from the animals kept the stable warm. Two wooden benches, one on the right side of the door and one on the left side near the pig sty, allowed the women to sit and knit or repair the family clothes. The children would sleep, cry, or scream, but in any case they kept warm.

On winter nights, the bedrooms were very cold. The window glass showed signs of outside frost. The family had a couple of bed warmers (*scaldaletti*). One belonged to my mother. It was a copper pot with many small holes around and a fastened copper lid on top. My mother would fill half of the pot with hot coals from the kitchen fire, then wrap it up in a heavy piece of cloth and put it between the bed sheets about fifteen or twenty minutes before going to bed. Those without a bed warmer would warm up a brick in the fireplace, wrap it up and put it between the bed sheets. Oven cooked bricks, when they were heated well, kept warm for quite some time, at least long enough to fall asleep.

Making a Living
on a Sharecropping Farm

Life on the sharecropping farm was hard for all of us. We grew mostly wheat and corn, and the crop yields were dependent upon the weather. We did have an irrigation canal crossing part of our land, but during times of drought very little water was available and the corn crop suffered. Major spring storms knocked the wheat to the ground, and hail knocked the grains out of the wheat heads, reducing production. Even in good years, after we shared half of the crops with the land owner, and after we set aside seeds needed for next year's planting and the amount needed for the family food, very little was left for sale. Lack of money was always the major family concern. The children were growing and needed more things. The money was never enough.

In order to earn extra income, which did not have to be split with the owner of the land, and which made it possible for the family to purchase a few extra things, the Patam family raised silkworms and sold silk cocoons, as most of the town sharecropping families did.

Raising silkworms was not a simple task. Every year, at the beginning of May, my grandfather purchased two ounces of newly hatched silkworms from a hatchery in a nearby town—just a handful, born from the tiny eggs of the silk butterfly. They made their appearance in the world looking like tiny dark colored bugs. As they arrived at the house, a bed, consisting of a small table covered with common wrapping paper, was prepared for them. The table was set up in a corner of our kitchen. The silkworms could not be raised outside in the open. To survive they required a relatively constant, warm temperature—warmer than the month of May in northern Italy would provide. Before the little creatures arrived home, the kitchen was disinfected. The walls were whitewashed. From the day they arrived and for about forty days thereafter, the kitchen fireplace was lit and the fire continued to burn with a low flame twenty-four hours a day.

The little bugs, as soon as they were bedded, had to be fed. They ate only mulberry leaves. Feeding them and cleaning their bed were jobs for the women of the house. The men, who spent most of their working days planting, cultivating, weeding and harvesting crops, found time to gather and bring home the mulberry leaves. Mulberry trees were generally grown in single rows between fields. In the spring, when their branches were full of leaves, they provided some protection to the wheatfields from the ravages of the strong winds.

During the first week of the worms' life, feeding took place every two hours. The mulberry leaves were chopped up and spread over the bed. The worms' appetite seemed insatiable. They ate continuously. As they ate, they made a mess of their bed. Pieces of leaves became inedible, soaked by a steady flow of body waste, and trampled by the eagerness of one worm to reach a fresh piece of leaf before the other. Cleaning their bed required someone to move each of the worms to a new bed, discard the paper, and start all over again.

As they ate, the worms grew. After a week of feeding, their bodies became fairly well formed. They had turned into caterpillars, about three-quarters of an inch in length. The color of their skin had turned gray. Soon they needed more space and a much larger bed.

In order to provide the needed space, the large kitchen table (our dining table) was moved outside on the porch next to the kitchen door. In its place, the men built a four-by-six-by-eight-foot wooden scaffold to support four or five bamboo tables tiered one above another, using material saved from year to year.

The small gray worms were then transferred to one of the bamboo tables. Each bamboo stick was tight close to the next. After the first week, feeding was reduced to four or five times a day. The mulberry leaves were then given whole. The worms devoured them. The men arrived home from the field with large sacks full of mulberry leaves. Slowly, day by day, the branches of the mulberry trees became leafless, no longer capable of breaking the wind.

The worms continued to eat and grow. At the end of the third week their bodies reached one and a half inches in length. The color of their skin had turned chalky white. Once again they needed more space. They took over

Silkworms have been raised in similar ways for many centuries throughout the world, as shown in this sixteenth century-engraving by Jan van der Straet.

another bamboo table. Their bed was cleaned anew by transferring them from one bamboo table to another. By the end of the fourth week, they grew to about two and a half inches in length. Their color turned a clear white, and their bodies became somewhat transparent and shiny. By now, they had taken over all the tables on the scaffold. For all practical purposes, they had driven all of us out of our kitchen. The family meals were now eaten outside the kitchen. The kitchen became off limits to all of us, except for the women in charge of feeding and cleaning the silkworms. At this stage of growth, cleaning their bed was of paramount importance. In a day, their bed would smell really bad. Mulberry leaves, trampled underneath the bodies of the worms, were soon covered with a green liquid body waste, in no time at all emitting a strong acrid smell, hard to describe—one has to smell it. Moreover, at this stage of their life, some of the worms died. Some of the dead bodies calcified while others rotted. The latter emanated a smell, a stench, even worse and more repugnant than the one from their soiled bed. It was imperative to remove the dead bodies as soon as they were found, not only to reduce the bad odor, but also to limit the damage that some of the contagious diseases affecting silkworms could have caused to the rest of them.

At the end of the fifth week, most worms had reached maturity. Their bodies had grown to three or three and a half inches in length, becoming shiny and quite transparent. Their color turned to light yellow. They stopped eating. At this point, the men of the house made small bundles of twigs loosely tied in an umbrella-like shape. The bundles were fastened in rows between two bamboo tables so that the base of the bundles was fastened to the lower table and the umbrella part would touch the underside of the table above. Each row was lined up about one and a half feet apart. Each bamboo table, when completed, looked like an artificial, well-designed Lilliputian forest. The silkworms, moving their heads up, down, and sideways, occupied the bottom of this forest. When they felt biologically ready, they climbed the bundle closest to them and settled on a twig. Most of them stopped in the umbrella area. Each one rested in a comfortable position and began to exude from the mouth a very thin thread of raw silk. As the silk flowed from their mouths in what appeared to be an endless stream, the worms continued to turn their bodies around until they had closed themselves inside a perfectly made cocoon—a yellow oval-shaped cocoon about one and three-quarters inches long and one inch wide.

When my grandfather announced that the silk cocoons were completely formed, all the members of the family, including the older grandchildren like me, picked the cocoons from the bundles that the men had carefully removed from the bamboo tables. The cocoons were deposited in tall, cylindrical wicker baskets furnished to us by the silk factory that was buying the cocoons. When the harvest was completed, the baskets were weighed and then transported on our own cart and horse to the silk factory. At the factory, a number of miles from our village, young female workers from the surrounding villages, most of them barely in their teens, spun the silk from the cocoons and made silk threads. The thread was sold to textile factories making silk cloth of stunning colors and designs. Fashion houses purchased the cloth to make beautiful silk clothes, to dress the royalty and the nobility of the time.

My mother worked for four or five years in such a silk factory, starting at about age twelve. At that time (1915), the minimum age for factory workers was eleven. She and two other young girls from her town of Torre de Roveri walked each Monday morning the five or so miles from home to the factory. During the day, she and fifty or sixty other girls, not much older than her, worked ten-hour days. Each girl was assigned a table, a large tin bowl, and a mechanical spinning wheel. Next to the table was a basket of silk cocoons. The bowl was filled with warm water. Eight to twelve silk cocoons, depending on the size of the desired thread, were transferred from the basket into the water. The warm water helped to soften the glue-like substance the silkworms produced to keep the cocoon firm. The young workers would then search and take the beginning thread of each cocoon, assemble them together, and feed them onto the spinning wheel. This produced a new thread, strong enough to make silk cloth.

At the end of the working day, the young workers, after a fast washing and a change of clothes, rushed to the cafeteria for a factory-provided supper. After supper and after a few songs, a few pleasantries and sometimes a few fights, they went to sleep in the factory dorm—a big room with two rows of small beds, and a nightstand next to each bed.

On Saturday afternoons my mother and her factory friends walked back home. Sunday was the day off—the day to dress up and go to church, the day to rest, to run around and to play. The meager salary each girl received was all turned over to the parents; the family needed every penny to survive. Economists, sociologists and psychologists who analyze child labor have concentrated on the harmful effects such labor causes the child. Little effort, however, has been made at analyzing the importance of child labor's contribution to the survival and the well being of their families.

The money we received from selling the silk cocoons was never very much. It never was enough to compensate for the extra work the members of the family had to go through to raise the silkworms or to compensate for the inconvenience and the smell those creatures would bring. From a purely economic point of view raising silkworms was not a profitable undertaking. That must be the reason that in more modern times this practice completely disappeared in all of northern Italy.

Raising silkworms was an extra activity that created overtime work for our family and for many peasant families in northern Italy. There were no fixed costs, and the variable costs, except for the small payment to the hatchery, consisted mainly of the labor cost. This labor was offered by members of the family without compensation. The sales of the silk cocoons, however, provided our large family the ability to buy a few things we otherwise could not have afforded.

Raising silkworms gave us children the opportunity to observe the complete life cycle of a butterfly. The children were allowed to keep a few silk cocoons for their own. We kept them in a shoebox in our bedroom. The box had a few air holes. The worms remained inside the cocoons in a chrysalis state for two months or so. For all this period they did not eat or move. After this period had passed, the stiff bodies inside the cocoons began to stir and undergo a complete transformation. From ugly pupas came beautiful white butterflies. They made a hole in the cocoon and came out inside the box. The females soon laid a bunch of tiny eggs. We opened the box and to our delight the beautiful silk butterflies flew out the bedroom window and disappeared into the sky, soon to die. But new tiny worms, when the time was right, hatched from the butterfly eggs, and the silkworm life cycle started again.

In the middle of June, after the silkworm operation concluded, the scaffolding was removed from the kitchen. Our life returned to more normal conditions, and the men started harvesting the wheat crop. The harvesting was all done by hand. One of the brothers would start cutting the wheat using a well-sharpened scythe. He would put his left hand on a small cross board on top of the handle and the right hand on another cross board in the middle of the handle. With a strong movement of his arms he would cut a swath of wheat of about two and a half feet wide and ten inches long. The wheat so cut fell in an orderly way at the end of the cut. He continued the same operation until he reached the end of the field. One at a time, the other brothers followed cutting swaths of wheat next to the first one. As they reached the end of the field, they went back and started again until the whole field was cut. After the wheat was cut, some of the women came to help the men gather the wheat in bundles. They tied the bundles and, if the weather was good, left them in the field for a day or so. If there was any chance of rain, the bundles were carted home and stored in the hayloft until the threshing machine came. After one field was harvested, the next field was cut until all the wheat crop had been harvested and brought home.

It was not until after the middle of July that the threshing machine came to separate the grains from the husk and the straw. The machine entered our courtyard through the big wooden door. Five men came with it. A noisy diesel engine, belching dark exhaust fumes, powered a few belts and three wheels on the left side of the machine. The bundles of wheat were fed into an opening on top of the machine, and the clean grains came out through a chute in front to be sacked. The wheat husk flew out the back into the air, eventually settling on the ground from where it was raked in a mound in a corner of the courtyard. A contraption at the rear of the thresher squeezed, bundled, tied and spit out the straw, which provided bedding for the animals throughout the year. For me and the other kids, threshing was an opportunity to play. We jumped over the mound of husk, hid around the bales of straw, ran around the thresher, and at the end we were just as full of dust and dirt as the men operating the machine.

A few hours in the morning and all of our wheat was processed. A few more hours in the afternoon and the wheat of the Sarzilla family was also threshed. After the machine completed its work, it left with its five workers. The next day, it went on to another farmhouse threshing the wheat of another sharecropper. As the machine left, the wheat in the sacks was divided fifty-fifty with the owner, a small amount was set aside for the church, and the rest was left to dry for a few days in the courtyard, then put into the storage room for us to eat with the surplus to sell.

After the wheat was harvested, some of the fields were plowed again and planted with *quarantino*, a fast-maturing corn, which gave very little yield but helped supplement our food supply and that of our animals.

The corn the family planted in the spring was harvested in the fall. When the harvest started, the men picked the ears from the corn stalks by hand, one at a time. The ears were loaded into a cart, taken to the house, and unloaded underneath the large wooden balcony that ran all across the back side, supported by brick and stone columns and arches as was typical of most farmhouses in our area. The balcony covered by the extended roof of the house served to connect the upstairs bedrooms with one another, and the lower part served to protect the corn, other crops, and farm implements from the rain. It was also a good place for us children to play when the rain and the mud made a mess of the courtyard.

The evening of each harvest day, the whole family gathered after dinner to husk the corn. We did not have enough chairs for everyone to sit. Grandma and Grandpa always sat on chairs, as did any pregnant women. The rest, including the children, sat on top of the mound of corn ears. The husking had to be done somewhat carefully, leaving a few of the inside leaves on the ear. These leaves were used to bundle ten to twelve ears together for hanging on the rafters, on the sides of the balcony, or on a specially built rack to dry. When the process started, my grandmother took out a rosary and led the family in prayer. After we recited the first fifty Hail Marys, one for each rosary bead, she began the next fifty until the husking was done.

After the corn had dried, it was unbundled and each ear was fed into a mechanical device, which had a couple of cogs attached to a large wheel with a handle. By turning the wheel, the cogs rotated and knocked the kernels from the cob. The kernels were then cleaned of any debris, sacked, divided fifty-fifty with the owner, with some set apart for the church, and the rest was set in the storeroom. It would be our main staple food for the next twelve months. We never did eat corn on a cob. First, we did not grow sweet corn, and second, eating such food was common in the New World but had not yet reached my part of Italy.

When the family needed a new supply of cornmeal, my father loaded a sack of corn on the cart, hitched up the horse, and took the corn to the local grain miller. A large waterwheel turned a mechanical grinder to mill the corn. The water flowed to the wheel through a small canal and was collected at the bottom in the same canal. During the milling process, the crushed corn was divided through strainers into three different products: a first quality cornmeal of a fine yellow color and texture, a second quality cornmeal, called *farinetta*, of poor quality, color and texture, and corn bran. The first quality meal was used to make polenta, the second was the main staple for our pig, and the bran was used as a food filler for the other animals.

We took our share of wheat that we did not sell to the same miller. The wheat was milled into flour and bran using a different milling machine than for corn. The miller was paid a few lira per hundred kilograms of corn or wheat. The women used the wheat flour to make pasta, ravioli, gnocchi, and some simple desserts. The wheat bran went mainly to Nino, our horse. Both the cornmeal and the wheat flour used for food were stored in bulk in separate compartments in a large wooden box, called a *madia*, kept in the kitchen. It was the only piece of furniture, besides the table and chairs, that adorned our kitchen.

The Patam family, like all the other sharecropping families in the area, did not waste anything. The furs of the rabbits were turned inside out, stuffed with straw and hung to dry on a peg in one of the courtyard walls. The bones of the yard animals and of the pig, after they were boiled and cleaned of meat, were saved and stored in a bucket. Unusable pieces of clothing and scrap metals of all kinds were saved. Once or twice a month, a *straccivendolo*, a buyer of all saved items, passed by with his cart to purchase furs, bones, and scrap metals. He paid cash and then resold the furs to clothes makers, the good bones to button makers, and the poor ones to fertilizer companies, the cloth material to companies supplying rags to mechanic shops, and metal scraps to wholesale scrap buyers. The goose down was cleaned and used at home to make pillows, and the soft and tender leaves of the corn cobs were used to stuff mattresses. The branches (and trunks of trees when available) were used as firewood. Leaves from the trees were collected and used as bedding for the animals in the stable. We bought very little, and little was thrown away. Sustainability was a word we did not know, but certainly we practiced it.

The Town Where I Was Born

The town of Grumello del Monte had a church built in 1744, twice as big as it would ever need. It had a schoolhouse big enough for the three elementary grades it offered. It had a two-story city hall and its own small cemetery with a gated entry and a six-foot wall surrounding it.

The town did not have a post office. Whatever mail the town received, and it must have been very little, was delivered by a postman from a nearby village. The town did not have a medical doctor, veterinary clinic, or even a pharmacy. It did have a midwife who, besides delivering babies in the town, provided her services to two other towns.

Whatever medical services existed at the time came from a doctor who had his office—actually a room in his residence—in a nearby town. He took care of the sick for three different towns and also served as coroner for all of them. In the morning he made house calls by bike or by carriage, carrying his medical bag. In the afternoon he spent as much time as needed to take care of the patients who came to see him. A pharmacy in the same town filled the doctor's prescriptions. All was very simple then. The doctor did not have a nurse. He did not keep any patient folders; the patient did. He did not have to file insurance forms or send out invoices. The government paid him each month according to the number of people he served. When they could, patients brought him a few eggs, a chicken, a bottle of wine, or some fruit and vegetables. He did not have the help of a medical lab. His diagnoses were his, and his alone. The coroner's reports he wrote absolved him of all mistakes.

For a major medical problem, such as a very serious accident, the unfortunate person was carried by horse and buggy to the nearest hospital, a trip of more than one hour. Most people, however, in the ordinary course of their life, no matter how sick they felt, did not want to be taken to a hospital. The hospital, they believed, was the place where people went to die. They want-

Grumello del Monte, circa 1920

ed to die at home, in their bed, among their people. Most of them did not make much use of the doctor's services. They took care of most aches and pains using their traditional home remedies. Hot linen-seed flour—boiling hot—wrapped in a cloth and laid on top of the stomach was used to alleviate cold, flu, and respiratory problems. Chamomile tea took care of stomach aches and belly aches. A necklace of garlic cloves hanging around a kid's neck got rid of tapeworms, which most kids picked up playing in the court-yard. Backaches disappeared with *ventose*: you took an empty water glass, lighted a match inside to eliminate the air, and then placed it on the location of the pain. It worked like a vacuum, sucking out the accumulated inflam-mation. Leeches were the best for bleeding. A mouth full of *grappa* (distilled wine), especially if it was aged with jensen root, took care of overeating and over-drinking. A tablespoon of castor oil cleaned the intestines. And there were other such remedies. The townspeople had a real aversion to calling the doctor. When a person was really sick and none of the traditional medicines worked, the doctor was called. Many times when the doctor arrived, it was too late; all he could do was prescribe morphine to relieve the pain, and call the town priest to administer last rites.

When a child or an adult was really sick, the family and friends prayed. They prayed at home, they prayed in the fields, they prayed in church. People were very devoted to God, and especially to the Virgin Mary. They would pray fervently, asking for help. When the land was dry, they prayed for rain. When it rained too much, they asked for the sun to return. When a big storm approached, they rushed to start a fire in the open air, burning some olive branches that the priest had blessed for that purpose on Palm Sunday. With that fire they asked the Lord to protect their crops from the approaching storm. Life at the time was simple, but it was hard, very hard, for most of the people, especially for the small farmers and the sharecroppers. Prayers gave them hope. Hope is all they had. When a family member, or a friend, or an acquaintance, or anybody else died, it was always the Will of God. No matter how young or how old the person, his or her time had come. Everyone believed that in death the person would go to heaven—the priest had said so—except for those, like some of my brothers, whose time came before they were baptized. They had to wait to go to heaven in a nondescript place called "Limbo," until the day of the Final Judgment.

People in the town did go to church; everyone did, every Sunday. In church, men sat in the pews on the right side of the altar. Women occupied the pews on the left side. Very young children sat with their mothers, and older children sat on the steps leading up to the main altar, boys on the right side and girls on the left. I am not sure when such separation of the sexes occurred in Catholic churches and why, but it was the case in my childhood. Going to church was the main, if not the only, social event. There were no church lunches or church dinners or any major organized activities. It was just a chance to wear your best, to see your friends, to meet other villagers and to hear your pastor read and explain the Sunday's Gospel. The Sunday Masses and all other Masses were totally in Latin. It did not matter much to the people. They only had a third-grade education. Most of them did not know much Italian. They spoke and understood their own dialect. The people in our village spoke their own version of *Bergamasco*, a dialect well known in the whole of the Bergamo province, but very different from the Italian language. People were taught Italian in school, but the two or three elementary grades they attended were not enough to learn much more than some rudiments of the language that were soon forgotten. Latin was good enough for them. They had memorized all their basic prayers in Latin and had no difficulties in repeating them over and over, even though they probably had no idea what they were saying. There was no question in their minds, however, that God knew exactly what they were saying and what they were asking. And they were not asking that much.

Most people in the village were born poor. They worked hard all their life just to grow enough food to keep hunger away, and to sustain them enough so they could continue to work until they died. And they all died poor, as they lived, and as they were born. Most of them were born there, they married there, they worked there, and at the end they died there. All were poor but never really unhappy. They accepted whatever God sent them. And, for what little they had, they thanked God. Three times a day.

They were poor, but they supported their church. At each harvest, they put some wheat, corn, or silk cocoons aside for the church. After each harvest, someone from the church passed by to collect the offerings.

The church did, in its own way, help the people of the village. It provided free baptisms, free wedding services, and free burial masses. It also provided last rites. The priest came every year to bless the house, the stable with the animals, and the fields. He always had the right words for the surviving spouse, parent, or child. He helped settle family disputes, village disputes, and disputes between sharecroppers and the landowner. In church at Sunday Mass, he reminded them in the words of Jesus "that it was easier for a camel to pass through the eye of a needle than for a rich person to go to heaven." It was comforting to them, as poor as they were, to know that.

People in the town died in their own home, assisted by their loved ones. At death, the person was dressed with his or her best clothes, and the body was laid on top of the bed. The bedroom was transformed into a funeral parlor, and the flickering light of a candle allowed family and friends to visit the dead person. Everyone asked God to have mercy and take the person to heaven with Him. The day of the funeral, the corpse was laid in a simple casket, built by the local carpenter. The casket was then placed on a table, properly covered with a black cloth, and located in the courtyard near the entrance of the house. Family, friends, and town acquaintances arrived just before the funeral starting time. All of them talked to one another of how good and how helpful the person had been in his life. They touched only on the good experiences. As the town priest arrived with all his helpers, the funeral started. The priest first blessed the casket. The four pallbearers, helped by some mourners, heaved the casket up from the table and onto their shoulders. The priest and his helpers, walking up front, started the procession. They were followed by the casket, by the members of the family, many of them crying, and by friends and acquaintances. The procession moved slowly from the house where it started to the church. When everyone had entered the church and the casket was properly posed on a specially built catafalque located in the middle of the church, the priest started the Holy Mass for the dead. The crying stopped. After the Mass, the priest walked around the casket to bless it, first sprinkling holy water, and then anointing it on each side with clouds of burning incense, flowing up toward heaven. After a last prayer asking God's mercy, the coffin was removed from the catafalque, brought outside the church, and the procession formed again to the town cemetery. Another prayer, another blessing, some more crying, and the casket was gently guided down to the bottom of the grave that the cemetery worker had dug in the ground, next to the last person he had buried. The body of the dead person remained in the ground for ten years or longer if the ground was not needed for someone else. When the grave was opened, the few bones left were transferred to the cemetery chapel, whose floor had an opening into a space below. It was the final resting place for the bones of the poor people. They were all together again, sharing the same space, one bone over the other. The few rich people of the town, two maybe three, built their own mausoleums and kept their bones all to themselves.

The Bell Tower

The town bell tower had been built before the church, in 1690. It had five bells, each with a different tone. Generally, a complete set would have had eight bells, used for various situations as described below. The three smaller bells (numbers one, two, and three) were added to the belfry after our family had left the town. Just below the belfry were three large mechanical clocks, one on each side of the tower, except to the north. The clocks had white backgrounds, with Roman numerals painted in black. Almost everyone in the village could see one of the clocks from their home. None of the peasants in the village possessed a clock or a watch. They all relied on the clocks of the bell tower and on the bells to let them know the time, day and night.

The bells were of extreme importance to the life of the villagers. The villagers knew the sound of each bell and the meaning it carried. At six o'clock in the morning, a soft, melodious sound came from bell number six. It was the Angelus—the wake-up call, and the first daily invitation to prayer, to thank the Lord for the good night sleep and to ask Him for the daily bread. At noon, the same bell told the people that it was time to go home, eat lunch, and thank the Lord for the food the good earth had supplied them. At six o'clock in the evening, the same bell reminded them that the working day was over, coming to a close, and that they should thank the Lord for all they accomplished that day. Men, women, and children did pray, even if only a short prayer, as the sixth bell invited them to do.

When one of the bells was played with a hammering tone it indicated that an emergency, or some kind of disaster, had hit the town. Someone's house was burning or a bad storm was coming. By word of mouth, the members of the village learned whose house was burning and rushed there to help, forming bucket brigades. No fire station or fire fighters existed in the town. Children, if not in school, rushed to see the flames devour the house, the barn, and the hay. The bell continued its sound until the emergency had passed.

Bell number five struck the hour, and a gentler sound by bell number four rang the half hour. Bell number five, played with slow, well-paced strikes, told us that someone in the village was dying. At that bell sound, people knew the priest of the town was bringing the sick person the last rites, and if possible the last communion. The priest, dressed in ceremonial vestments, carried the Host in a chalice and walked to the sick person's home, preceded by an altar boy carrying the cross, and followed by another carrying an umbrella-type canopy that he kept above the priest's head to protect the Host from rain, dust, and whatever impurity could contaminate it. The bell sound invited the people in the village to pray for the dying person.

Bell number seven, rung slowly, announced that the sick person had died. The same bell with the same sound told the people that a funeral was taking place. Bell number eight was referred to as the *campanone* (the big bell). It was played alone on special feast days.

All the bells were played together, in a concert-like fashion, every Sunday morning and on major Catholic feast days. They played and played. The sound was one of celebration and of joy. They announced the Sunday's High Mass during which the celebrants, the church choir, and the parishioners all sang together, praising the Lord with as much voice as they could muster.

The bells did not play by themselves. Each bell was attached to a rope, which reached the ground of the bell tower. A capable bell ringer pulled the right rope just so at the correct time. Every village had its own bell ringer. Some could create quite a concert playing various melodies. Our town bell ringer was also the church custodian. He had very little schooling but had learned to get the proper sounds out of each bell. He taught other interested people how to ring them, and when it was necessary to play all the bells together one or two other people would help him. Each bell was made of a composition of tin and copper. Different sizes and different combinations of the two metals produced different sounds.

Along with the church, bell tower, school building, city hall, and castle, the town had a railroad station, a unique gift for a small rural town. Trains on the Bergamo-Brescia line stopped there. The availability of the train made it possible for the town's surplus farm workers, especially the young ones, to work in the big cities. A job in the big city, even a low-paying one, was the best way for most young people to escape the *mezzadria* trap.

The Food We Ate

We were poor, had no electricity or running water in the house, but so far as I remember, we had enough food to keep hunger away. The cow provided us with milk for seven or eight months a year. The vegetable garden provided fresh produce for a good part of the year. We raised rabbits, chickens, and a few geese to have meat and eggs, and we were able to raise a pig.

A few male chicks, not more than two or three a year, were castrated at about two months of age to become capons. They were caged and fed corn until they grew big and plump. Later in the year they would become our best Christmas and New Year dish. We kept two or three hens and a rooster every year to bring forth new chicks. We ate the others. My grandmother would kill a chicken in the courtyard using a sharp knife to cut a deep incision across the lower part of the neck. Blood poured out from the wound and in no time at all the chicken was dead. We ate all parts of the chicken. The feet were boiled, the intestines were cleaned and fried, the meat was stewed, the bones were boiled to make chicken broth, and the heart, liver, kidneys, and lungs were chopped up and added to the stew.

We raised a few geese, the noisiest of all of our courtyard creatures. Every spring at the market we bought a few goslings, and they ate together with the chickens and shared the courtyard. As the fall came, my grand-mother or one of my uncles would nail them to a board. Then they were force fed mostly a mixture of water and *farinetta* (second quality corn-meal). In France goose breeders would immobilize and force feed them to obtain the maximum amount of liver for *pâté*. We just wanted more fat and meat. As winter approached the geese were killed, the meat and fat cut from the bones, the intestines cleaned and fried, and the bones boiled for broth. The meat and fat were partially cooked, cut into pieces, and stored in a ceramic urn. During winter, goose meat packed in its own fat stayed edible for a good two months without refrigeration. The cold kept the bacteria away.

Every year, on a Monday in April, my grandfather and my father would traveled to a nearby town that held a weekly market where live animals were bought and sold. They bought a young pig, two or three months old, weighing around twenty-five pounds. When they arrived home, the whole family ran into the courtyard, especially the children, to see the little pink pig. The adults spoke favorably about the small, squealing animal, to the delight of my father and grandfather who felt that their selection, from among other piglets they saw and haggled over, met with everyone's approval. Of course all the children touched the little pig, some pulling its tail, some trying to lift it, and others just poking.

The little pig did not appear to enjoy the festive welcome. It did nothing but squeal. It was the first time to be separated from its little brothers and sisters, and the piglet was very disoriented. After everyone looked and touched, the pig was taken to the stable that would be its home for the next seven months. Its place was in the right corner in a four-by-four-foot pen, with a bed of straw atop a hard concrete floor, and a wooden trough to hold the food.

After the pig entered the pen, no one paid much attention to it, except for the person feeding it and cleaning the bed. Twice a day the pig was fed, mostly scraps from the family table mixed with warm water, and some milk while young. When the pig grew older its meals were a mix of warm water, *farinetta*, and corn bran. As months passed, the pig grew, and by the end of November it reached two hundred pounds. The time had come to slaughter it, usually in early December, and that was a day of excitement. Neighbors came to help or just to look. The children watched the whole operation from some distance. As in other peasant families, we children grew up conditioned to accept the killing of animals for food. We grew up spending many hours playing in the courtyard, and it was in the same courtyard that Grandma killed the chickens, ducks, and geese. It was in the courtyard that Grandfather killed and dressed the rabbits. Killing the pigs just required some extra people to share the work—most importantly a butcher, whose job was to kill the pig the proper way, and to direct the process necessary to produce sausages, salami, bacon, and other products the pig provided. No part of the pig was ever wasted.

On the appointed day, the butcher arrived at the house with his bag of tools: meat grinder, assorted knives, knife sharpener, large wooden mixer, and small packages of spices. The spices included black peppers, salicylic acid, rock salt, and garlic. The family greeted the butcher, and immediately he gave orders to start the process.

The two-hundred-pound pig, freed from the pen, rushed out of the stable into the courtyard. Three or four men ran in pursuit, cornering it and grabbing it by the legs. They took it to one side of the courtyard, close to a scaffold erected the previous day. The men threw the pig to the ground and held it down. Its head turned up; the butcher grabbed a sharp, mid-sized knife, and promptly cut the jugular vein in the squealing pig's neck. This was the best way to kill it without much pain. The blood, flowing profusely from the neck, was collected in a bucket, with some warm water to prevent clotting. After a few more grunts the pig was declared dead.

Men then doused the dead body with buckets of hot water, to clean the skin and soften the hair covering the body. The butcher used a thin sharp knife to shave and clean the whole body. After cleaning, the men tied each of the pig's rear legs to a rope. Two men lifted the pig's body up while a third man tied one leg high on the left scaffold post, and then the other leg on the post at right, leaving the head of the pig to dangle motionless a foot or so from the ground. Its eyes were spent, but wide open.

As the lifeless pig hung, the butcher (there was at least one in each village) selected a mid-sized knife and slowly made a deep cut in the belly until all the intestines were made bare and started pushing out in the open. Men removed the intestines and placed them temporarily in buckets filled with water. The butcher continued cutting vertically through the body to expose the kidneys, liver, heart, lungs, and stomach. Each organ was duly removed and stored in containers.

I watched all the action taking place, along with the other children, family members, and some neighbors. Our faces did not show joy or excitement; we were somber. We watched each movement of the butcher attentively. We did not scare, or experience nightmares. We were used to the killing in the courtyard. A very good depiction of butchering a pig in a peasant courtyard, although short and lacking the gory details, is seen in Ermanno Olmi's movie *The Tree of the Wooden Clogs*. The film was shot in rural northern Italy, not very far from our village, and described peasant life at about the time of my childhood.

After all the innards were removed, the body and head were split in two. The two parts were untied from the posts, brought into the kitchen, and deposited on an old table we kept on the porch. Our large kitchen table became the butcher's working table, with his meat grinder in place, and this is where most of the meat was processed.

The butcher produced three major products, and a few minor ones. First, lard was removed from each half of the pig's body. The lard covered the whole back of the pig. The two slices of lard were covered with rock salt and laid on a flat surface for a number of days until the salt had penetrated deeply. Then it was wrapped in cheese cloth to protect it from flies and insects, and hung from the rafters of the storage room. When it was ready to eat, the men of the house cut a thin slice, put it on the grill over hot coals in the kitchen fireplace, and after a few minutes ate it with polenta, in the early morning for breakfast, or later for lunch. The women cut slices to use as a condiment for the evening soup. The lard lasted almost the whole winter; the salt, cold weather, and our strong appetite for lard kept it from ever going rancid.

After the lard, the butcher cut away the two strips of bacon covering the pig's belly. Each strip was turned inside up and covered with a mix of salt, whole black pepper, and a few cloves, then rolled up, tied with kitchen string, like a big *salame*, and hung from a nail on one of the rafters of the store room, next to the lard. It was ready to eat after a few weeks; we ate it at lunch, mainly raw or fried with eggs, sometimes with polenta, or to supplement a plate of pasta, and it was always a good dish when we had guests.

After the butcher stripped the lard and bacon from the carcass, meat and bones remained. The butcher carved the meat from the bones, and divided the meat into three separate piles. Pieces carved from the pig head and other poor quality cuts formed one of the piles in the corner of our kitchen table. The best quality meat—filet, loin, and rounds—was set aside for salami, and the rest became sausage.

As the butcher carved up the pig, with the help of a couple of the family's men, the women worked steadily, but carefully, cleaning the pig's intestines. The first step was to squeeze out their contents as much as possible without breaking them. Each intestine was then filled with warm water, squeezed out again, and turned inside out—then cleaned again and reversed again. They were ready to be filled with sausage and salami meat.

The butcher always started first with sausages. He took the meat that had been reserved, ground it, and placed it in the wooden mixer, a long box without a top. (In some years, if my grandfather could afford it, he bought a few kilograms of beef to grind up and mix with the pig meat.) To the ground meat, the butcher added salt, a little red wine, some whole black pepper, salicylic acid as a preservative, and some finely ground fresh garlic. He mixed it all together by hand, working vigorously and continuously for a good ten to fifteen minutes, to make sure that the sausage flavors were thoroughly mixed to taste the same throughout.

After mixing, the butcher removed the blade from the grinder and attached an elongated funnel, to which the cleaned small intestines were attached. Ground meat was fed into the machine, and the crank propelled it into the intestine. The butcher used his hands to squeeze and guide the meat inside the intestine until the whole length was uniformly filled. Putting the filled intestines on the table, he took string to make a knot every six inches to create individual sausages, linked together in chains of five to six feet each in length.

Next the butcher started on the salami, following the same process. He ground the meat, with some fat attached, mixed it with the same basic ingredients, and pushed it through the grinder into the cleaned large intestines. Each *salame* was limited to one or two feet depending on the length of the casing, and tied with string every half inch or so to keep its shape and dry properly.

The small amount of poor-quality meat remaining was mixed with salt and pepper and wrapped in cheesecloth. We called it what is translated in English as head cheese. This is what we ate first, after the liver, kidneys, and heart.

The ribs and other bones were salted and covered in cheesecloth, and laid in the storage room to use for broth.

The sausages and salami had to dry slowly to be preserved. To dry they were hung from bedroom rafters on the second story of the house, usually in my grandparent's room. A brazier full of hot coals was set on the floor below, and slowly drops of fat would form on the outside of each casing;

later some would fall onto the floor of the room. In fifteen days or less the sausages and salami were dry enough and ready to eat, and could remain for a few winter months without refrigeration.

The blood that flowed from the jugular was mixed, the same day or the next, with bread crumbs, Parmesan cheese, small yellow chopped onions from the garden, salt, and a little nutmeg, to form a blood cake. This was cooked in the frying pan, with a lid covered with hot coals in the fireplace. It was our primitive oven, and after forty or forty-five minutes the cake was ready to eat.

I remember the blood cake was very good, and it was loaded with protein—something we kids needed badly. Even after we left the farm, my mother continued to bake blood cakes during the pig-killing season. She bought blood from farmers in the area we lived, knowing that I was fond of such food. The first few summers I returned to Italy from my new home in the U.S., my mother continued to surprise me with a blood cake, which I eagerly ate. Later she stopped; it had become more and more difficult to obtain fresh blood, as fewer and fewer farmers killed pigs at home. The supermarket had arrived, and it became cheaper and more convenient to buy sausages, salami, lard, and bacon there.

Like most peasant families in northern Italy at that time, our staple food was the lowly "polenta." Our 50 percent share of the corn crop was enough to provide us with cornmeal year round. If one year our yield fell short, we borrowed what was needed from another farmer. Polenta was to us like rice to the Chinese.

There was always enough polenta to satisfy everyone in the family. What was leftover was eaten in the evening with soup or in the morning with milk. I seldom saw or ate bread when I was a child. Bread for us was a luxury. We did have wheat flour, but we used it to make noodles for the evening soup, and to make other pasta. We did not have an oven, and it was difficult to make bread in the fireplace. We did not have money to purchase bread at the store, except on special occasions.

Every morning around eleven, my grandmother put water and salt in a big pot hanging in the fireplace to boil. As the water boiled, she added the cornmeal. She continued stirring the mixture with a barkless wooden stick, assisted by one of the daughters-in-law, until the polenta was properly cooked. After forty minutes of stirring on the hot fire, the polenta was ready to eat. The polenta was poured out of the pot onto a special wooden board (*taiera*) in the middle of the kitchen table, and it looked very much like a big cake. It was hard enough that it would stand up by itself but soft enough that it could be sliced using a string tied to the handle of the board. Everyone at the table cut a piece of their choice by passing the string underneath the polenta and pulling it upward.

When the polenta was ready, lunch was ready; it was our most important meal. The polenta was generally served with chicken or rabbit stew, or pork sausage in the winter. Our vegetable garden provided potatoes and carrots as filler for the stew. The stew always had abundant gravy; with polenta, gravy always went a long way. When meat was scarce, we children satisfied ourselves with polenta and gravy. The whole family could never sit together around the big kitchen table. It was not big enough, and there weren't enough chairs to go around. Most of the time, the children sat on the floor.

Supper consisted almost always of a bowl of soup, a kind of minestrone. It started with a piece of lard cut up and fried in a big pot. Chopped vegetables in season were added after most of the lard had melted. Water and salt were added and the whole thing was allowed to boil for an hour or more. Homemade *tagliatelle* (noodles), prepared by the women ahead of time, were added to the boiling mixture. A few more minutes and the soup was ready. The grown-ups used a big bowl and thickened the soup with leftover polenta. We kids ate from smaller bowls, enough to fill our stomachs.

Sometimes, on Sundays and on feast days, the women used wheat flour to make tagliatelle, ravioli and gnocchi for lunch. It was something special that the whole family really appreciated and enjoyed.

For breakfast we each had a bowl of hot milk filled with pieces of polenta, when available. If not, Grandma boiled the milk, adding *tagliatelle* or rice. It was a milk soup, especially good on cold winter mornings. On special occasions, often on Sundays, Grandma fixed *bolfadei*, a mixture of cornmeal, wheat flour, salt, and water cooked for about thirty minutes. It was served in a bowl and each person added an amount of milk he or she liked. We kids loved it.

Milk came from our own cow. After giving birth to a calf, she gave milk for about seven to eight months. My grandfather milked her early in the morning, and one of the women milked her in the late afternoon. For three or four of those months, the cow gave more milk than the family used. We kids did not drink milk during the day, except for what we had at breakfast. What we did not use we gave to neighboring families whose cows were dry, and they returned the favor when our cow was dry. We kept track of the exchange, and discrepancies were paid with other foods. We were all just as poor; a chicken or eggs in trade for milk was a fair deal.

We bought very little at the grocery store or at any store for that matter. We bought essential goods: oil, vinegar, salt, some low-quality cheese (with major flaws from the aging process), some dried fish (*baccalà*) for the Friday dinner, sugar, and little else. The grocery store, about the size of our kitchen, was located a few houses down our street. The owner, a kind and burly person, white apron tied just where his belly ended, served all the customers himself. He sold groceries on credit to us and to most of his other customers, keeping a book of debits and credits, one page per customer. He trusted all of his customers, mainly sharecroppers, to pay their debt, and they always did. At harvest time, at the sale of some wheat, or corn, or silk cocoons or some other cash sales, the family paid the grocer first.

Christmas dinner was the best dinner of the year. Christmas was an important church day, but it was also an important family day. We children looked forward to it with a lot of excitement. We did not get presents at Christmas, but it was one of the very few dinners at which we had bread and dessert. The family women made an abundant amount of ravioli stuffed with meat and covered with butter and cheese. They also prepared stuffed capon, plumped up for just this meal. Bread, bought at the store, replaced polenta that day, and the dinner ended with a homemade dessert.

Easter was another festive day. Preparation for Easter Sunday, however, lasted all week long both at church and at home. During Easter week the whole family went to church every evening for retreats, sermons, prayers, stations of the cross, confirmations, and benedictions, all in preparation for Easter Sunday. High Mass was sung by the town's church chorus, accompanied by music from the church's pipe organ. At home, the women used that week to clean everything in the house. All pots, pans, and skillets were taken from the kitchen into the courtyard and scrubbed, scrubbed, and scrubbed until they shined like new. The pantry was cleaned as were the cornmeal and wheat flour boxes. They searched for little worms, moths, and spiders, and killed any found. It was spring cleaning and there was no better time for it than Easter week. On Easter Sunday, the dinner was elaborate, but not as opulent or ever as good as at Christmas.

Our family did not produce wine. My father bartered some from the local wine bar in exchange for some transport services, and at times my grandfather got some from his sister, Dola, whose major crop was grapes. Some was obtained in exchange for corn.

All the men in the family drank wine—locally made young wine. They drank it at the bar on Sunday afternoon or evening where they played card games, betting wine instead of money. Playing cards at the wine bar or playing bocce ball were the only entertainment the men of the town could afford. They drank wine at home on special occasions, such as the end of a good harvest, the baptism of a child, or the profitable sale of a cow. Sometimes they also took some wine with them when going to work in the fields. The women drank very little wine, and mainly at home.

I was five when I drank wine for the first time. Once in a while my father took me with him in the fields, possibly because he wanted to spend more time with me. While he tilled the soil with horse and plow, I followed him up and down the field until I tired. I then went to rest in the shade of a mulberry tree. There I played with the many little creatures coming out of the earth all around the place. One very hot day, after a few runs up and down the field, I rested in the shade of a tree where my father had placed our lunch, a bottle of water and a half bottle of red wine. After a while I became very thirsty. As my father did a few minutes earlier, I grabbed the bottle of wine and drank a good amount of it. As the wine did its job on me, my stomach emptied and I fell asleep. My father, seeing what I had done, and seeing the bottle tossed on the ground still oozing wine, lifted my limp body on his shoulder and brought me home. He put me in bed and I did not wake up until the morning after. The experience kept me away from wine until the age of eleven when I started working at my uncle's wine bar.

The Way We Dressed and Played

After we passed the mummy stage of infants wrapped in swaddling cloth, we kids almost never wore new clothing. Until the age of eight I never wore an outfit that was purchased new, and I feel sure that was the case for my cousins and for most of the kids in the town. One thing I remember is that we kids never made use of underwear. A pair of short pants, an old shirt, and a sweater when the temperature required it was all we needed at home, at play, and at school.

The young men of the town dressed neatly when going to church or when visiting their girlfriends on Sundays. They would wear a pair of well-ironed pants, a clean shirt, and shoes, all locally made by town artisans. The town did not have a clothing or shoe store. The youth's mother or sisters took good care of each garment, and one or two sets of each item were made to last until the young man would marry.

Most married men in sharecropper families, including mine, had only one good suit in their armoire. (Wall closets did not exist in farmhouses.) It was the suit they had worn at their marriage ceremony, and it was the suit they would wear at a relative's wedding, at a funeral, or at Christmas. It was more often than not the suit their bodies would be clothed in when placed in the funeral casket. Aside from that special suit, each man had a limited number of work pants and shirts that the women kept usable by constantly mending them, adding patches of material, not necessarily of the same cloth or color, and washing them when soiled.

Women of the town kept their wedding dresses for special occasions, but they also had one or two other dresses to wear for church on Sunday. Almost all them had a black or very dark dress to wear at funerals and for many months after a member of their family had died. When going to church and inside the church they also wore a hat or a veil. At home they wore a blouse, a long skirt, and an apron with a large pocket. The women in the Patam family were not different from those in the village; they all dressed the same. One thing I remember is that my mother, grandmother, and aunts each had a nightgown they brought with them when they married. None of our women ever wore a bra. I am not sure if bras existed at that time, or if there was no money to purchase them. Young unmarried ladies wore simple dresses, made by the local seamstress. No dress, even the wedding dress, was ever bought in a store—they were locally made. Women from sharecropper families did not wear or own jewelry, except for the wedding ring. Each of them, however, on their wedding day, brought to their new home a dowry consisting of bed sheets, pillowcases, towels, and a nightgown or two. These were things they had spent much time embroidering, things they would use over and over, again and again.

Sharecropper weddings were very simple. The groom, dressed in a dark suit, waited for his bride at the main entrance of the church. The bride, wearing a nicely fitted dress, entered the church first and walked to the altar accompanied by her father. The groom followed, accompanied by his mother. He knelt at the altar next to his bride. The twenty or thirty invited guests followed them into the church and took their places in the front pews. The parish priest married them and read to them the three articles related to the duties and responsibilities of married couples contained in the Italian civil code. The ceremony then continued with the Holy Mass. When the Mass was over, the newlywed couple signed the marriage certificate and left the church together, both with glorious smiles. As they exited the church, guests and friends greeted them by throwing handfuls of confetti at them (candies made of sugar, egg white and almond). We kids delighted in picking up and eating whatever confetti we could find on the ground. Many kids knew when a wedding was taking place. For many of us, wedding candies were the only candies we were fortunate enough to eat.

After the ceremony and the greetings were over, the wedding party walked to the local wine bar and restaurant for the reception and dinner. Everyone ate and drank as they had never done before. As the wine began to take its toll, everyone sang. They sang popular songs, and drank, and sang, and drank until their voices and their sense were no longer with them. Then the women, many still sober, dragged their husbands home.

Women, like my mother, who decided to marry into a sharecropping family, knew that they would have to join the husband's family. They knew that they had to help prepare the family meals, help wash the family dishes, help feed the animals, and do many other chores. They knew all of this before getting married, because the sharecropping agreement tied their husbands to the land and to the farmhouse they would occupy. They knew, as my mother did, that marrying into such a family life would be hard. What most of them did not expect and did not cherish were the fights that took place almost daily in such large families. My extended family did not escape from this curse. Fights were almost a daily occurrence among family members: brothers against brothers, brothers against sisters-in-law, sisters-in-law against sisters-in-law, and everyone against my grandparents, who could not keep much order in the house. What did they fight about? A myriad of things. Money: none of them ever had enough. Work: one was accused of working less than the others. House chores: you were not contributing enough, or not doing things well. Children: your child did this or did that, and the like. At times, one member of the family would not speak to another for days or weeks. I cannot think of anything that could have kept the family together except for a strong and deep love among each of the married couples, and the overall necessity to stay together. The young spouses (my mother was barely nineteen when she joined the family), after a few weeks, and maybe a few tears, adjusted to the ongoing chaos and learned how to make the best of it. Separation or divorce were very much unknown in Italy at the time. The family, the church, and the state kept everyone together until death made them part.

The Wooden Clogs

I do not remember at what age my parents bought me a pair of new shoes. In a large family like ours and with so many relatives and acquaintances around, used children's shoes were probably almost always available. Whatever shoes we had, we only wore for church. At home we played barefoot, and when walking to school we wore homemade wooden clogs. Everyone wore wooden clogs: men working in the fields, and women working at home or going to the grocery store or to the water fountain. The clogs were relatively easy to make and lasted a long time. My grandfather was good at making them, and he made them for all of us. He took the trunk of a poplar tree, sawed it into different pieces, split each piece in the middle, and with a special cutting tool sculpted the pieces of wood to fit the size and shape of the foot of each person. After the wood was prepared, he nailed on top an appropriate strip of cloth or a piece of rubber from an old tire, and the clogs were ready to wear. Those homemade wooden clogs must have inspired Ermanno Olmi, one of the great Italian film directors, to direct the movie *The Tree of the Wooden Clogs*. As I mentioned earlier, it depicts rural life around the time and place of my childhood. The film tells the moving story of a northern Italian sharecropping family evicted from the land because the father cut down a tree to make a pair of wooden clogs for his son who was to start elementary school.

At the age of ten, when we moved to the town of Seriate and the family finances improved, we purchased wooden clogs at the store. At eleven, as I started middle school and had to travel to Bergamo, I began to wear shoes. I had no choice.

The Way We Played

Toys were never a part of my childhood, nor that of my cousins, nor for most children in our town. On Christmas day, there were no Christmas gifts to open. December 12, the feast day of Santa Lucia, was the day children were given presents. For the Patam children an apple, an orange, a piece of chocolate, and a few candies were all they ever got. At the age of four, I received a toy horse. It was very small, made of paper maché, with the four legs glued to a piece of wood, which had four small wheels. I do not remember my reaction to such an unusual gift, but I feel sure I must have shown it to all the children in my neighborhood. It was not until I was eleven that on the twelfth of December I received my second unusual gift, from one of my uncles. It was a French-Italian dictionary. I had just started the sixth grade, and the study of French was required.

The lack of toys did not keep us kids from playing. Until the start of first grade we played in the courtyard chasing one another, or chasing the chickens and ducks that used the courtyard as their playground. When it rained, we played under the covered porch or in the hayloft. During the cold, snowing, winter days we were confined to the stable, which the animals kept warm but which had little room for us to play. It had only enough room for us to fight, cry, and scream at one another.

As we entered grade school, playing soccer became our favorite pastime. Soccer for us boys was the only game in town. It was not an organized game. There were no uniforms, no coaches, no referees, no screaming parents, just us kids. The schoolyard, the city square, or an empty lot were readily transformed into soccer fields. Two good size rocks at one end of the field and two at the other end served as goal posts. We formed teams of five or seven players from different parts of the town and kicked the ball, any kind of ball we could find, up and down the field for hours.

We did not have toys, but we did not feel the need for toys. We did not ask our parents to purchase toys. Toys were things we did not use, and therefore there was no urgent desire to have them.

Later in my life, as I traveled and worked in many developing countries (some of them very poor), very few children had any toys, but they did not suffer from it. They just played like we did before and after school. They enjoyed kicking a ball or playing soccer in improvised soccer fields, in empty lots or in city streets, just as we did. The only thing they needed was a ball, not necessarily a soccer ball, but any kind of ball. Young girls played with a homemade doll that they put to sleep in a shoebox and dressed with leftover pieces of cloth, the same as our girls did.

Remembering how we children spent so much time playing without toys, without guidance and without fancy equipment, and observing children at play in poor countries, I have concluded that in many respects it is easier to be poor in a poor society than to be poor in a rich society. This is true because many individual desires tend to be influenced, even conditioned, by the society one lives in. The children in poor societies rarely asked their parents for toys, new shoes, or new clothes, because none of their peers possessed them. Poor children in rich societies see such things all over the place, especially toys resting in the front or backyards of many houses they pass. They would like to have similar toys and wonder why they cannot have them, at least some of them. They ask their parents why they cannot have toys, or a bicycle, or something else they have seen at someone else's place. Parents listening to the pleas of their children might give up some food to buy toys. The situation is even worse today; call it the "technological divide." Parents know that the children of middle- or upper-class families own computers and are concerned that if their children do not have one they might fall behind at school, or may not be able to keep up with their friends. They make sacrifices until the children have what their peers have. In poor countries very few children, even today, have a computer or even a cell phone. Their parents are not, at least not yet, subject to the pressure felt by poor families in rich countries to provide their children with the latest inventions of the information technology age. The "demonstration effect," however, may soon equalize the burden of poverty all over the world, as children in poor societies become more aware of what the wealthy have elsewhere, and grow unsatisfied with their inability to catch up.

The Breakup of the Patam Family

The Great Depression of the 1930s hit Italy very hard. Unemployment was rampant, prices were falling, especially for agricultural commodities, and the life of the sharecropping families became even more miserable than before. Some of the younger people began to leave their families searching for a job, any kind of job, in the bigger cities.

Our family started breaking up at the end of 1932. I was barely six years old. My grandfather could not keep the family together any longer; my grandmother had died, and the family discipline started breaking down. My two married uncles with children could no longer see any future in sharecropping, and as their children increased in age and in number they started looking for a better way to make a living. The family, by now, had surplus labor and their departure would not have affected the sharecropping agreement. Everyone agreed to the brothers' departure, feeling that a city job would be good for them, their families, and maybe for the rest of us since it would leave fewer people to share the produce of the land. It was clear to all that, after many years of sharecropping, the family did not have any money, savings, or future.

My uncle Attilio was the first to leave. Through a town acquaintance who had left earlier, he was able to find a job at the Breda Steelworks in Sesto San Giovanni, an industrial town on the outskirts of Milano. He was the smartest of the Patam family. His formal education stopped at third grade, but he was the one who helped my grandmother with the family finances. More than anyone else he felt the hopelessness of the sharecropper life. For a short while, he commuted by train to his new job. When he had enough money, he rented a small apartment on the ground floor of a building near his job and brought his family and belongings there. My father helped him to load things, mainly his bedroom set, on a cart, which our horse Nino pulled from our house to his new residence. It was a sixty-mile round trip, a two-day journey for Nino and my father.

My uncle Attilio had four children: Lucia, Lina, Maria, and Luigi. The apartment had only a large bedroom and a very dark humid kitchen with a concrete floor. Two of the kids slept in the parents' bedroom and the other two in the kitchen. My uncle had applied for government housing, but he was told that a place would not be available until a new building was completed.

My aunt Nini, Attilio's wife, was the sweetest person in the Belotti family. She was delighted to have her own place after seven years of marriage. The place was not that comfortable, but she made it livable. A few years later, as the job at the Breda Works became more secure, they moved to a larger apartment on the second floor of a decent building where the sun could enter the rooms and brighten their existence. During their stay in Sesto San Giovanni, they had four more children. One died at birth and the other three, Giovanna, Anna, and Irene, survived. Aunt Nini died a few years later. She was in her fifties. My uncle Attilio continued to work at Breda until his retirement at sixty. He spent most of his retirement days at a local bar playing cards and drinking a moderate amount of wine. He developed diabetes, which he was not able to control. First, a local surgeon amputated one of his legs, then the other, and finally a stroke put him out of his misery forever.

My uncle Luigi was the second to leave the family. His brother Attilio helped him to get a job at Breda Steelworks. The new government enterprises that Italy created during the depression needed steel to build the many infrastructure projects underway to fight the depression. The Breda Steelworks, the largest Italian steelmaker at the time, was hiring new workers. Most came from rural areas. The factory provided a dorm for the newcomers, and later helped them to obtain government housing in town. After Luigi was assigned an apartment in a government housing complex, he took his wife Carolina, his two children, Vittorio and Gianna, and loaded them together with all their belongings on the family cart. Our horse Nino, guided by my father, pulled the loaded cart to their new place.

Luigi and Carolina had two more children, Francesco and Pierino, at the new residence. Luigi continued his work at the Breda factory until his retirement at sixty. Like his brother Attilio, he led a simple life during his retirement. Raising four children consumed all of his salary, leaving no savings.

The meager government pension he received enabled Luigi and Carolina to pay the rent and buy enough groceries to survive. He also developed diabetes. Maybe he did not know any better, or his doctor did not stress the importance of following a proper diet, or maybe the doctor, at that time did not recognize the disease until it was too late. As the disease progressed, his right foot was amputated. From that day on, he did not walk out of his apartment. Every day, he sat on a high wheelchair next to the kitchen window and looked out onto the street below. Neighbors passed by to say hello or chat a few minutes with him. He had a good word for everyone. He always kept a mug of wine next to him, and from time to time, slowly, he quenched his thirst with it. He never did give up his wine. He drank it with much pleasure but never in amounts large enough to become drunk. All four children had married and moved out of the house. My aunt Carolina, one of my favorite aunts, took care of him. She fed him, washed him, and put him to bed. My mother and I visited her many times. Carolina never did complain about her suffering. She was doing the best she could for her husband, but she could not deprive him of his wine. Before dying, he lost his other foot, and later a stroke robbed him of his speech. He died at his home in his apartment—the only apartment he had ever known.

After the two brothers left the family, things did not improve in the Patam household. One of the remaining brothers, my uncle Beppo, did not go to school—he started first grade but never finished it. He was just not up to the school challenge. There was something wrong with him; he could not express his thoughts very well. He was very attached to my father and did everything my father asked him to do. He worked in the fields, and he also worked at home. He kept the stable clean as well as the courtyard, the porch, and the stairs. He did many of the things his brothers could not do or did not want to do. He never worried. He never possessed a thing of his own, not even his bed. On Sunday my grandfather or my father gave him a small allowance. He spent it at the only bar in town.

The youngest of the brothers, my uncle Valento, was in his early twenties and was not very much interested in working the land. He worked a few hours or a few days here and there, but contributed very little to the welfare of the family. My grandmother, when she was still alive, protected him. Most of his brothers were not happy with him, and the sisters-in-law did not get along with him. For them, he was another cause for frequent family fights. They prepared his food, and washed and mended his clothes, but they rarely talked to him.

The departure of my aunts Nini and Carolina left my mother alone to take care of the family chores. My grandfather and my father helped, but most of the cooking, the mending, the household work, and much of the cleaning was hers to do. She married my father when she was barely nineteen, in the year 1921. She left her village of Torre de Roveri, with a fairly simple but comfortable life. At the age of twelve she had started working in a silk factory and worked there until she was fifteen. When her older sister died at nineteen of the Spanish flu, she was forced to quit her job and help her mother with the family chores. Her father and her three brothers were very hard working men but were also very demanding. Her mother, never in very good health, needed help. Her other sister was still in school. During the last three years before she married she worked hard. Her life was not very easy, but it was pleasant and was enriched by the many friends of her age living in the farmhouses that surrounded her home.

Rosa left her family to marry my father, joining a large family whose many members she did not know. I do not think she ever totally adjusted to her new life. The fights, screaming, poverty, and disorder, as well as the in-laws, and the lack of friends she could talk to and unload her hurt feelings, must have made her life miserable. I feel sure she must have wanted to leave the Patam family very badly, even before Carolina and Nini did.

Aside from the family fights and deprivation, my mother suffered greatly from the death of her children. She married in 1921, and by the end of 1926 she had given birth to four children. The fourth was named Mario in honor of the Virgin Mary. She had lost the first three, and she hoped the fourth would survive. He did survive long enough to write this story. My survival, however, was not guaranteed. One day, in 1930, at the age of five, I became very ill with a very high fever and breathing problems. My father hitched Nino to the cart and rushed to the pharmacy in the next town to post the request for the doctor to come check on me. As the next morning arrived, my parents waited for the doctor to pick up his calls from the pharmacy, and make his way to our house in whatever order he determined among his other visit requests. My fever had not diminished and my breathing had become more and more raucous. While waiting for the doctor, my aunt Nini prepared a hot cake of linseed flour, wrapped it with a towel, and put it over my chest. It was a common remedy used at that time to reduce cold congestion, but it did not seem to help. My whole family must have prayed very hard that morning, because a doctor arrived. It was not the local doctor who came late that afternoon, my mother later told me, but a pediatrician, a Dr. Ugo Frizzoni. He was the cousin of Vittorio Frizzoni, the owner of the land my mother's father supervised.

My mother was well known to Dr. Ugo Frizzoni. As a teenager, after she left the silk factory, she babysat his children on many occasions when he and his family visited his cousin Vittorio, whose large villa was adjacent to the house occupied by my grandfather. Dr. Frizzoni was a well-known pediatrician who had founded a children's clinic in the town of Pedrengo, near the city of Bergamo. He was returning home from visiting a sick child in the town of Sarnico, a few kilometers east of our town, and stopped in to visit my mother. He had heard from her father that she had lost her first three children, and he wanted to talk to her and find out more about her children. As he arrived, and after my mother got over the excitement at his sudden appearance, she took him upstairs to take a look at me. His diagnosis was quick: "Rosa, your son has pneumonia." He took a sulfa drug from his bag and administered it to me right away, and left some for my mother to give me later. Sulfa drugs were new then, but the medicine worked and I survived.

After my birth in 1926, my mother gave birth to five more children and adopted one. They were all boys like the previous four. They all died very young, some barely out of my mother's womb. I got to know very few of them; what I remember is a table on the porch outside the kitchen covered with a white sheet, and a small white coffin lying in the middle of it. I remember people from the neighborhood walking through the main door of the farmhouse and silently gathering around the table, saying a prayer and offering their sympathy to my grieving mother. I also remember one of the town priests arriving at the house with two altar boys. He blessed the little coffin, and then started the funeral procession to the church. Only twice I followed my little brothers to the church. In church, there were a few prayers, another benediction with holy water and incense, and the procession took the little bodies to the cemetery. A small grave in the children's section swallowed the little white coffins. The next day our lives continued as before. Every year, from the age of three to eight, this scene repeated. I was told that whenever my mother realized she was pregnant, she always cried because she worried about getting the money to pay for the funeral expenses.

At the age of six, my parents enrolled me in the first grade. There was no kindergarten in town. The Catholic sisters provided limited preschool facilities, but very few families made use of them. The elementary school building was on the main square of the town, close to our home. A pencil and a notebook were all we needed to take to class; there were no textbooks. The teachers wrote what we needed to learn on the blackboard. Homework consisted of repeating over and over the day's lecture. Learning to read, write, add, subtract, multiply, and divide was all that was expected from us. By the end of the third grade we could do all of that. The hardest task for us kids was learning to read and write in the Italian language. For most of us, Italian was a foreign language. At home, at play, and at work we spoke the Bergamasco dialect, one of the most difficult of the many Italian dialects that Dante Alighieri refers to in his book, *De Vulgari Eloquentia*. My parents eventually learned to read and understand Italian, but they never really spoke it.

The town school offered only the first three elementary grades. The Italian government at that time required that all children complete the third grade or stay in school until the age of eight. After the third grade it was very difficult for the town children to continue school. None of the surrounding towns offered the fourth or fifth grades. Larger towns did, but not many of the families could afford the cost of the transportation, books, clothes, or shoes to continue their children's schooling. Moreover, it was not something most parents were eager to do. None of the children I played with went to school after the third grade.

I was one of the very few lucky ones, and my luck was all due to a horse.

As I mentioned earlier, my family had a horse. We called him Nino. My father loved him. He used him to plow the land, prepare the soil, plant the seeds of corn and wheat, and do whatever other work was necessary to run the family farm. My father fed him, brushed him, and took good care of him. He used Nino to earn a few extra lire by transporting a few things for the local grocery store and for the town wine bar. He also used him on special Catholic feast days, either in our town or in the surrounding ones, to carry a large container full of *biscotti*, candies and other sweet treats he had bought from an out of town distributor, and sold just outside the church where the celebration was taking place. A few times he took me with him. He sold much of what he had, but I do not know if he ever made any money selling candies. I do remember that not long after he had started, he stopped doing it. There were too many competitors—some of them with larger and greater offerings than his.

One Monday morning, when I was in the middle of third grade, my grandfather took our horse Nino to the market and sold him. He used the proceeds to buy two oxen. He always maintained that the supervisor of the Gonzaga land forced him to do it because one can plow the land more deeply with two oxen than one horse, and the change would bring about higher crop yields.

My father became so upset at the loss of Nino that he decided to leave what remained of the Patam family. We left in November 1933. November was the month sharecropper families would move; the crops were all finished, and new contracts would be signed.

It was not possible for my father to get a factory job at that time. The country and much of the rest of the world were still suffering from the Great Depression. His two brothers were hanging onto their jobs at the Breda Works, but no new hiring was taking place. In 1931, the Mussolini government had taken over the largest Italian commercial banks, most large steel producers, the Alfa Romeo automobile plant, and many other firms. It transformed them into state enterprises even before John Maynard Keynes wrote about such policy in his *General Theory*, but after Pope Pius XI in 1931 argued for such policy in his encyclical, *Quadragesimo Annum*. Jobs were probably saved, but no new jobs were created at the time.

Torre de Roveri and Pasta Hill

The lack of factory jobs convinced my father to move to the town of Torre de Roveri, my mother's town, also located in the province of Bergamo. It was about the same size as the town we left. Many of its inhabitants were also sharecroppers. At one time, most of the land and houses were owned by three noble families: the Count Della Rovere, for whom the town was named, the Count Astori, and the Pasta family, who owned most of the hill on the northeast side. When we arrived, the Count Della Rovere had passed away and the palace had been transformed into the town city hall. The Astori palace, in the center of the town, was occupied by the elderly countess and her daughter. The Pasta family had left the town, and the property on Pasta Hill (*Colle di Pasta*) was owned by a Swiss family headed by Vittorio Frizzoni, who had hired my maternal grandfather Francesco. At first, Francesco was hired as a farm worker and soon thereafter he was appointed as supervisor for all of the Frizzoni estate, which included seventeen sharecropping families, their farmhouses, a large piece of land which the owner maintained under direct cultivation, and a big wine cellar.

The town of Torre de Roveri had a large church and a bell tower like any other rural town in northern Italy. It also had a bakery, a cheese and oil store, and a grocery store that also sold fresh meat, salt, and cigarettes. All three stores provided credit at no interest to their customers. The town had a wine bar, but it did not have a doctor, a pharmacy, a clinic, or a post office. These services were available in a town a few kilometers to the south. It did have a well-trained, very good and gentle midwife who visited pregnant women and delivered babies in the town and in one of the surrounding towns. Most important for me, the town elementary school provided a fourth grade education.

We moved to Torre de Roveri where my maternal grandfather had offered my father a job as a farm worker. He needed someone to help farm the land under the owner's direct cultivation. The work was hard, it was seasonal, and the pay was low, but it was a job my father could do and do well.

We arrived in Torre de Roveri with no money, but because my father had a job we were able to rent a small apartment not far from the center of the town, and we were also able to buy groceries on credit. A few days after we settled down, I returned to school to complete my third grade, and in the fall of 1934 I started the fourth grade.

The apartment we rented consisted of a bedroom and a medium-sized kitchen. The kitchen had a fireplace and an electric light bulb hanging from the center of the ceiling but no electric plugs. The apartment did not have running water nor a bathroom. Drinkable water was available from a fountain in the courtyard of the building where an outhouse was also located. This last structure was shared with two other families, as well as the customers of the wine bar and bocce ball court located on the ground floor of the building. The owner of the wine bar, who also owned the building, kept it fairly clean.

My father's salary was only seven lire (the Italian currency at the time) a day—less than fifty cents each day. In order to make ends meet, all three of us had to pitch in. In his spare time my father walked the forested hills above the land he was cultivating and gathered dead wood for our fireplace. He convinced the owner of the building to allow us to build two rabbit hutches against the northern wall of the building. In a short time we were able to add rabbit meat to our menu. The rabbits were fed only grass that my mother and I cut from the banks of a small creek flowing close to our building, and from the sides of the road that passed the front of the house.

At the beginning of the summer, when school was out and the farmers were harvesting their wheat, my mother and I spent many hours, sometimes whole days, going from one harvested field to another to pick up the heads of wheat that had fallen to the ground and been abandoned by the owner. It was hard work; it required a lot of searching and bending. The straw was high and not much wheat was left on the ground. Besides, we were not the only ones doing this work. Other women and children would also pick the wheatfields; it was a common undertaking all over rural Italy. An Italian poet, Mercantini, wrote a patriotic poem titled *"La Spigolatrice"* ("The Gleaner"). At the end of the wheat harvesting season, my mother and I had accumulated as much as fifty or sixty pounds of wheat, which my father took to the miller to turn into flour. My mother used this to make pasta, and once a week she used some of it to make bread in the fireplace, something she had learned to do.

As the summer came to a close and fall arrived, my mother would rise early in the morning, prepare my breakfast, and walk up the hills behind the town and reach her father's home. It was grape harvesting time. She would spend the whole day helping her brothers harvest grapes, the major crop of all seventeen sharecropping families under her father's supervision. The harvest lasted seven to ten days. During that time, every day she left the house very early in the morning and returned home late in the evening.

The grape harvest was a time of long, hard workdays, but it was also a joyous time. Many young women left their mountain homes and walked many hours, even a whole day, to reach their host families, sharecroppers who needed extra help. These mountain girls, sixteen to twenty-five years of age, strong and beautifully built as if they were born from the mountains themselves, spent the day harvesting grapes, and much of the evening stomping and crushing the grapes barefoot with their skirts tied up high on their waists. The vats full of grapes were located in cavernous cellars attached to my grandfather's house. Each vat was assigned to one of the sharecropping families, and one was reserved for the grapes harvested on the land under the owner's direct cultivation.

As the young women stomped the grapes, they sang with all the voice they could muster. They sang local songs, mountain songs, joyous songs reverberating throughout the cellar. Soon everyone joined in the singing, creating a truly festive atmosphere. They all started to forget how hard they had to work for a meager return.

After crushing, the grape must was moved to fermenting vats. After fermenting, the stems, skins, and whatever else was left were transferred to a large hand press, where the last drop of juice was squeezed out and collected. (The wine produced using the press was mostly for the sharecropping families themselves to drink). The stomping vat was then washed out and everything was made ready for the next day's harvest. At the end of the harvest, the young ladies returned to their mountain homes. They were paid very little; they were provided with food and a place to sleep, usually a haystack, and each one was given as many bunches of grapes, still attached to the branches, as she could carry. My mother did not get paid but every evening she came home with a few bunches of grapes, which my father tied up in a bundle and hung on a nail in one of the rafters that held our kitchen ceiling. We would have enough grapes to eat until the end of the year.

After the grape harvest was over, my mother and Rita, the lady next door, went in search of chestnuts. Late in the fall the prickly shells opened up and let chestnuts fall to the ground. This is when my mother and her companion would get up early in the morning and walk for two or three hours until they reached the public forests on the high hills northwest of the town, where many chestnut trees prospered among ferns and beech trees. Each carried a small burlap bag, and as they walked from tree to tree they picked up chestnuts from the ground, sometimes having to smash open the prickly shells to retrieve the shiny brown chestnuts. After a day of work, they returned home with twenty or twenty-five pounds of chestnuts each. The next day and the next day after that, they returned walking through a different part of the forest, bringing home more chestnuts to eat during the winter months.

Gathering chestnuts was the final task our family, and many other families in town, pursued before the cold winter set in. Chestnuts were a very good food supplement. Both kids and grown-ups liked them. They could be eaten boiled, roasted, or raw. They could be dried and ground into chestnut flour, which could be used to make chestnut pies or cakes. For many mountain dwellers, chestnuts were the staple food for part of the year until potatoes and corn replaced them. Like potatoes and corn, chestnuts helped the mountain people survive, and helped our family to improve our diet.

During our first summer in Torre de Roveri, as the work in the vineyard slowed greatly, my father was offered a summer job working in the excavation of tunnels for the building of a new railroad near Cuneo in the northwest mountains of Italy's Piedmont region. He took the job, worked hard, and brought home some money. He used ten lire of his savings to buy a sofa-bed, which we put in the kitchen. I was eight and had completed the third grade. It was my first bed—I finally could sleep all by myself. (I still have that sofa-bed in my summer place on Lago Maggiore in northern Italy. My children and grandchildren are making good use of it.) My father returned to Cuneo again the next summer and was able to save a little more money.

Torre de Roveri was good to us. It was there that I completed fourth grade. If we did not move there when we did, I would probably have never continued my education. It was there that my parents were able to buy me a bed and my first pair of new shoes. It was there, on the occasion of my Confirmation, that I wore my very first suit.

Grandfather Chino

Torre de Roveri turned out to be very good for us, but also for my mother's family. The Frizzoni family, the owners of Pasta Hill, greatly trusted my grandfather, allowing him to administer their estate without much interference. He was the one who decided when the grapes were ready to be picked, when a new grape vine or new grape variety was needed to substitute for an old one, when the wine was ready for sale, when a farmhouse needed to be repaired, and many other decisions small and large. The sharecropping families held him in great respect. They asked his advice not only about farm operations, but also about running the household, discipline of children, and purchase of tools or farm animals. A group of nearby family heads would come many evenings to his house. They sat around the kitchen table and played cards with my grandfather. No money was ever involved; it was just a way to spend a pleasant evening, especially during the long winter nights. Such a peaceful scene in some other area must have been what inspired Cézanne to paint his series "The Card Players." Overall, my grandfather was very honest. He never took advantage of his position to enrich himself. He died almost penniless at eighty-four.

Grandfather Chino was born in the small village of Zandobbio in the province of Bergamo in 1858. His family owned a small farm, much of it hilly terrain. His formal education ended after third grade. According to my mother, following third grade he worked on the family farm, caring for the pigs and rabbits. After a year of helping the family, he tired of his job and he tired of eating polenta every day. One day, at the age of nine, he heard that a baker in the town of Seriate was looking for a boy to deliver bread to his customers. Without telling his parents, he ran the ten or so miles from his home to Seriate. Upon arriving at the Fosti bakery, the owner told him that he had hired a boy his age the day before. He was very disappointed, but the baker told him that a bakery in Santa Caterina, a suburb of Bergamo about three and a half miles from Seriate, was looking for a delivery boy. He rushed there and got the job. He was allowed to sleep on a mattress underneath the stairway leading to the owner's living quarters. He got up at four o'clock every morning and started delivering freshly baked bread, walking from one street to another, back to the bakery to reload, and out on a third and fourth street until all the deliveries were made sometime in the middle of the morning. His pay was just a few cents a day, but he was provided with three meals a day and a place to sleep. His parents had been looking for him, but he did not want to tell them where he was because he was afraid they would come and take him home. One day, a family neighbor, who was in the same area selling his home-grown cherries, saw him and told him that his parents were looking all over for him. He pleaded with the neighbor not to tell his parents where he was—but the neighbor did. His father rushed to see him, and Chino pleaded to let him stay at his job. The father asked him, "Why is this job so important to you?" He replied, "I like it and I can eat all the bread I want." His father let him stay. The baker was happy with him and promised to look after him.

Chino (pronounced Keeno) was the nickname for Francesco. As a kid he was called Franceschino, or Chino for short. He stayed with the baker for a few years and learned how to make different forms and shapes of bread. When he was still young, he immigrated to Switzerland where he worked in a bakery in the city of Gallen. At twenty he returned home, married Pierina, a young lady from his town, worked on the family farm and had three children (my mother was the second). Life on the family farm did not fulfill his expectations, so he returned to Switzerland and found a job in a pastry and confectionery store. He returned home three or more times a year with his pockets full of candies for the children. After he felt sure his job was secure, he moved his family to Torre de Roveri and rented a house not far from the center of town. During this Swiss period, he fathered three more children. Tired of traveling back and forth to Switzerland, he agreed to take a job with the Swiss family of Vittorio Frizzoni, who owned the former Pasta estate. The estate included a big villa with a beautifully manicured garden, and much of the hills surrounding it; the villa was the family's summer residence. The rest of the year they resided in the city of Lugano, in southern Switzerland.

At first my grandfather worked at many jobs under the direction of the estate supervisor. When the supervisor was fired under suspicious circumstances, Mr. Frizzoni appointed him to take the job, and a close bond developed between them. They treated each other with trust and respect that lasted until my grandfather died in 1942.

Grandfather Chino was very strict with all the members of his family and also with the sharecropping families—strict but just. None of the children or grandchildren addressed him with the familiar form in Italian or dialect. We all used the formal terms as we would address a priest, mayor, lawyer, or any other important person.

The trust between my grandfather and the Frizzoni family was such that it passed down to all the members of his family. Eventually, at one time or another, all of them worked for the Frizzoni. My uncle Nildo kept the gardens manicured. He also cultivated vegetables and fruit to provide the Frizzoni family with fresh produce during their summer stay. In addition, he supervised the workers cultivating the land under the owner's direct cultivation. He took over my grandfather's job after he died. My uncle Bernardo became the Frizzoni family's driver and followed them to Switzerland. My aunt Vittoria became their cook wherever they went. My uncle Giuseppe became one of the seventeen sharecroppers, and also provided the milk they needed when they were in town. My aunt Gina (Nildo's wife) saw to it that they had enough eggs and poultry meat during their summer stay. My mother helped with cleaning and babysitting the Frizzoni children. She, however, married young and did not work for them. At times she helped Vittorio Frizzoni's elderly father, Antonio, and he gave her an eighteenth century imperial dresser as a wedding present, which she took with her to Grumello del Monte. It was a valuable piece of antique furniture, recently stolen from our summer house in Lesa, Italy.

I do not know much about my grandmother, Pierina, Chino's wife. While living in Torre de Roveri, my mother and I visited her family quite often, especially because we always returned home with some extra food, mostly eggs, milk and fruit. During these visits we saw very little of my grandmother; she was always in poor health. My aunt Gina, a very strong and hardworking person, had taken over running the household, and my grandmother was either in bed or sitting in the small living room next to the kitchen. It was considered her room, and one could always find her sitting there, mostly by herself. Sometimes one or more of the grandchildren entertained her, but she would tire of them quickly. In the last few years of her life, before she died at sixty, she did not sit with the rest of her family during meal times. One of her sons or daughters-in-law brought food and a small bowl of wine to her in bed or in the small living room. I never knew what ailed her. One day, her heart stopped working and she died. I always felt she must have been a good mother and a good stewardess of the family finances. She raised six children to adulthood without much help from her ever-wandering husband. My mother always spoke fondly of her.

At the end of the summer of 1935, a few days after my father had returned from his second summer working in the mountains above Cuneo, he received a note from his brother Attilio informing him that Breda Steelworks was hiring again. He rushed to Sesto San Giovanni, and on the recommendations of his two brothers he was offered a job with the firm. It was a difficult job in the steel foundry, but the pay of nineteen lire a day was almost three times that of a farm worker. He felt the job was secure, long-lasting, and was not affected by weather or seasonality. He took it.

Seriate

My father, however, decided not to move the family to Sesto San Giovanni. At the same time that he started working there, my uncle Bernardo tired of his job as driver for the Frizzoni family, and decided to use part of his savings to open a wine bar (*osteria*) in the town of Seriate, about three miles from the city of Bergamo. He rented an old three-story building; the ground floor housed the bar, the first floor had two bedrooms and a bathroom he used for himself, and the second floor had a small apartment with a kitchen, a small bedroom, and a larger one. He was not married at the time and could use my mother's help. He invited her to come to Seriate where she and the family could occupy the apartment on the second floor of the house. My mother jumped at the idea, and in the fall of 1935 we moved to Seriate.

Seriate was a much bigger town than Torre de Roveri. It was more industrial than rural. It had two chemical plants, a fairly large and well-known textile plant, a manufacturer of farm and construction utensils, a horseshoe maker, and various repair shops. The main street through town featured a bank, various stores, four bakeries, a pharmacy, and two large eighteenth-century villas (one belonging to the Countess Ambiveri and the other to Count Piccinelli). Across from Villa Ambiveri, a three-story building of some grace and beauty, lay the Seriate elementary school. It was named after Cesare Battisti, a hero of the Italian Risorgimento (the nineteenth century "resurgence" that moved the country toward unification). My mother rushed to enroll me in the fifth grade. The school had just started a few days earlier. Thanks to our horse Nino, I was now entering the fifth grade.

The apartment over my uncle's wine bar was not much different from the one we just left in Torre de Roveri. It had the same electric bulb coming down from the middle of the ceiling in each of the three rooms, and no plugs in the walls. It had a fireplace but no running water; a fountain in the courtyard provided water. I was ten, and had a small room all to myself. With the money my father saved from his last Cuneo job, we were able to purchase a used stove. It had a cooking top with three different-sized burners, and a hole on the right side large enough to insert a copper container to provide the family with hot water. It would burn wood or coal. The stove was the most important addition to our kitchen furniture, and it came with a sizable oven. The apartment, however, still lacked a bathroom. An outhouse, located at one end of the outer corridor atop the stairs that led to the apartment, served our needs and those of the building's owner, who occupied the east side of the building. At that time, most old buildings, even in the bigger cities, featured such appendages on one or more of the outer walls. A cast iron tube carried whatever was dropped in the appropriate hole to a septic tank below. I lived in that apartment until the day I left for the United States.

The End of the Patam Family

A few weeks after we arrived in Seriate, the rest of the Patam family broke up. My uncle Valento married, found a job in Sesto San Giovanni, and settled with his family in Tagliuno, a village not far from Grumello del Monte. He and his wife Linda had four children: Maria, Luigi, Roberto, and Ubaldo. Before he reached the age of sixty, he suffered a heart attack. Two years later he had another one and never recovered from it.

My uncle Beppo was taken in by my grandfather's sister, Dola. She owned a piece of land on the hill just above the Gonzaga's castle. She really did not need any extra help. Dola was a very generous person, and I think she felt sorry for him. She realized that none of his brothers could care for him. They had large families, very little space, and no money to feed another person. He spent the rest of his life with his aunt Dola and her family. He worked at whatever he could do, with no pay except for food, a bed, and a small weekly allowance spent at the village bar playing cards and drinking wine. Once a month or so, generally on a Sunday, he walked from Grumello del Monte to Seriate to visit us. He had lunch with us and then walked back home. My father gave him some of his clothes if he had any to spare, and a few lire. I always felt sorry for him, and, if I had not already spent it, I gave him my puny allowance for that Sunday—an allowance just enough to purchase a small cone of ice cream or a slice of watermelon from one of the vendors outside the town church.

Uncle Beppo did not last long, and was the first of the brothers to die. Like his two oldest brothers and his mother, he had severe diabetes. He probably did not find out about it until it was too late. I do not think he had ever seen a doctor until he was recuperating in a health clinic, where in a short time he died.

After my uncle Valento left and my uncle Beppo moved in with aunt Dola's family, my grandfather remained alone in the farmhouse. He could not stay there because he was not able to continue farming. Moreover, the sharecropping contract with the Gonzagas required that at least three male adults be available to work the land. My grandfather had to go, but he did not have a place to go to. His first two sons had large families and did not have room for him. His sister Dola had already agreed to keep my uncle Beppo. He did not get along with my uncle Valento and his wife. Their family was also getting large. He had a brother in Bergamo, a retired train engineer with ample room for him. They were not in contact, and life in the big city would have been very difficult for him. My family was the only choice left. My father invited him to join us; my mother, after some crying, agreed to take him in. She did not mind the extra work, but we did not have a room for him. Also, she had hoped that some of the other sons would have taken turns caring for him.

My grandfather arrived at our place with all of his belongings in a two-by-two-by-four wooden box. He had two bed sheets, a couple of shirts, a pair of pants, and a coat. He did not have a penny with him. At his arrival, my parents bought a used bed, moved my bed into their bedroom, and my grandfather was given my small bedroom. When he arrived, he was already suffering from liver disease. Every month or two, his liver flared up. He screamed, took some medicine, and as the pain disappeared, his skin became yellow. The family doctor gave him some more medicine, but to no avail. A month or two later the same thing happened again. Soon, morphine killed his pain, and then his liver stopped functioning altogether. He died in his bed; it was October 1936, and he was seventy-four. After his funeral, I returned to my small room. It now contained my grandfather's wooden box. It is still with us, in our vacation home, now full of toys and games for our grandchildren.

I know little more about my grandfather Belotti and his early years. His name was Antonio, and he was born in Grumello del Monte in 1862. His family may have had some money because he had a brother who became a railroad engineer and owned an expensive apartment in one of Bergamo Alta's palaces. My grandfather had little to no contact with him or his children who attended university and had important professional positions in Bergamo. My mother and I visited his brother's family a few times, but the Patam family was never mentioned in those conversations.

My grandfather's sister, Dola, owned a large piece of property on the hill just above the Gonzaga castle. I have always wondered why my grandfather's siblings had done so well while he had done so poorly. He never owned anything. He worked all of his life, but in the end he did not even have a bed to sleep in or enough money to pay for moving to our home. I know even less about my grandfather's wife, Luigia. She was the matriarchal head of the Patam family, but I was only five when she passed away. I do not know her story. I remember she was a fairly large woman who always wore a blouse and a long skirt, almost down to her feet. Her preferred colors were dark gray and black. Her hair was combed by the wind. While she was healthy, she ran the Patam clan with a strong hand, but she could not keep it from breaking up. The grandchildren were growing in size and number, and the money from the farm was not keeping up with their numbers or their needs.

Grandmother Luigia's story must have been a simple one of work, hardship, and death. She saw many of my little brothers dying. She must have suffered greatly, as my mother did, to see so many grandchildren taken away in little white boxes. Before she reached the age of sixty, she was diagnosed with diabetes. The doctor visited but could not help her. In a short time, her right leg became gangrenous, bringing horrible pain. She screamed so loudly. Her bedroom was next to that of myself and my parents, and I could hear her screams. Toward the end, even the shots of morphine no longer seemed to help. The screams ended with her death, a relief for her and for all of us. I was only five, but I felt her pain and the relief. Those screams are something you never forget.

Grandmother Luigia's funeral was the first I attended. When I got up that morning, I put on my best clothes and went downstairs. I sat on the bottom steps and I watched what was taking place. The large doors of the farmhouse were wide open. People, lots of them, came in. One at a time, they stopped next to our kitchen table, paying respects at the open casket. There lay my motionless grandmother dressed in her best, to be seen and lightly touched by each visitor. As they passed, each made the sign of the cross. At the appointed time, the priest, altar boys, and the person carrying the cross arrived. The priest led everyone in prayer for the deceased. After the prayers, the casket was closed, and the procession with the cross, altar boys, priest, casket, and mourners, in that order, moved toward the church. In church, a funeral Mass was celebrated, and a few songs asking God to grant rest and peace to the deceased were sung. The priest gave one more blessing with holy water and then with incense, and the procession left the church in the same order toward the cemetery. The casket was laid on top of a concrete table at the entrance to the cemetery. After another benediction, the body in its casket was gently given back to the earth. At the end, many returned to our home, enjoyed some food and wine, and relaxed recounting the good memories and deeds of my deceased grandmother.

After we moved to Seriate and my father started working at the Breda Steelworks, our standard of living began to improve. My father commuted to work, and every week he brought home his salary and gave it to my mother. We spent little of it because my mother was working with her brother at the wine bar, and we could eat all of our meals there except on Sunday when my father was home. The apartment we lived in did not have much, but for the first time we had a real stove with an oven. It kept the apartment warm during the winter, and on very cold winter days there was no better place to warm my wet feet than to sit in front of the stove, open the oven door, and put my feet inside. The lack of electric plugs did not bother us, because we did not have anything to plug in. After a few years in Seriate, we were able to purchase a new kitchen table with four chairs and a credenza.

My uncle's wine bar was successful. A few years after he started it, he transformed it into a regular restaurant and added beer on tap (*Birra Italia*). The restaurant was very successful, and the name was changed to *Birreria Seriate*. By this time my uncle had married. His wife, Lina, was from Torre de Roveri. She was the second of seventeen children, and had a very strong personality. When she arrived at the restaurant she took over the kitchen. Cooking became her passion. She was very good at it and kept the job until she turned eighty-five. My mother worked in the kitchen with her off and on until age eighty-two. My father, while he was working at the steel plant, spent his spare time helping in the restaurant. On very busy days, especially during weekends, I also helped my mother in the kitchen, or my uncle at the bar. A few years later, my uncle expanded the restaurant and added a new dish on the menu, *faraona sotto cenere*—guinea hen cooked under hot coals. The dish became the restaurant's calling card. It attracted people from Bergamo and other towns. The name of the restaurant was changed again to *Ristorante La Faraona*, the name it still bears today.

My Elementary and Secondary Education

The move to Seriate was a very lucky one for me; it offered me the opportunity to complete fifth grade. Seriate was only three miles from Bergamo, the seat of the province. Bergamo had various middle schools and high schools, and I could reach the city by bike or streetcar. The move made it possible for me to continue my education, which I could not have done in our previous towns.

My fourth- and fifth-grade teachers

I do not remember much about my first-, second-, or third-grade teachers, but I do remember well my fourth-grade teacher in Torre de Roveri and my fifth-grade teacher in Seriate. My fourth-grade teacher was a very solidly built woman in her late thirties. Her hair was red, her eyes blue, and her voice strong. She was a disciplinarian, as most teachers were at the time. She liberally enforced classroom discipline by a good spanking, and if that was not enough, by a few good slashes across the body with the ever present stick. Spanking at school, at home, and even in church during catechism lessons was well accepted by the community. It was the way to enforce proper behavior.

The school in Torre de Roveri had only four grades and four teachers. There was no principal to send the bad kids to for punishment, and no psychologist to help parents or kids. It was all in the hands of the teachers. No doubt my fourth-grade teacher knew what she was doing. She must have had lots of experience dealing with kids of that age.

My fourth-grade class had approximately thirty kids, ages nine to twelve. Some were diligent, attentive, and studious. Some just wanted to complete the fourth grade and say goodbye to school, and some were there because their parents insisted they should stay in school. I was there because my parents wanted me to complete the fourth grade. I was nine, what else could I have done?

Of all the students in class, I was the one, it seemed, who received the most spankings from the teacher. I always sat in the front row because I could see the writing on the blackboard much better than from other rows. (Years later, at seventeen, I realized I needed glasses.) I was very close to the teacher's desk. Many times when I saw her coming toward me, I left my desk and ran around the classroom. She ran after me, to the delight of the other students, cornered me, and beat me up. What was my crime? I was diligent, I always did my homework, and my grades were very good. The only thing I remember that likely upset my teacher was that I helped other students answer questions the teacher asked them—a sort of reverse cheating.

Grading in both elementary and secondary education in Italy was then, as in most schools even today, based upon a combination of oral and written exams. During oral examinations the student called upon would leave his or her desk, stand in front of the class, and answer the questions the teacher asked. Since I always sat in the front row, I was near the students who were standing to be interrogated. I do not remember my motivation, but when I realized the student was running into difficulty answering a question, I would try to help him or her out with a word or a sign or in other ways. Whenever the teacher noticed my helpful efforts, she would get upset, and after her threats did not stop me, she would beat me up. Her beating did not keep me from doing the same thing the next day or the next interrogation period. I must add that the students never asked me to help them either in or out of class. As I grew up, I never resented my fourth-grade teacher for beating me up, as I was certainly at fault.

My fifth-grade teacher, a Mrs. Maffeis, was also a strict disciplinarian. She however did not use her hands. Next to her desk she had a long flat measuring stick. Her punishment was to call a misbehaving student in front of the class, ask him or her to extend the hands forward with the palm up, and she would hit both hands with the stick. One day, I do not remember what I did, but I incurred her wrath and I received my share of slashes. My hands really hurt. After the beating, I must have told the teacher something she did not like, because she suspended me for the next day. She sent me home with a note to my parents, which I decided not to give to them. The next day I went to school. I did not go to my classroom, but I stayed in the schoolyard to play marbles with a couple of other students who were also suspended or decided not to go to school that day.

Some of my classmates informed the teacher that I was in the schoolyard, and she asked me to come into the classroom. She beat me up some more, and she sent me home. This time she sent a note to my parents through a student—a girl—living next door to us. After my mother read the note, she also beat me up, and very solidly at that. I never resented my mother for doing that. For what I can remember, every kid in my neighborhood was subjected to the same treatment, some more than others. Our parents could not punish us by depriving us of certain treats. We had none.

Beating was accepted by the community, and schoolteachers made use of it often, but some of them may have overdone it. For example, one day, the year before my fifth grade, a fifth-grade teacher in the same school grabbed one of his misbehaving students and lifted him up for a minute or so outside the classroom window on the third floor of the school building. The whole town learned about this incident, and the townspeople were still talking about it one year later, but the teacher continued to teach. He had a reputation of being an excellent teacher, and he was well liked and respected by the community.

During fifth grade many of us children spent time after school at the parish recreation center (*oratorio*). The priest in charge helped us with our homework and also provided playing cards, a ping-pong table, checkerboards, and the like. The center had a full-sized soccer field used by young adults, and a small one for grade school kids. I played many games, but I must confess that I did not play any of them well. Most of the time I was on the losing side.

It was in Seriate's parish recreation center in the summer after fifth grade that I met Monsignor Angelo Roncalli, who in 1959 would become Pope John XXIII. He was born in 1882 into a farm family who for many years had worked a piece of land in the small town of Sotto il Monte in the province of Bergamo. At twenty-two he was ordained a priest. During World War I he was appointed as chaplain in the Army. After that he joined the Vatican Diplomatic Service and spent ten years as Papal Ambassador to Greece and Turkey. In 1925 he was made a bishop, and continued his diplomatic work in

Bulgaria and then in Paris. In 1953 he was made Cardinal of Venice, and six years later he was elected Pope. He chose the name John, he said, "because that was my father's name—Giovanni—and also because Saint John the Baptist was the patron saint of my own parish."

When I met him that summer, he was visiting, as he was accustomed to do during his vacation, one of his very good friends, Monsignor Carrozzì, the pastor of our parish in Seriate. They had studied for the priesthood together in the Bergamo seminary (now named after John XXIII), and had become lifelong friends. That summer he visited the recreation center and participated in some of our activities, in spite of his great girth, including playing a bit of soccer. He talked to us children in very simple terms about his job, and he had a good word for all of us. He said he would pray for us, and asked us to pray for him. Monsignor Roncalli came from a peasant family, and his growing position in the church did not keep him from showing his humble upbringing. He loved the people from his land, and he loved talking with them.

When he was made Cardinal of Venice, on special occasions he traveled to Bergamo. In returning to Venice he asked his driver, who was my aunt Lina's cousin, to stop at the restaurant. He remained in the car and my aunt brought him a cup of coffee. On one such day, he brought her a cake.

I did not have a chance to meet Monsignor Roncalli after that summer. The day he was made Cardinal of Venice I was a student at Midwestern University. The day he was elected Pope, I was at the University of Texas in Austin studying for a Ph.D. in economics, and the day he died I was teaching at Santa Clara University in California. He did not last long as a Pope, only four years. However, he became known as the "Good Pope," not so much because he carried out his papal duties well—which he did—but because throughout his life he was a good, loving, and humble person.

After fifth grade, I went through all of middle school without corporal punishment. The same was the case with my friends. In fact, as we moved from the fifth to the sixth, seventh, and eighth grades, teachers rarely used corporal punishment, and the students seldom grossly misbehaved. Grades, good grades, had become very important. The law at that time required the completion of only the fifth grade, where it was offered. After that most students did not continue school. I continued because my parents felt I was too young to do anything else.

After the fifth grade, Italian students who desired to continue their education had a choice of the type of middle schools they wanted to attend. Usually the student and parents consulted with friends and acquaintances before choosing. They could choose the *scuola media*, a middle school that would prepare them for a secondary education; or they could choose the school of *avviamento commerciale* (commerce school), which consisted of three years each of Italian, math, a foreign language, and business-related classes, which included typing, shorthand, basic bookkeeping, and the like. The curriculum was directed at preparing students for secretarial and office work. The third choice was the *avviamento industriale* (industrial school), to prepare students to work in industry.

My parents chose the *avviamento commerciale* for me. They felt another three years of schooling would be all the education I needed to get a reasonably good job. The school I attended was located in the lower and newer part of Bergamo. It was in Via Garibaldi, about three and a half miles from my home in Seriate. When the weather was good, I rode a bike. When it was poor, or the ground was covered with snow, I went by streetcar. Classes started at eight thirty in the morning and ended at twelve thirty in the afternoon, Saturday included. The curriculum was fixed—no class choices.

My first year of *avviamento commerciale* was a complete disaster. Because of the many school changes I went through and the fragmented education I received, I was not really prepared for a big-city school. I was doing poorly and was losing interest in school. Most kids I knew, including one of my best friends, had stopped at fifth grade. Most of them already had jobs. They worked in small shops, construction work, shoe repair places, bakeries, and the like. Most of them were in apprentice positions, but they had jobs. My friend was working in a small shop making wooden clogs. I thought I could do the same. That year I flunked three subjects: French, math, and history. During that summer my parents sent me to private lessons in French and math. I studied history by myself. In September, I repeated the exams in those subjects, but I did not pass one of them. I had to repeat the sixth grade. My parents insisted that I did. Repeating sixth grade was one of the good things that happened to me. I felt ashamed but I got over it. From then on, I started doing well academically. I began studying and learning.

The next three years of middle school were very much uneventful. In the middle of the seventh grade, as World War II was approaching, the army took over our building and the school was moved to the top of Bergamo Alta, in Citadel Square, across from a twelfth-century Benedictine monastery. The program did not change, but the move added two extra uphill kilometers to my daily commute and an extra hour of streetcar travel during the snowy winter.

During my middle school years, after I had completed my homework, I worked at my uncle's restaurant, helping my mother wash and dry glasses, dishes, pots, and pans. On Sundays, when some of the restaurant customers played the game of *mora*, an outlawed finger game in which each player called out the combination of fingers he and the opposing player would put on the table, I stood on the road in front of the bar and reported to my uncle if the *carabinieri* (the national police) were coming. They were easy to spot because they were in uniform and traveled by bike. The game, generally played by four people split in pairs, was fast and furious, and the finger counting was not always accurate, giving rise to major fights among the players. The fights were much intensified by the great amount of wine the players had been drinking. In some cases one or more players sustained serious injuries from these fistfights. By the time the police reached the bar, if they did, the *mora* players had stopped calling numbers and had started playing cards. A set of cards was always on standby. The game of *mora* today, at least in public places, seems to have disappeared.

During this period, besides working at my uncle's restaurant, I spent part of one summer taking a course at the local post office, learning Morse code— a potential entry into a very desirable post office job. I also spent most of another summer working as an apprentice (without pay) in a Bergamo firm, SACE, which produced electrical machinery and devices. Apprentice work was the best road to a permanent job. Neither effort, however, led to a job.

In the summer of 1940 I was almost fourteen and had completed three years of *avviamento commerciale*. I did not have a job, but I was looking for one. One day that summer, my father was returning home from work on the train and met Dr. Cesare Tombini, who had a villa and a farm in a town next to Grumello del Monte. My father and his horse Nino had done some work for this man a few years earlier. Dr. Tombini was, at the time, the director of the Istituto Tecnico Agrario of Treviglio and of the Scuola Tecnica Agraria in the same location. At this encounter, my father asked him if he had any suggestions about his son Mario's future. Dr. Tombini did not hesitate a moment. "Send him to my school. He can complete the Scuola Tecnica Agraria's two year program and become a *fattore*" (a farm overseer and administrator). My father knew that a *fattore* could live well, by working hard, and sometimes taking advantage of his position. Moreover, his father-in-law was one of them. He accepted the invitation right away, and on arriving home announced the news to me and my mother. I did not have much choice, and that September I started at the Scuola Tecnica Agraria of Treviglio.

Treviglio was midway between Bergamo and Milano. The school was about twenty kilometers (twelve miles) from my home. To get there by eight thirty each morning, I had to get up three hours earlier, eat breakfast, run to the Seriate railroad station, take the six o'clock train to Bergamo, change trains in Bergamo, arrive at Treviglio Est station, and walk three kilometers to school. Three other students and a professor of Italian, all from Bergamo, followed the same travel routine. At four thirty in the afternoon we did the reverse, and I arrived home about two hours later. It was a twelve-hour travel and school day, six days a week.

The Scuola Tecnica Agraria's two-year program was intensive and hard. Classes went from eight thirty to twelve thirty. Lunch in the school cafeteria was served from twelve thirty to one, with recreation for a half hour afterward. We usually played soccer. From one thirty to four the students worked in nearby fields owned by the school. The academic curriculum consisted of two years of Italian, two years of accounting, one year of sciences (physics and chemistry), two years of agronomy, one semester of biology, and one semester of *agrimensura* (land measurements, drainage, irrigation design, and maintenance).

The afternoon work, supervised by some teachers and upperclassmen, encompassed most of the agricultural practices of the time. It included spading (a lot of it), hoeing, planting, pruning, harvesting, cutting grass, feeding cows, rabbits, and chickens, and other agricultural and farm operations. It was heavy work, but I learned a lot, and it turned out to be extremely useful in my future consulting work—as well as providing me with a lifelong hobby.

The food in the school cafeteria was almost entirely produced on the school farm. So was the wine the students were allowed to drink at each meal (a quarter liter per person). Whatever we drank or ate was free.

Mario at age seventeen

During my second year at the agricultural school, the second World War had begun to hit Italy hard. The railroad from Bergamo to Treviglio and Milano was bombed and damaged several times. Some days we could not go to school because the train did not run; some days we were late to class. On other days the trains going home did not arrive and we had to walk six miles or so to catch the streetcar in Stezzano, which ran to Bergamo, and another streetcar on to Seriate. Some days we bicycled to school. I survived all the disasters and completed the program. In fact, I did particularly well.

At the end of my second year, I received a job offer form Dr. Zapparoli, the director of the Curdomo (Bergamo) Agricultural Experimental Station.

69

He was one of the best plant geneticists in Italy. He needed a replacement for his assistant who had been called into the army. I took the job, and for a year I worked under his direction on a project to develop hybrid corn for eventual introduction in northern Italy. The experimental station was also working to improve potato yields and to increase the strength of hemp fibers. That was my first real full-time job. I was almost eighteen, the war was going on, and food was scarce for all of us—everything was rationed. Luckily, the experimental station was of great help to its workers. The corn and potatoes we produced were distributed among us, alleviating much of our families' food shortage. The hemp plants were chopped and composted. None of us knew that the top part of the plant (*cannabis sativa*) could be dried, made into a cigarette, and smoked.

I did enjoy the job at the experimental station, but it lasted just over a year. In September 1943, the Allied troops conquered Rome, and Italy signed the armistice. Central and northern Italy were taken over by Germany, and a few months later the station closed down for lack of funds. I had to find myself a new job, and I soon did. The job was as an assistant to the administrator of a large landowner and financier, Dr. Giulio Zavaritt, whose offices were in the city center of Bergamo.

My new job did not require much expertise. I went from one farm family to another to have the head of the family sign rental, lease, or sharecropping agreements. I collected rent in money or in kind when due, and I did whatever other tasks were directed to me. One of these that I enjoyed took place at the end of spring into part of summer; on certain days, I was sent to visit Dr. Zavaritt's young cattle herd grazing on Bergamo province's Prealps. To reach the moving herd, I rode my bike to the town of Nozza, and from there walked for two or three hours following different trails until I found the herd. The purpose of my trip was to bring the two cow herders cornmeal and salt for their polenta, and on my return to replenish my backpack with cheese and butter, to bring to our office in Bergamo. Northern Italy was still at war at that time, and dairy products were precious to all of us.

Working in the Zavaritt office and observing the work of the administrator and office secretary, I felt I needed more education. I quickly enrolled at the Istituto Mascheroni, a private institution offering accelerated evening courses that would lead in two years to examinations at the public Istituto

Tecnico Commerciale for the professional diploma of *ragioniere* (accounting). It was the same diploma the office administrator proudly hung on the wall behind his desk. It took me three years to earn this diploma. Besides the courses offered at Mascheroni Institute, I had to take an exam covering three years of Latin language and another exam covering two years of civil, international, and commerce law. My formal Italian education ended with this diploma. I had legally graduated from the Istituto Tecnico Commerciale, I was twenty-one years of age, and I had a job—a job that allowed me to combine my agricultural and business training.

At the time I completed the Istituto Tecnico Commerciale, secondary education in Italy was practical and served the country well. Students who completed middle school and wanted to continue their education could enroll in a five-year program in specialized professional schools such as the Istituto Tecnico Commerciale, the Istituto Tecnico Industriale, the Istituto per Geometri (construction and housing trades), the art academy, and the music conservatory. If the student's goal was to teach at the elementary level, he or she enrolled in the Magistrali, or teaching schools. If, however, the goal was to obtain a university degree, the student enrolled in a classical or scientific lyceum. The choice of school or program was made at the tender age of fourteen. No matter the choice, after graduation the student could always enroll at a university in the primary subject of his or her professional school, or by examination in other subjects. After a student had made his or her choice of school, the five-year program was fixed. Everyone had to follow the same courses for all five years; there were no sport teams or other activities in any of the schools. Each of the programs was very comprehensive and required a great amount of work. Some students dropped out before completing the program.

Growing Up Under Fascism

I do not remember much about Fascism in the early years of my life. On October 28, 1922, the Fascists, led by their founder Benito Mussolini, marched on Rome and dissolved the Italian Parliament. King Victor Emanuel III, powerless but concerned about the social unrest plaguing Italy at the time, accepted Mussolini's coup and the new Fascist totalitarian government.

Mussolini was known as *Il Duce*: the leader, the commander-in-chief. At the age of eight, as I completed the third grade, the mayor of Torre de Roveri gave me a booklet with excerpts from speeches Mussolini had made on various occasions to the Italian people. In reading the booklet, I realized that many catch phrases such as "it is better to live one day as a lion than one hundred years as a sheep" or "it is the plow that prepares the soil, but it is the sword that defends it" were taken from these speeches and painted in large characters in black and white on the walls of many buildings, including one on the south face of our apartment building.

I do not know why, but I decided to read those Mussolini speeches aloud on the balcony of our apartment to the people passing in the street below. I am sure I did not understand anything I was reading, but I read those words with excitement in my voice and large gestures with my hands as an Italian orator would have done. I soon regretted very much that I had ever done such an odd thing for a boy of my age, because the people of the town bestowed upon me the nickname of *Duce*. As I walked past the school, to church, and every place else in town, young and old began to refer to me as *Il Duce*, Mussolini's title.

I became so upset about the nickname that I found myself constantly fighting anyone who was calling me *Duce*, especially my classmates. The main problem I encountered in all the fighting was my size: I was thinner and smaller than almost everyone in my class. I always lost. Many times I found

72

myself laying down, covered with mud and sometimes blood, in the ditch at the edge of the unpaved road that passed in front of our elementary school. As seems natural with kids, the madder I got, the more obstinate the others became, and the more beating I received.

Fortunately, after completing the fourth grade, we moved to Seriate. There none of my new classmates knew me, and none of the grown-ups had ever seen me before. I did not read aloud any more of Mussolini's speeches, and I happily lost my nickname. I did not, however, escape Fascism.

In order to register for the fifth grade, I was required to join the Fascist party, at least that's what we were told. From that time on we were brainwashed, really brainwashed. In 1935 Mussolini started the *Sabato Fascista*, the Fascist Saturday. The young people in the town were organized in four different age groups. During the school year, each group was required to meet every Saturday afternoon in the courtyard of the Fascist house, usually located next to the city hall. The members of the youngest group, from four to eight years of age, were called *I Figli della Lupa*, The Sons of the She Wolf, one of the symbols of the Roman Empire. They wore white shirts and short black pants for the boys and white shirts and short black skirts for the girls. A sash across the front and the back of the shirt embellished both uniforms. They did not do much at their Saturday gatherings. They were taught a few Fascist songs, read some Fascist stories, and learned about Fascist principles encouraging love of party and country

The next group, from eight to fourteen years old, was called *Balilla*. Balilla was a young boy from Genova elevated to hero's rank in 1746 during the French invasion of the Italian Ligure coast, when he indignantly threw a rock at the occupying troops and sparked a riot that eventually led to the French retreat. The Balillas wore black shorts, and a distinctive hat that was black, round, and somewhat sloppy with a black cord and tassel coming down almost to the chin. They were trained to march in coordinated steps as soldiers do, and were taught Fascist doctrine. They sang Fascist songs, including a song titled *"I bimbi d'Italia si chiamano Balilla"* (the boys of Italy are named Balilla). The Balilla movement turned out to be Fascism's most important way to indoctrinate Italian young people to support the party. It started in 1935, and by 1937 almost every town in Italy had a Balilla group and a Balilla house.

The third group, ages fourteen to eighteen, was called *Avanguardisti*, the avant-garde. They wore a quasi-military uniform and spent the afternoon marching and doing paramilitary training.

The young women had similar organizations. From eight to fourteen years of age, they were called *Piccole Italiane*, and from fourteen to eighteen they became *Giovane Italiane*. They were also taught the Fascist doctrine, but most of their Fascist afternoons were devoted to learning how to cook, raise children and make clothes.

The members of a fourth group, ages eighteen to twenty-one, were called *Giovani Fascisti*—the young Fascists. Through participation in the other groups and through other deeds they had earned the right to wear the black shirt. They would organize, take charge, instruct, discipline, and lead the younger groups. They were getting ready to join the Fascist military and the Fascist hierarchy.

These various groups would be required to march in uniform through the main street of the town and to the main square every time there was a Fascist celebration, commemorating the days of the founding of Fascism, the founding of Rome, Veterans' Day, etc. The marches during the Fascist regime were no different from those I later saw on television under Russia's communist regime, Hussein's Iraq, or North Korea's Kim Jong Il. Saturday meetings, patriotic songs, marches, and celebrations, ending with the ever present Fascist speaker, were all directed at building patriotism in the younger generations—a patriotism, however, closely tied to Fascism, which soon became hard to separate.

A second way the Fascist government tried to brainwash the minds of the young was to require junior high and high schools to introduce a mandatory course called the Fascist Doctrine, for one hour a week. The textbook for the course carried the same title. It was an expanded version of what was taught on Saturday afternoon, and was usually taught by a member of the Fascist hierarchy. The course explained how the Fascist state was organized, how the new economic, social, and political institutions were supposed to function, what each new institution was supposed to accomplish, and how the Fascist corporate system—an assembly of representatives from worker corporations (unions), employer corporations, and government—was supposed to eliminate worker strikes and maintain labor peace. A myriad of other information was all aimed at showing how superior the Fascist state was relative to other forms of government.

Students like myself would read and study the Fascist Doctrine to fulfill the requirement without paying much attention to the message. I am not sure how much of the doctrine remained with us even in a subliminal sense. I have never learned exactly how the Fascist state was supposed to function, but the fact that Fascism was depicted as the best system kept us from learning anything about alternative systems. A large photograph of Mussolini hung in each classroom, as in most offices, but I do not think it ever inspired any one of us to join his regime.

To captivate students, every time Mussolini spoke to the nation, which turned out to be quite often, the Fascist education ministry would order all schools to gather students and teachers in the school playground to listen to the speech. We were always happy to miss class on those occasions. I do not think any of us paid a lot of attention to what Mussolini was saying. Maybe the teachers were listening, maybe not. At the end of every speech someone would shout *"Viva Il Duce"* (long live the chief), and the audience in the courtyard would repeat *"Viva Il Duce."*

All of this attention to the nation's youth, with a certain degree of coercion, and the presence in the schools and outside the schools of Fascist symbols, was aimed at shocking the youth from political indifference to slowly embrace the superiority of the Fascist state. Winning the hearts and minds of the youth was of primary importance for survival of the totalitarian regime.

I do not know how many high school students were strongly convinced to become active members of the Fascist party. Quite a few were. At the same time, however, there developed a passive acceptance among youth of everything the Fascist government was doing, such as making strikes illegal, occupying Ethiopia and Albania, helping Franco's Spain, and even the alliance with Hitler's Germany. It was not until the last year of World War II that Italian people and many Italian youth started rebelling against Mussolini and Hitler. Many of them formed rebel brigades, hid in the Italian Alps, and fought the Fascist and German armies. As the war ended, Fascism ended with it.

Under the Fascist regime brainwashing was not limited to the youth. It encompassed the whole population. Fascist propaganda permeated all corners of Italy, and was addressed to all people. Young minds were more vulnerable and easier to penetrate than older ones. As Fascism came to power, all newspapers were subjected to censure. No editorials, no articles criticizing the regime in any way were allowed. Some major newspapers, such as *Il Popolo d'Italia*, were totally in the hands of the regime. Copies of this paper were posted in selected locations in every city of the country.

When radio became an important means of communication, the regime took control of Italy's airwaves. For all practical purposes, unless you owned a shortwave radio and could secretly listen to it, and very few Italians to my knowledge would risk getting caught, you could listen to only one news station: the state-run station. With all the media under Fascist control, what one would read or hear every day was Fascism, Fascism, and more Fascism. Half of what you could read or hear were tirades against the enemy of Fascism—freedom, democracy, capitalism, consumerism, and the League of Nations. The other half consisted of praise to the leaders of the Fascist government, their new projects, and the changes the Fascist government instituted for the benefit of the people.

Many members of the Italian intelligentsia, who could not stand the loss of freedom, left the country. Some of those who tried to raise their voices were exiled. Many others remained in Italy and kept silent. A few were imprisoned or assassinated.

Mussolini's goal was to bring Italy back to the glory of the old Roman Empire. He used many of the Roman symbols. The main symbol of Fascism, depicted in every corner of Italy, was a bundle of twigs tied together with an axe. It indicated strength in unity. Such a bundle of wood in Italian is called *fascio*, thus Fascism, and its design was very close to the symbol sculpted on the walls of the Roman Senate. The Roman She-Wolf, the Roman salute, the Roman steps, and other symbols were incorporated one way or another in various aspects of the Fascist government. Roman symbolism helped Mussolini create diversion; it helped him to get Italian minds, especially the young ones, to focus on the promise of a new Italian greatness and away from the harsh reality of everyday life.

Totalitarian governments can last for a long time. They fail mainly for two reasons: first, they fail because of a country's internal desire for freedom. After citizens satisfy their basic necessities, they begin to long for freedom—to travel anywhere in the world, to study and to work at what they like best, to write and to speak their own mind. Or second, in some cases, insignificant events trigger pent-up emotions enough for people to rebel and to bring about a government change.

In the summer of 1975, I found myself working as an economic consultant on a large vertically-integrated fruit and vegetable project in the middle of a major agricultural area of Bulgaria, then a communist country.

One evening at the Tremuntium hotel in the city of Plovdiv, I met four professional women from Communist East Germany: a teacher, a dentist, an engineer, and a junior architect. They were good friends and traveled together during vacations. Their complaint was that they could not travel outside Eastern Europe and Russia. They wanted very much to visit the U.S., especially San Francisco. Their passion was so intense that on the map of Bulgaria they used for their trip, they had crossed out the names of the major Bulgarian vacation spots and had replaced them with names such as San Francisco, Las Vegas, Lake Tahoe, Virginia City and Sacramento. As they traveled through Bulgaria, they visualized themselves traveling in the *Bonanza* territory of central California. *Bonanza* was one of the TV shows East Germans were allowed to see. Freedom to travel is what they wanted.

Overthrowing a regime internally through political rebellion is very difficult when a totalitarian regime controls the police, army, and court system, and has trained spies and enforcing thugs. But it can be done. One has only to read *History as the Story of Liberty* by the Italian philosopher and historian Benedetto Croce to learn that it has been done many times. In more recent times, however, powerful dictators have been brought down by external forces. Dictators like Hitler, Mussolini, and Saddam Hussein could have remained in power for many more years if outside armies did not eliminate them and their regimes. They survived while their territorial or political ambitions remained confined within the borders of one country. They fell when their grandiose schemes led them outside their original borders.

World War II

It is hard to understand the horrors of a major war unless you have lived through it. I was about fifteen when Mussolini decided to enter World War II on the side of Hitler's Germany, with the silent approval of our King, Vittorio Emanuele III. What a terrible war and what a waste of money and lives.

One of the first bombs to hit Italy fell about two hundred feet from our house in Seriate. It was a small bomb that created a slight crater on the road in front of our home. All the windows were shattered, but there was no further damage to our building and no injuries to any of us. The same airplane, however, dropped another eight bombs, one after the other, in a straight line. Not much physical damage was done to any buildings, but two young people, a boy and girl, were struck by the third bomb. Both died, their dream of love shattered. It was an airplane from a squadron of nine English RAF planes that lost its way toward its objective: the Milano industrial complex. It was late in the night, and I was in bed sleeping. I did not wake up as the glass from every window shattered; my mother woke me up. I went downstairs in the courtyard and joined a group of neighbors. I stayed for about an hour and then returned to bed.

From that day on it was one air alarm after another. There were three targets relatively close to us that the allies wanted to take out or impair: the Orio Military Airport, the Palazzolo railroad bridge on the Oglio river, and factories around the city of Milano. The Orio Military Airport, only about two miles from our home, was bombed many times and made inoperable for most of the war. The Palazzolo railroad bridge was bombed and more or less destroyed eighty-one times during the war, and each time it was repaired, in different ways using various materials, just long enough for one or two trains with military supplies from Germany to cross. This kept many members of the Italian Engineer Corps stationed next to the bridge for the duration of the war. After 1942, as the war intensified, the industrial periphery of Milano was bombed almost every night. Each bombing was preceded by the sound of a siren. The alarms eventually became so frequent that it was impossible for us to sleep in the house. At first, as the evening turned dark, we took a blanket or two and slept in the cornfields next to the house. Later, we decided to move back to Torre de Roveri where my grandfather offered us a room. There were no targets there worth bombing. While there, my mother and I worried a lot about my father who was still working in the Milano industrial zone at the steel plant, where he slept most every night. The move made it more difficult for me to go to school, adding at least forty-five minutes each way to my commute.

We could not get much information about the destruction and casualties caused by all the bombs. Newspapers and radio were strictly controlled by the Fascist regime. We did know by word of mouth that the airplanes were causing great damage and many casualties. The so-called collateral damage was extensive. In Italy and elsewhere in Europe most zoning laws allowed factories to be built next to houses, churches, and schools. Bombing a factory meant destroying not only the target but whatever was next to it. As a fifteen- or sixteen-year-old I could not help but visit some of the bombed areas. From the house we could see the sky light up during the bombing, as well as the smoke after the bombs had done their damage. One day, at noon, a group of airplanes bombed the Pirelli tire factory on the outskirts of Milano. One of the bombs hit a nearby elementary school. One hundred children were reported killed. Another day, at three o'clock in the afternoon, the Dalmine Works, a manufacturer of bomb casings and other war materials for the Italian and the German armies, was bombed and almost completely destroyed, just a few miles south of Bergamo. I jumped on my bicycle and visited the horror scene with a friend. Thousands of workers (up to three thousand, we were told) either lost their lives or were injured, some badly. I will never forget the sight of those workers lying on the floor inside and outside the walls of the various factory buildings. Blood and corpses were everywhere. They were all good people, and good workers. They did not ask for a war. They just did what they were told to do. What a sacrifice war imposes on everyone. It does not matter who wins or who loses; it does not matter if the war is just or unjust, everyone pays. Similar scenes occurred in many other parts of Italy.

During World War II, the Italian civilian population also suffered from food shortages. Everything, from bread to meat to potatoes to sugar, was rationed. Once a month we ran to city hall to get our monthly coupons. What we could purchase was never enough. The black market flourished. Money could buy you extra things. One of my aunts smuggled cigarettes from Switzerland and sold them at higher prices at the port of Genoa. Another aunt sold contraband sausages and other meats. She would buy long strips of sausage from local farmers, wrap them around her body beneath her clothes, and sell them in Bergamo. I myself would ride my bike to some rural area at two or three o'clock at night and bring home a small sack of potatoes. For almost two years, our family survived on cheese and boiled potatoes as our main staples. However, I never stopped going to school. There were a few absences when the trams or trains were not running, but no intentionally missed days.

All the sacrifices the Italian people made during the first year of the war were not enough for Mussolini. He wanted more. He felt sure that Germany, Italy and Japan, allied strictly together in the Axis Pact, would win the war in the end. But he needed more money to pay for it, and he asked Italian women to help. In a speech filled with large gestures and great oratory, he asked the women of Italy to show their patriotism and love for Italy by giving the fascist state their most precious jewel: their gold wedding ring. In return, they would receive a ring made of stainless steel and a certificate proclaiming their noble gesture to help Italy fight its enemies. It was hard for our mothers, grandmothers, and sisters to offer the government the most significant evidence of an important event in their lives. Besides, for many, like my mother, it was the only major piece of jewelry they owned. The call for the ring was not obligatory; women did not have to do it. However, most of them feared the consequences of not complying. Many husbands convinced their wives to do it. Married women of prominent families in town set an example by donating their rings first. There was a list of who gave, and it was easy to learn who did not. As a consequence, many women gave up their gold rings, often with tears in their eyes and a heavy heart. Some who could afford it bought a new gold ring and turned that in, keeping the original close to their heart. From that point until the war was over, all Italian women, whether they had given their gold rings or not, wore ugly stainless steel rings where gold bands were supposed to be.

On September 8, 1943, the Americans and the British troops reached Rome from Sicily, and forced the King of Italy, Vittorio Emanuele III, to sign an armistice. The government was dismantled and Mussolini was arrested. All the government powers were taken over by the Allies. For us, however, the war did not end. The Germans freed Mussolini and put him in charge, at least nominally, of the north-central part of Italy still in their hands. They formed a republic (*Republica Sociale Italiana*) with a government made up of Fascists still loyal to Mussolini. We referred to this as the Republic of Salò, the city on Garda Lake where the government was based. The war for us continued for another year and a half, a period when shortages became more acute, and bombings and civilian suffering continued.

On April 21, 1945, Germany signed the armistice that concluded World War II, and a new tragedy struck Italy. It was the cry of revenge. Mussolini, his mistress, and some of his collaborators were shot in Dongo (in Como province) as they were trying to reach Switzerland. Their bodies were hanged upside down in a square in Milano. At the same time, many young and old members of the Fascist Party, accused of taking part in this or that Fascist crime, were dragged into the main squares of cities and towns and shot to death. No proof, no evidence, no judges, no juries, no tribunals, and no processes. Someone would shout an accusation, and someone else would shoot. Fortunately, such killing lasted for only a couple of weeks. After that, order returned. In my town of Seriate, eight people so accused were taken from their homes, brought against a wall in front of the church, and shot to death by a group of partisans commanded by a lieutenant from Seriate, Dr. Fasana. Later, troubled by what happened that day, he joined a lay Catholic order and spent much time in Africa caring for the poor.

As the war ended and the killing stopped, after a short time of celebration and euphoria, we returned to school or work. We were young men and women who had seen and suffered many horrors and tragedies, but soon we stopped talking about the war. Soon we forgot about the hard time, the bombing, and the deaths. We forgot about the body parts strewn around a school, a factory, a derailed train, or a collapsed building. Some of the soldiers were our fathers or our brothers, and some returned home, but some did not. We forgot them too. My God, how easy it was for us to forget all of those things. The war? Who started it? Why? Who benefited from it? Who won? Who lost? Why did Hitler decide to occupy Austria in 1938, and then Poland in 1939? What did the Polish people do to him to merit his ire? And all the other European people whose soil he trampled? And the Jewish people? What had they ever done to him to deserve such a horrible end? What did Italy's Mussolini expect to gain from joining him? Is it the nature of dictators to be obsessed by power, and to use such power to kill, to conquer, to subjugate, to expand, and to want more and more until the catastrophes arrive and many innocent people perish with them? History is full of dictators. Why do we let them appear again and again on the face of this Earth? Is Saddam Hussein, a bloody tyrant like few others, going to be the last one? Why did he invade Kuwait? Why did he kill thousands of Shiites and Kurds and millions of Iraqis and Iranians in a futile war? Why did he not devote his time and efforts developing Iraq's vast resources and great agricultural and tourist potential? If he had done so, he would still be alive today, and the Iraqi people, all of them, would have benefitted handsomely from the richness of their country—richness that belonged to them.

Why is Kim Jong-un of North Korea starving his people to build up a strong army and produce nuclear bombs? What is he going to do with them? When will his people revolt against him?

How quickly we forget our past. Why even study history, ancient, modern, or any time between, when we so easily forget the history we make, the history we live, and the history that has just marked our lives and forcibly changed them?

With the end of World War II, a new era dawned in Italy. A few old statesmen returned from exile, and some younger ones sprang up from the returning guerilla outfits and from different parts of Italy. Many new political parties emerged. Among them, the strongest were the Christian Democratic Party led by Alcide De Gasperi, the Italian Socialist Party led by Pietro Nenni, and the Italian Communist Party led by Palmiro Togliatti. In 1945, a provisional government was formed including all major parties. A new Italian Constitution was written founded on liberty, democracy, and a parliamentary form of government, and was approved by voters on June 2, 1946. Parliamentary elections were held, and in July 1946 a new government was formed, led by De Gasperi and his Christian Democratic Party. A new democracy was born.

It was a government devoted to reconstruction and reconciliation. The war had greatly damaged Italy's social and economic infrastructure. Roads, railroads, bridges, schools, and factories were damaged, destroyed, or poorly maintained. The task was great, and the Marshall Plan helped immensely. Italy rebuilt and recovered. One lesson was learned: no matter how great the destruction, suffering, and loss, people all over the world do not give up or succumb to the forces of evil; rather, they start all over again. They easily forget the past, and they always rise up to build a new future.

Dr. Giulio Zavaritt

After a few days celebrating the end of World War II, I returned to my job in the offices of Dr. Zavaritt on Via Verdi in Bergamo, one of the most beautiful cities of northern Italy. A year earlier Dr. Zavaritt had offered me a full-time job, after a few questions about my past and my future plans. We had met in the summer of 1942 when I was an apprentice under his land supervisor in the city of Gorle, a mile or so from Seriate. Dr. Zavaritt owned a few thousand acres of farmland in Gorle and surrounding cities. He also owned a very large villa in Gorle; the villa was originally part of a fourteenth-century monastery. Attached to the villa was a farmhouse for two farmworkers' families. There were three large stables for horses and cattle, and a large courtyard for agricultural machinery and farm implements. A wine cellar and other storage rooms were part of the main villa itself.

Next to the wine cellar was the office of the farm supervisor. The office had a large old desk and a bookshelf loaded with accounting ledgers, one for each of the farmers under his supervision. The ledgers contained the yearly financial and production numbers, and also personal and family information for each tenant or sharecropper. The leases usually lasted nine years, with agreed yearly payments comprised of thirty kilos of wheat, thirty kilos of corn, and a half kilo of silk cocoons for each *pertica* (seventh of a hectare). Of course, when the payment was due, the farmer could pay the equivalent market price of the commodities. It was a good system, which avoided price speculation on both sides.

I worked during the summer of 1945 in this office, and that is where I met Dr. Zavaritt and his family, who spent most of their summers at the villa in Gorle. The villa had two stories, and was beautifully furnished with antique furniture, old paintings, and magnificent chandeliers. The dining room and two large drawing rooms opened onto a sizeable concrete terrace overlooking a three-acre garden. The garden centered on a small lake, which was fed by a creek running from one end of the garden to the other. Three men devoted almost all of their time to cultivating, planting, and harvesting a variety of fruit and vegetables for the family use, as well as growing a myriad of flowers that provided a glorious display of colors for much of the year.

Dr. Giulio Zavaritt inherited the land and the villa in Gorle. The estate had originally been purchased by his grandfather, who moved to Bergamo from Switzerland in the early nineteenth century. This purchase, as Dr. Zavaritt's daughter Carla explained to me, resulted from a historical accident not generally found in popular history books. When Napoleon, Emperor of France, invaded Italy and conquered Rome in 1809, he decided to expropriate the property of the Catholic Church that was not strictly devoted to basic ministry. This decree included the land and villa in Gorle, which at the time was part of the Diocese of Bergamo; the Bishop of Bergamo used the villa as his summer residence.

The reigning Pope, upset by Napoleon's expropriation of the Catholic Church's property, issued a papal ruling condemning Napoleon's action, and decreed that any Catholic person purchasing such property would be excommunicated—deprived of the Holy Sacraments and therefore denied entrance into heaven. The Pope's action opened an invitation to many Swiss residents who were not Catholics to descend into northern Italy and purchase the expropriated properties, probably at bargain prices. Dr. Zavaritt's grandfather was one of them.

The Zavaritt family belonged to the Valdese Church, founded by Waldo di Lione, who lived from 1130 to 1217. Waldo had become upset about many of the Pope's doings, so he defied the Pope and established his own Protestant church with very strict ethical rules and great compassion for the poor. A group of Valdese Protestants from Switzerland eventually settled in Bergamo. Some became landowners, some industrialists (especially textiles), some professionals (doctors, engineers, and architects), and some bankers. They built a Valdese church in Bergamo, and the church finances were administered by Dr. Zavaritt. Working in his office, I met many church members who would come to the office regularly to pay their share of church expenses.

In addition to his land holdings, Dr. Zavaritt owned a few rental buildings, a small button factory, a small hydroelectric power plant, and a hotel and spa resort. He also owned shares of stock in several enterprises including the Banca Popolare di Bergamo, of which he was a member of the board of directors.

Regardless of his wealth, Dr. Zavaritt was very kind and generous, and never ostentatious. He owned a car and two horse-drawn carriages, but almost never used them. He had a driver, used mostly by his five children. He commuted from Bergamo to Gorle on a bicycle, rain or shine. He walked or biked to business meetings in the city.

Dr. Zavaritt cared deeply for the poor. He made a list of the people he helped, and every Saturday morning the people on the list lined up in the courtyard of the villa at Gorle and waited for him to arrive. At ten o'clock he arrived from Bergamo riding his bike. He opened a storage room on the ground floor of the villa and greeted his poor one at a time. He knew their names and asked each one how he or she was doing. He asked about the health of their wives or husbands or other family members. He made notes in his book, and gave each person some cornmeal, potatoes, beets, or whatever was in season. He also gave them a few lire depending on need or in an emergency. When someone on the list died or stopped coming, he added a new person in need to his list. He could have helped his poor by sending someone to take care of them each week, but he insisted on doing it himself. There was joy in his eyes as he helped them.

Besides taking care of the poor on his list, Dr. Zavaritt funded much of the yearly expenses of a forty-child orphanage run by his eldest daughter, Enrica. It was housed in one of the buildings of a thermal spa complex he owned in the town of Trescore Balneario, ten miles east of Bergamo. He helped his daughter Carla, whose husband died in World War II, to adopt more than twelve children. He was also a generous donor to other charitable organizations and to his church. One of the principal tenets of the Valdese Church was to help the less fortunate through personal involvement and generous assistance. Dr. Zavaritt and his family were great believers in what the church asked its members to do. They put their money, their time, and most importantly their hearts into doing it—an example worth imitating

Dr. Zavaritt's wife had died several years before I joined his administrative staff. To take care of his children and household, he hired a governess, Mrs.

Murri. She was a highly educated person who belonged to the same church and was a widow with one son, Waldo. She stayed with the Zavaritt family until her death.

My acquaintance with Mrs. Murri was instrumental in my immigration to the U.S.

Mrs. Bea Kuteman-Harris

It was a beautiful spring day in 1948. I was working at my job in Dr. Zavaritt's office. The office was located on the ground floor of the Zavaritt residential palace. The work was light for me that day, and in the middle of the morning, as I sometimes did, I walked out of the office into the garden-courtyard of the palace. Cyclamens, daffodils, and pansies were all beginning to show their spring colors. The Prealps, beyond the city, had just freed themselves from the winter snow. A green carpet was beginning to cover them.

As I was admiring this beautiful corner of earth, two of Dr. Zavaritt's daughters (Carla and Silvia), Mrs. Murri the governess, and a fourth lady whom I did not know, entered the courtyard. Mrs. Murri introduced the lady to me as Mrs. Bea Stone from Texas. "Pleased to meet you" I said, delicately taking her hand. *"Il piacere é tutto mio,"* she answered in Italian. Nothing more after that. The four ladies crossed the courtyard, entered the palace, and went upstairs to the family living quarters. I went back to the office.

At noon, as usual, I jumped on my bike and headed home for lunch—a routine very common in most Bergamo offices at the time. At three o'clock, I would return to the office until seven or later.

My trip home was about thirty minutes. That day, however, it took me longer. I was going more slowly than usual. I was thinking about Texas. I had never met anyone from Texas before that morning. Before my eyes I was seeing big Texas ranches, cattle drives, cowboys, Texas farms, whatever I had seen in movies. I felt it would be great to see that part of the world. Mrs. Bea had a ranch, the office secretary had just told me. Maybe I would be able to see her again and ask her some questions about Texas and the ranch.

Mrs. Bea remained in Bergamo as a guest of Mrs. Murri for about a week. One morning that week, I saw her admiring the flowers in the courtyard. I walked out of the office, approached her and said, "Hello." She answered,

"*Buon giorno*" and then asked me the Italian names of the various flowering plants the gardener had sowed in abundance alongside the courtyard paths. I gladly named the plants and repeated them once more as she asked. I knew very little English at the time but I made an effort and asked her about Texas and about the ranch.

"Texas," she answered, "is a very large state, much larger than Italy. It has many farms, many ranches, many oil wells, much natural gas, and many wealthy people. People drive big cars not only on paved roads but also on dirt roads and even off roads. Texas," she continued, "is a fast growing state. New people are coming every day and they will continue to come. We still have a lot of room." I was impressed. I thought it would be a great experience for me to visit such a place—spend some time in this new world and then return home and share my experience and my Texas stories with my family and friends. That morning, I summoned all of my strength and decided to tell Mrs. Bea that I would like very much to spend some time in Texas. Was there any way she could help? I felt that I had good credentials. I could assist in running a farm, looking after a ranch, and also do office work. I felt sure that, if asked, Mrs. Murri and Dr. Zavaritt would vouch for me.

At this time, I had not explored any of the consequences that my departure for Texas would entail. It was just a thought, an idea, an impulsive feeling of youth. I was twenty-one years old. I was happy with my job, my parents, my town, and my friends. I did not want to leave any of them. I just wanted to take a sabbatical, so to speak, spend some time in a different world, and learn new things. Spending time in Texas intrigued me.

Mrs. Bea did not appear excited about my inquiry. In fact, she showed very little interest at all. She did not know anything about me, and I felt sure she had probably been asked the same question by others in her travels. However, she did not say that she would not help me.

As she started walking toward the main entrance of the Villa, she said, "I cannot promise anything. When I return home I will see if there is anything I can do." The conversation ended there.

Mrs. Bea was born in 1900 in Mineola, about eighty miles east of Dallas, Texas. Her grandfather served as the German consul in South Carolina. After his consulate service was over, he settled in Philadelphia. His son, R. B. Kuteman, at sixteen left Philadelphia for Texas. There, he worked for the family of the governor, the Honorable Mr. Hoge. He invested his savings in timber-land, married, moved to east Texas and established a lumberyard. Texas was growing, houses were being built, and the lumberyard became profitable. He saved and later bought an eighteen-hundred-acre ranch. He built a ranch house, bought some cattle, and soon after he built a group of houses which formed the beginning of a new northeast Texas town he named Ringgold. He had three children, Jim, Robert, and Bea.

At the age of sixteen, Bea married a young man by the name of Murphy. They had a daughter, Mary. Soon after, they divorced. It must have been an unhappy marriage because she never talked about it. Mary married and had a daughter, Kathy, who in turn married Temple Dixon, a senator in the Texas legislature. They had four daughters, now all married with children.

In 1925, Bea decided to spend some time in Milano, Italy. She wanted to improve her piano playing and her singing. Milano had a great opera house, La Scala, the best in the world. It also had many artists connected with La Scala Opera Company who gave private music and voice lessons. She trained with one of them.

While in Milano, Bea met and fell in love with an Italian young man who was working at one of the major Italian banks in the vicinity of the opera house. His name was Waldo Murri, the son of Mrs. Murri, Dr. Zavaritt's governess. They married and moved to New York, where Waldo found a job with one of the big New York banks. Soon after, they moved to Dallas, Texas. In Dallas, Waldo obtained a job at Southern Methodist University as a profes-sor of Italian, and Bea helped manage the Ringgold ranch. There, they had a son, Robert. A few years later they left Dallas, and after a short teaching job in Sherman, Texas, they moved to St. Charles, Missouri, where Waldo taught at Linden Wood College. He died at St. Charles shortly thereafter. Robert was five at the time and Bea returned with him to Dallas, Texas.

A few years later, Bea married Mr. Stone from Wichita Falls, a city north of Dallas and only about a thirty-minute drive from her ranch in Ringgold. She was still married to Mr. Stone when I met her in Bergamo. She had come to visit Mrs. Murri, her ex-mother-in-law and Robert's grandmother, for whom she had great admiration and great affection.

I did not see Mrs. Bea after the day I talked to her in the courtyard. A few days later, I was told she had returned to Texas. Remembering my short conversation with her, I felt that a trip to Texas would never be part of my life voyage, and that Mrs. Bea would forget about me. After all, she did not even ask for my home address. Anyhow, it was just an impulse of youth. I continued with my work, my studies, and my life. Soon, Texas was no longer on my mind.

A few months passed after my encounter with Mrs. Bea. No letter from Texas came, and I honestly expected none, when one day an airmail envelope addressed to me at the office in Via Verdi showed a Texas return address. It was from Mrs. Bea. It was very short. It said, "Dear Mario, if you are still interested in coming to Texas, we will be glad to give you a job. Signed, Bea." Simply, Bea.

It was a shock. I did not share my elation with the other office workers. I did not want Mr. Bonini, the office manager, to start looking for another assistant, at least not yet. At home that night I discussed the letter with my parents. My father was very enthusiastic about this potential job in America, as the U.S.A. was referred to by most Italians at that time. My mother did not show much enthusiasm about the whole idea. I had a good job and she did not think it was a good idea to give it up, even for a short time. Moreover, Texas—she had never heard of it, and it was so far away. However, she, did not block the idea, and wanted me to do what my father thought was best for me.

The next day I informed some of my friends of the work offer from Texas, and a few days later I gathered my birth certificate and my identity card and walked to the Italian government office in charge of issuing passports. I showed the letter from Mrs. Bea to the officer in charge and I asked for a passport I could use to go to the U.S.A. I orally translated the letter for him into Italian. When I finished, he lifted his hand, looked at me and said, "There is no way that you can go to the U.S.A., at least not for a long time. You must know that the U.S. government has immigration quotas for each nationality, dependent upon the number of people already living in the U.S. from that country. Italy's quota is only five thousand a year and there are at least one hundred thousand Italians who have applied to go to the U.S. before you." I went back to my office very disappointed. I had not told anyone in the office that I was planning to leave, and I did not need to tell them my that hope for a trip to America had vaporized.

I did tell my parents and some of my friends what I had learned from the passport office. My father was just as disappointed as I was. My mother showed some disappointment, but I felt that inside she was relieved at the outcome. I continued my job in Dr. Zavaritt's administrative office as if no letter from Texas had ever arrived. I wrote a letter to Mrs. Bea telling her how it was impossible for me to come to Texas as long as the quota system was enforced. I thanked her for her help and for being so nice.

Everything for me returned to the way it had been before I met Mrs. Bea. Texas with all of its riches had moved much further away.

Marisa

The year before I met Mrs. Bea, I joined a group of friends and acquaintances in a new mountain climbing club (the still active *Societá Alpinistica Seriatese*). The purpose of the club was to help the town youth to love and appreciate mountain sports. Because of my job at Dr. Zavaritt's office, I was somewhat familiar with the Bergamo Prealps, and I was soon appointed secretary of the club. My duties were to organize mountain climbing excursions during the spring and the summer, and skiing trips during the winter. It was also my responsibility to hire the needed buses and to manage the club finances. The members of the club would meet once a week to make plans for the next trip, to sing mountain songs (the church organist—Mr. Morris—provided the music), and to recount the experiences of earlier trips. It was a lot of clean fun for a bunch of young people, mainly from working families, most of them working or still in school.

On one of these trips I met a young lady, Marisa. What I remember is not her beauty, but that she was intelligent, full of life, and very likable. She was also the sister of two of the original founders of the club. She loved skiing and mountain climbing, and participated with her brothers in almost all the trips I organized. I soon fell in love with her—skied next to her, ate at the same table, climbed the mountains staying close, and helped her in some of the more difficult climbs.

Marisa's home in Bergamo was not very far from the office where I worked. She lived with her parents on the third floor of an elegant apartment building, and she was usually home by herself in the afternoon after school. She attended the Scuola Magistrali in preparation for an elementary school teaching degree. Many afternoons when leaving the office for an errand, if time permitted I would visit her. She was always extraordinarily kind to me, but she never showed any readiness to accept me. She never turned down

Societá Alpinistica Seriatese at Ponte di Legno in December 1947
Mario is standing fourth from right, and Marisa is second from right

my offer of engagement, but at the same time she never accepted it. I would visit her, talk to her, laugh with her, and propose to her, but I could never get a yes or no answer from her.

Marisa Onetto grew up in a family of professional people. Her father was a well known accountant with an office in the center of the city. Her mother moved with the society's best. I grew up in a peasant family. My father had a journeyman job at a steel plant. My mother cooked and washed dishes at my uncle's restaurant. I had a good job but it was only as a secretary or assistant. I wanted very much to improve. I was studying to become an accountant, like her father, and like my boss. I was going to school at night and I was getting close to my goal.

Marisa's behavior toward me indicated that she liked me a lot. I felt she had good feelings about me, but she was not ready to engage in a deeper relationship. I felt that our relationship would get better after I completed the Istituto Tecnico Commerciale and received my accounting diploma. In the

94

meantime, as long as she did not throw me out of the apartment, I planned to continue to visit, mountain climb, and ski with her.

One evening, at a meeting of the club, the Onetto brothers approached me and proposed a business deal. They had learned that one of the largest poultry farms in Milano's periphery was up for rent, and asked me if I would join them and rent the place. Given my agricultural background, they suggested that I could manage the overall activity. Carlo, one of the brothers, and the owner of a dental laboratory, would take care of all the machinery including the incubators, and also take care of sales. Franco, the other brother, a medical student, would take care of the various chicken diseases. Carlo, the promoter, worked out a lot of profit schemes with pen and paper. We would start with a certain number of chicks, leading to so many hens, which would bring in revenue from all the eggs produced, as well as sales of chickens, yielding substantial profits per year.

Of course, none of us had ever been involved in raising chickens and knew almost nothing of how to operate a business. I was, nonetheless, intrigued by the proposal. The idea seemed good; the profitability appeared excellent. The location of the property could not have been better, and my affection for their sister was still strong. I visited the place and found it remarkably well designed and well organized. At the center of the farm there were two beautifully designed buildings, one for the owner and the administration with a large egg incubator in the basement, and the other with various bedrooms for workers and members of the staff. The two buildings were surrounded by many chicken coops, each one of them with a small fenced yard where the chickens would spend their time during the day. For shade, there were apple, pear, peach, persimmon, plum, and fig trees, aligned along paths between the chicken coops. Fruit trees abounded around the houses and other open space. At the very entrance of the lot near the gate was a concrete fruit stand, where people stopped to purchase eggs, chicken, and fruit. The main chicken breed there was the White Leghorn, the most productive of egg layers. There were also a few Rhode Island and Plymouth hens. The whole operation appeared quite alluring.

I decided I should join the Onetto brothers, not only because I was attracted to the place and the opportunity it represented, but also because working with Carlo and Franco on a daily basis gave me what I believed was a good

The Valmonte chicken farm, as shown in an old brochure

opportunity to remain close to their sister Marisa. Moreover, by that time my hope for an adventure to the U.S.A. had vanished.

To join the new venture I needed two thousand lire, and I had to give up my job at Dr. Zavaritt's administrative office. I did not have any money. What I made I gave to my parents. My father, who approved of my new undertaking, gave me five hundred lire. I borrowed equal amounts from my uncle Bernardo, from the managers of the office where I worked, and from Dr. Zavaritt's farm supervisor.

As soon as I had accumulated the necessary funds, I quit my job, and with the Onettos I went to Milano and signed a three-year lease on the property. A week later, we moved to the farm and started to work raising chickens, a whole lot of chickens.

It was hard work. More money was needed. To save on expenses, I brought my mother to the place. She would cook breakfast, lunch, and dinner for all of us. My father, who was working in a steel plant not very far from the farm, would come after his job to work in the orchard, taking care of the trees.

We ate eggs in the morning, at lunch, and at dinner. Any chicken disabled in some way found its way to our kitchen. Fruit and vegetables came from the farm itself.

Marisa and her father visited us most weekends for a few hours. Her father looked briefly at the accounting books, and took a stroll around the farm and the vegetable garden. Marisa spent some time with the young chicks, talked with her brothers, spent a few minutes asking me questions about the various farm activities, and then sat down to read. Both of them had lunch with us, and after lunch they headed home. I was too involved in running the place and I never found the right time or place to ask her for something more than her friendship. I was also greatly concerned that she would not give me the answer I expected.

For the first few months, the chicken farm was running well. The coops were getting fuller. We easily sold all the eggs we produced. The incubators provided hundreds of new chicks every month, and the fruit we produced was readily sold at the entrance stand. We were not making money yet, but the outlook was good for future profitability.

The enterprise never became profitable. One day we discovered a dead hen in one of the coops. It was the chicken flu. We rushed to vaccinate all the chickens, but many died anyway. It was a complete disaster. Revenues fell. A few months later, we did not have enough money to pay the rent. We decided to give back the farm to the original owner and return home. The return was very painful. I had failed, lost my job, and had surely lost Marisa— my inspiration to join the business venture. I squandered a good part of my parents' savings. I had to return the money I borrowed—when and how I did not know. Worst of all, I had to explain to my friends that I had failed.

I slowly recovered from my first entrepreneurial shock. I learned that love and business did not mix well. I did not rejoin the mountain club. I did not try to see Marisa again. I felt too embarrassed to visit her, see her, or talk to her again. I looked for a new job. I found a temporary one as the assistant to the director of my former agricultural school. I ate and slept at the school. I received only a small cash compensation, but I was happy to have a job and to stay occupied.

Obtaining a U.S. Visa

It was the fall of 1949 and it was the beginning of the Italian economic miracle. Jobs of all kinds became available. I was not happy with my job at the agricultural school, and besides, it was only a temporary job—one I took while looking for work more in line with my studies. Milano was the center of the Italian financial system, and it seemed the best place for me to find a good job. I journeyed to Milan and visited a few banks, the largest employers of *ragionieri* (accountants), but they had no positions open. Maybe sometime in the future, I was told. I took care of a few chores for the school and headed home. A few days later, I returned to Milano on another school errand, and on my return I passed in front of the United States consulate building. Over a year had passed since my last letter to Mrs. Bea. The sight of the consulate building reminded me of Texas. I felt that there was no better time for me to leave Italy and all of my troubles behind, and start anew in a country many Italians loved and admired. I decided to enter the consulate and ask how to get a visa to enter the U.S.A. I was greeted by a kind young woman. In response to my question she answered, "The only way you can go to the U.S.A. is to apply for a student visa. To receive this visa," she continued, "you must take an English exam, be accepted at an approved university, and pass a physical examination."

At home that weekend, I wrote a letter to Mrs. Bea in Texas. I explained to her that the only way I could come to Texas was to come as a student, but to do so I had to be enrolled in a university. Could she help?

I did have all the needed education credentials. I had studied three years of English at the Istituto Tecnico Commerciale where I had obtained my accounting diploma. I was not, however, interested in continuing my studies. I felt sure that if I could enter the United States, I could get a job and skip the university. I needed money to pay back the people who had given me loans for the chicken venture.

Two months after I wrote to Mrs. Bea, I received her reply. It was short. It said, "You have been admitted to Midwestern University in Wichita Falls. We expect you soon. Bea." I was stunned. I could not contain my joy. The road to the USA had suddenly opened. I was accepted at an American university. I did not know anything about it. I was not asked to send school transcripts, take an English exam or submit any other documents. "I was enrolled," said Mrs. Bea. Her words were good enough for me. Soon the families in my neighborhood and my friends in town knew that I was bound for America—for us it was the great, bountiful country where many fortunes were made.

A few days after Bea's letter arrived, I applied for an Italian passport. A month later it was ready. It was the beginning of 1950. My next step was a visit to the U.S. Consulate General in Genova. I showed them all my letters, my passport, and my admission to Midwestern University, and I asked for a student visa. The employee who took up my case left for a moment and returned to his desk with a thick book. He leafed through the book once, then again, then a third time. Finally, he spoke: "Midwestern University," he said, "is not on the list of U.S. approved universities for foreign students. We cannot issue you a visa." I felt my world falling apart. My dreams shattered once again. Maybe I was not destined to go to America either to work or to study.

I returned home that day and I told my mother what happened. She felt sorry for me. On the other hand, she had never shown a lot of enthusiasm at the idea that her only son, after so many others had died, would leave home for such a distant place. I had lost a lot of my enthusiasm about being able to cross the Atlantic but I decided not to give up, at least not yet. "Dear Mrs. Bea," I wrote in my letter to her, "Midwestern University is not approved for foreign students, please find me another university." I mailed the letter and I waited for the answer.

One week, two weeks, three weeks and no letter from Texas arrived. By now, I was without a job. I did not feel like looking for a job. I spent my time reading, studying English, helping my mother at the restaurant, and going out with my friends at night. I waited for the mailman every day. No letter arrived from Texas. Two months must have passed when the postman delivered an airmail letter from the U.S.A. It was not from Mrs. Bea but it was from the registrar at Midwestern University. The letter said "The name of the university was recently changed from Hardin Simmon College to Midwestern University and it was approved by the State Department to admit foreign students."

The next day, I got up early, ran to the train station and jumped on the train for Bergamo, changed trains to Milano, and again to Genova. From the train station, I ran to the U.S. consulate to get my visa. The employee found Hardin Simmon College on the list of approved institutions. He then told me, "it will take some time before we can issue you a visa and when it is ready we will notify you by letter." I completed the necessary application forms and headed home. It was a very good day.

I waited and waited for the student visa. I did not have a job and I was not going to look for one. Again, I spent my time reading, helping my mother and my uncle with the restaurant, and spent most evenings with friends. During this period I also became acquainted with a young lady from Seriate. Her name was Tilde (short for Matilde), and she was the daughter of Mr. Santo Maffi, the mayor of the town and owner of the only pharmacy. To obtain my Italian passport, I needed a document from City Hall which had to be signed by the mayor. The city clerk prepared the document but the mayor was not available to sign it. He went to the office just once a week to sign papers. I was in a hurry to get things done and I decided to go to his home, above the pharmacy. His wife greeted me and asked me to wait a few minutes. They had two daughters, and one, Tilde, was sitting at the dining table working on her math homework. She was a high school junior, seventeen, had a gentle smile, and was reasonably good looking. I helped her to find the answer to one of the problems she was working on. Soon thereafter, her father came. He signed the document. I thanked him profusely. I said goodbye to Tilde and left.

While waiting for the visa, I met Tilde a few times on the main street of the town as she was returning from school. One day as I walked with her to the pharmacy, her mother invited me upstairs. I told her I was waiting for a student visa to go to the U.S. She was impressed. Meanwhile, Tilde sat at the table and started working on her math homework. She asked me a question, and I sat next to her and explained to her how she could solve the problem. From that time on my presence in Tilde's home became more frequent and I began to feel some attachment to the seventeen-year-old. I was twenty-three.

Finally a letter came from the U.S. consulate. It was a shock. There was no visa. Only a terse note: "Sorry we cannot issue you a student visa because you were a member of the Fascist Party and the McCarran Act states that anyone that belonged to the Fascist, Marxist, Communist, or Falangist parties cannot enter the United States."

Me a Fascist? What were they talking about? On September 1943, the Fascist government was overthrown, and the King of Italy signed the armistice with the Allies; I was not yet seventeen. I had never held a party position, never participated in party meetings or in any political activity, and did not join any party associations or organizations. I only did what the educational system required us to do. Enrollment in the party was required to go to school, even at the elementary level. It was automatic as far as I can remember.

Before the age of nineteen, I was drafted into the army of the new Italian Social Republic formed in northern Italy after the armistice, and headed by Mussolini who had been freed by the German SS from his prison. I spent three days at a recruitment base in Brescia. After that, I returned home and never went back. A few months later, the war was over. That was the extent of my involvement.

What was I going to do now? I felt that my dreams of working or studying in the U.S. had vanished again. The law is the law. Who could help me now? What difference could it possibly make to the U.S. government if one more foreign student did not reach their shore? Midwestern University could undoubtedly survive without me. Mrs. Bea? What could she do? Besides, my twenty-fourth birthday was coming close. I had spent over two years trying to get to the U.S. I felt it was time to give it up. At twenty-four, wasn't I getting too old to enroll at a university? What about my career in Italy? After all, I had always planned to spend a few years in the U.S.A. and then return home. That is what I promised my mother, my friends, and also, Tilde.

During the next few weeks, I started looking for a job. Job opportunities were opening up. I filed a few job applications in Bergamo, mainly with banks. I visited Milano and its financial businesses a few times. Without the right work experience, and especially without knowing the right person to pull strings for me, a job in Milano seemed impossible.

My visits to Milano, however, turned out to be very significant in restarting my quest to enter the U.S. One day there I learned that Miss Margaret

Truman, the daughter of the U.S. president, was speaking to the students at the University of Milano. I went to listen to her speech. I do not remember most of what she said, except this: "There is a need to increase the friendship between Italian and U.S. students through exchanges, especially at the university level." She promised she would work to make it happen.

That evening I took pen and paper (I did not have a typewriter) and wrote a letter to Miss Truman. "Dear Miss Truman, I am referring to your speech to the students of Milano University. You talked about increasing exchanges between American and Italian students. I have been accepted at Midwestern University in Wichita Falls, Texas. I have a sponsor (a very kind Texas lady), I have spent over two years trying to get all the necessary documents and I have not been able to obtain a student visa because of the McCarran Act. I want you to know that when Fascism was overthrown I was not even seventeen and that I have never participated in any political activities or joined any Fascist organizations except for what the education ministry required all students to do. I am very eager to continue my studies in the United States. Could you kindly help?" I do not have a copy of that letter but those words are very close to the originals. I do not remember why, but I put a recent photo of myself (the one I used for the passport) in the envelope with the letter.

Several weeks passed, and one day in late 1950 I received a letter from the U.S. consulate in Genova asking me to report to their office. I did, and was asked to see the employee handling student visas. I sat at a desk across from him. He showed me a letter. It was in my handwriting. Many words were underlined in red pencil (all of my English errors, I was told) and at the bottom of the letter, in handwriting, there was a note addressed to someone asking this person to look into my case. I could not read the signature from across the desk, and they did not give me a copy of the letter. I assume that Miss Truman passed my letter on to someone in the State Department, and from there it went to the consulate in Genova.

The consulate employee asked if I had written a letter to Miss Truman. I said yes. He also said that the McCarran Act had been modified and it was possible for me to get a student visa. The consulate would issue one as soon as I passed a physical exam. He gave me the name and address of a doctor close to the consulate and made an appointment for me for the next day. I passed

The Vulcania, *May 1951*

the exam, and finally was issued a student visa valid for attending Midwestern University. It was valid as long as I remained a student in good standing.

On the 24th of May 1951, my father and my aunt Lina accompanied me to Genova. Tilde and her mother came to see me off at the Seriate train station. My mother stayed at home crying. The train arrived. I kissed Tilde, said goodbye to her mother, and jumped on the train with my suitcases. I waved my hand from the window to Tilde and to the town that was now passing by. I spent the night in Genova, and the next morning walked up the plank of the *Vulcania*, the ship that would take me to America.

The Vulcania *and Meeting Rose*

The *Vulcania* and her sister ship, the *Saturnia*, were passenger lines that regularly took passengers from the Italian port city of Genova to New York and vice versa. It was an eleven-day trip. The ship had three passenger classes—first, second, and third class. I had a third-class accommodation, which put me in a cabin with two bunk beds on each side of the two main walls. The bathroom next to the cabin was shared with the occupants of another cabin. Parts of the open spaces on the lower decks of the ship were occupied by triple-bunk beds, which I presumed were the sleeping places for holders of special reduced-cost tickets, and probably for the lowliest crew members. I did not have a chance to check the first- and second-class accommodations. There were about fifteen hundred other passengers traveling with me on the voyage; three or four hundred of them were going to Canada to help with the harvest of sugar beets, I was told.

As I stepped on the *Vulcania*, one of the sailors took me to my cabin. I selected one of the bunk beds, placed my few belongings on it, and returned to the top deck of the ship where everyone else seemed to have gathered. It was the thing to do. From there I was able to see my father and aunt on the dock looking up to see me one more time. As the *Vulcania* slowly started moving, Italian patriotic songs reverberated on board the ship. Some of the passengers sang, but most waved furiously to their relatives and friends below. Many on deck and on land were crying, not knowing if they would see their departing sons or daughters or parents or friends again. There was much happiness in the air but also deep pain inside.

As the *Vulcania* increased its speed and distanced itself from Genova, the people on the top deck became very quiet; they wiped the last tears from their eyes and slowly dispersed, each heading to his or her cabin. I did the same. The ship's first stop was Naples. More people came on board and more provisions were loaded on the ship. We had four hours to leave the boat and see Naples. Even though I had never seen Naples, I decided to join a group of passengers and see Pompeii, the Roman city buried by the Mount Vesuvius volcano and brought back to light by Italian archaeologists. It was an impressive sight, one I promised to return to because our time was too short to take a good look at the place.

At dinner time, the passengers were divided into two groups, one eating earlier than the other. Each passenger was also assigned a table. At dinner that evening I sat at my assigned table; the next day at lunch, I sat at a different table, where a young lady named Rose and her mother Carmela happily welcomed me to sit with them. They were emigrating to the U.S. to join their husband and father who had emigrated the year before and had settled in Oakland, California.

The next day, the *Vulcania* stopped in Palermo, Sicily. A few more people came on board. Rose and I took this opportunity to visit Palermo's cathedral, the tomb of many Norman kings. After the short outing, we returned to the ship. The next stop was Gibraltar. It was night. No new passengers came on board, but a lot more provisions did. The morning after, we woke up in the Atlantic Ocean. The *Vulcania*'s smooth voyage in the Mediterranean had now turned into rough, endless ups and downs that sickened many passengers, including me. I do not remember having seen or talked to any other occupants in my cabin. Maybe there were none.

In spite of the ocean turbulence, for Rose and I the voyage to the U.S. turned out to be very much like a pleasure cruise. We ate at the same table, played the same games, associated with the same people, and spent much of our waking time together. Her mother made sure that we would not spend the nights in the same cabin. Rose was sixteen, almost seventeen, the right age for a girl to fall in love. As the *Vulcania* crossed the Atlantic, we continued to spend a great deal of time together, sharing each other's past, and talking about each other's future. I felt she was becoming attracted to me, and I was beginning to feel attracted to her. We did form an affectionate bond—a bond strong enough to remain with us even as we separated, a bond which eventually moved us closer and closer together until it turned into a fast, enduring love.

As the *Vulcania* arrived in the port of Halifax, Canada, all the sugar-beet temporary immigrant workers disembarked. Passengers going to New York

Mario at age twenty-four in 1951

were not allowed to leave, and I was very happy to stay on board. It was the last day I could spend with Rose, and for the first time since we left Gibraltar I felt good, really good. The ups and downs of the ship had stopped, and my sea sickness had magically disappeared. The next day we would be in New York; Rose and I would separate. Texas was all I could think about. As the *Vulcania* sailed for New York, the atmosphere on board had totally changed. At dinner that night many concerns were suddenly transformed into great excitement and great expectations. Many dreams were turning into reality. Passengers started exchanging addresses, invitations, and best wishes as if all of them had become instant friends, lovers, or even relatives. Rose and I also exchanged our addresses and our wishes and pledged to write to each other. Finally, in the morning the *Vulcania* reached New York. The city impressed me greatly with its many skyscrapers, so much higher than buildings I had seen, as well as with its vast expanse, and with its many cars. At that moment I felt that America was much bigger and much richer than I had ever imagined her to be.

The *Vulcania* ended its voyage in the New York harbor. What a difference between our departure in Genova and our arrival in New York. As the *Vulcania* dropped its anchors and we crowded the top deck looking at the city below, anxious to walk on American soil, we did not hear music or songs or people waving and welcoming us to our new country. Everything seemed very quiet, everyone occupied with what they were doing and where they were going. For New Yorkers the *Vulcania* was just another boat, with a new batch of people crowding its port from distant lands. Those of us on board were happy anyway. For most of us, New York was only our first stop. We were happy but also anxious about what lay ahead.

Ellis Island

As the *Vulcania* docked at the port of New York, a dozen U.S. immigration officers came on board. Each of them carried a light folding table and a briefcase. They lined up the tables on the top deck. Each officer put his briefcase on top of the table, took out a few pieces of paper, a pen, a pencil, and a small box with an ink pad and an official stamp, then sat down and started to work. They had over a thousand passengers to process, a few of them just tourists but most immigrants. I had a student visa. I had not met any other student visa holders among the *Vulcania*'s passengers, though there could have been others.

The passengers began to assemble on the top deck, carrying their hand baggage. Inside it, I felt sure, they had their most precious possessions: family photos, friends' addresses, medals of their favorite saints, and immigration papers. They did not form a line; Italians do not like standing in line. They always like to be first, to go ahead of the guy before them. Soon a single line becomes double, then triple, then an unruly mass of individuals trying to pass ahead of each other. On the *Vulcania*'s top deck they just assembled behind the ropes the immigration officers had installed, each pair of ropes leading to one of the tables.

I arrived on the deck with a small handbag, and joined Rose and her mother. We had decided to take the same train from New York to Chicago, where I would change to a train to Saint Louis, and then another train to Wichita Falls, Texas. Rose and her mother would change trains in Chicago for Oakland, California.

Because of our travel plans, I offered to carry one of Rose's two bulky handbags. The three of us went through the same immigration officer, mother first, Rose second, and I third. The two of them showed their papers. The officer looked at the papers, then at them, nodded his head, stamped the papers and welcomed them to the U.S.A. It was my turn. I showed the officer whatever documents I had. He looked at them, then at me, then at the papers again. He was not satisfied; something was missing. He spoke with the officer at the next table. They nodded at each other. He said something to me that I did not understand. I only had three years of high school English. The immigration officer was my first encounter with everyday spoken English. I did not understand him at all, and I could not utter even a simple English sentence. I felt uncomfortable, lost, and concerned. Finally, the officer told me to move to a corner of the deck and wait there. I gave Rose her handbag, kissed her, said goodbye, and walked to the corner.

I waited and waited in the corner, until all the passengers had disembarked. In the end the group in the corner had grown to about twenty or so. None knew enough English to know why they were not allowed to disembark, to freely reach the land of their dreams, and to meet their relatives or their spouses or their new employers. They remained quiet; they did not even show their unhappiness to each other in Italian, Sicilian, Ligurian, or Venetian. They were all good citizens, hardworking and smart people. Deep down they knew that things would turn out all right. They waited so long in Italy and worked so hard to get a visa that they thought it impossible that they would not be allowed to enter the U.S., and I felt the same way.

After the top deck was cleared, two officers approached the group. "Come with us," they said. We followed them down the plank and into a paddy wagon, which carried us to another side of the port. A boat was waiting for us; we embarked and after several minutes landed at an island. Ellis Island. It was June 6, 1951, four o'clock in the afternoon.

There must have been more than a thousand people there—white, black, Italian, Chinese, Latin American, and seemingly most other ethnic groups in the world. There were men, women, and children, there were old and young, people of all ages. Some of them were there for a few days, some for months, and some even for years, I was told.

As our group arrived on the island, we were given an orientation to the place, and were instructed on how to conduct ourselves. First we were led into a large room, the Great Hall. It served as a kind of living room for the immigrants who landed there, and was filled with men, women, and children of all races. Some were sitting on benches, some were standing, and

some were moving about. Many were talking, telling one another their stories. Their voices were low, almost whispering. None were smiling. They all
looked very tired; their faces and especially their eyes showed a lack of sleep.

The Great Hall, I learned, was two hundred feet long by one hundred feet
wide, rising fifty-six feet to a vaulted tile ceiling, held up by two rows of large
columns. It looked to me like a big European cathedral without the altar,
organ, and pews. The people I saw in there, I am sure, prayed to God to help
them to get out of there—as I did.

Leaving the Great Hall we entered a large dining room where a thousand
people could be fed in one shift. Most of the room was filled by long, narrow
tables and chairs, like the ones you would see today in a large soup kitchen.
The food was served cafeteria style on metal trays with partitions so that the
gravy would not mess up the salad or fruit. Next we climbed a long staircase
to a huge dormitory room. In fact, there were two large dormitory rooms,
one for men and another with a separate entrance for women and children.
The hygienic facilities were located along the wall that separated the two
dormitories. The shower stalls were open for everyone to see, and the toilets
did not have locks on the doors.

At the end of our orientation, we were shown the immigration offices to
the left of the main entrance to the Great Hall, and a foreign exchange office
to the right. We were told that Ellis Island was opened on January 1, 1892,
as an immigration station, and since 1919 had also served as a deportation
center. Deportation was a word none of us wanted to hear. Before we were
allowed to disperse, we were assigned a number. It was the number of our
bed, but also served as an identification number. Our names did not count
any more. A number was all that was needed. Mario and all the other Marios
in there were re-baptized and given a number name.

At the end of the orientation, still holding my small handbag, I walked
into the big hall and sat at one of the benches. I was very tired. I had been
sick for many days on the *Vulcania*, from the day the ship crossed the Strait of
Gibraltar into the Atlantic Ocean until we arrived in Halifax, Canada. I was
also very emotionally drained. I was supposed to have been on my way to
Texas, but was instead on Ellis Island. I had never heard of Ellis Island before
arriving, and did not know why I was there—surrounded by so many different faces that I had never seen before.

It was six in the evening. I was tired; all the offices were closed. Nothing I could do would get me out of there that evening. Even if I could have gone out, what would I have done in New York? I did not have any money; I did not know anybody. No train for Texas would leave late at night. I took another look at the Great Hall and at the people. I got up and decided to get something to eat. The dining room was open, and evening dinner was being served.

My first meal at Ellis Island was a total disaster. In Italy, my mother and my aunt Lina cooked at my uncle's restaurant. They prepared very good food, and I ate there most of the time. We ate Italian bread, pasta of all types served with the best Italian sauces, veal prepared in different ways, succulent roasts, various Italian cheeses, espresso coffee, and good wines.

In the cafeteria line, when my turn came I picked up a metal tray, aluminum fork, spoon, knife, and paper napkin. I started with two slices of white sandwich bread. I did not take the soup. It did not look or smell like anything I wanted to eat. I took some mashed potatoes, sweet potatoes, sweet peas, stew meat with vegetables, a metal cup of water, and one of coffee.

I could not eat the sweet potatoes. It was the first time I tried such food, and I could not eat them. The bread was a sure disappointment. I ate a piece of meat with the stewed vegetables, and drank the water. I left the coffee untouched; I did not like its color. I took my tray with the leftovers to the collection site, left the dining room, and went upstairs to bed. I could not take a shower. In fact, I did not take a shower during my three days and two nights at Ellis Island. I could not bring myself to show my nakedness to hundreds of people, or even to one for that matter. I did stand naked once years earlier when many young men were called up by the local military district, so that their doctors could determine our physical fitness for the army. I stood naked in line with others of my age for this ritual, but I felt embarrassed and did not like it one bit. And I liked it even less in the male dorm on Ellis Island.

I did not sleep much my first night at Ellis Island. How could I? The fact that I was tired did not help; it made matters worse. I wanted to close my eyes and sleep but my mind did not let me. I continued to wonder why I was there—in a big dorm occupied by hundreds of people who could not sleep, like me. What questions would I be asked in the morning? What answers would I be prepared to give? And if they did not like my answers, or did not believe me, what then? Did I have to go back to Italy? How? Who would pay for my ticket? I only had fifty dollars in my pocket to purchase a train ticket from New York to Wichita Falls, Texas, and a few dollars to buy whatever else I needed for the voyage. And what about my sponsor, Mrs. Bea? She was supposed to be at the Wichita Falls railroad station to meet me, and welcome me to the great state of Texas. What would she think happened to me when I did not show up at the station? Did anybody advise her of my side trip to Ellis Island? How could I sleep with all these questions for which I did not have answers?

The morning came as it always does. The dorm came to life, with the spring sun pouring through the high windows. People were getting up, and lines started forming in front of the bathrooms. The smell of bacon and scrambled eggs filtered through from the kitchen downstairs. I got up and decided not to stand at the bathroom lines. Instead, I walked downstairs to the Great Hall and used the facilities there. I did not shave that morning; I could not. I went downstairs for breakfast, but eggs and bacon early in the morning nauseated me. I dipped some bread in a bowl of hot milk and that was enough for me. It was as close as I could get to my regular breakfast. It satisfied my stomach much better than the evening dinner.

After breakfast, I walked out to the garden of Ellis Island. It was not well maintained like an Italian garden, and was not well planned and full of a variety of bushes and plants like an English garden. It was more of a park than a garden, with good spots and poor spots, but no flowers that I remember. It was surrounded by a tall metal fence, but it had a view. From the garden, I could see the Statue of Liberty. This view gave me renewed hope, a feeling that things would not be as bad as they first had appeared; I am sure that everyone who spent time on the island felt the same about this view.

I spent some time contemplating the statue. It was not sculpted by a Greek master, nor by Michelangelo or Canova, but for the people of Ellis Island it must have been just as beautiful, as if it had been sculpted by any one of them.

I returned to the big hall. I wanted someone to talk to. I wanted to know why I was there and what I had to do to get out of there and catch a train to Texas. In the hall I noticed that one person was sitting at each of the tables lined up at the side of each column. I also noticed that each table had a sign with the name of a country. I went around until I found the Italian table. Sitting there was an older man, maybe in his sixties. He was listening to a short-wave radio, and like all the other persons sitting at their countries' tables, he had lived at Ellis Island for a good while and was very experienced in the ways of the place.

From this unfortunate man I learned that a person whose immigration documents were missing, or incomplete, was required to complete them before he or she could leave the island. In case this was not possible, the person would be repatriated. In many cases it was a matter of days before the documents were in order. In some other cases, I was told, it had taken months; in some other cases the documents remained incomplete and deportation was due. For many people, repatriation was not an easy undertaking.

The first obstacle in going home was the return ticket. Most people at Ellis Island, like me, had spent all their savings and even their families' savings to get to the U.S. The U.S. government was not interested in paying for the return fare, except in rare cases. The immigrant's government was not happy to do so either. After all, these countries felt that the U.S. had provided most of these people with an entry visa and should pay for their return. Second, the immigrant had left his or her country feted by his or her family and friends with congratulations and best wishes. Everyone expected them to do well—to make a fortune. Everyone knew that America was the land of opportunity. How could he or she go back to the same family or friends? How embarrassing to have to return poorer than before. Going back was the last thing immigrants wanted to do. They asked for more time. They asked for reviews. They asked their governments for more documents. They asked for letters of recommendation. They looked for new sponsors, for new employers, and even for a spouse. For many of them, the stay at Ellis Island turned out to be short. For some of them, it was quite long.

I asked my newfound friend how to figure out why I had been taken to Ellis Island. I told him that I had a student visa from the U.S. Consulate in Genova, and that I was enrolled at Midwestern University in Wichita Falls, Texas, and that I was sponsored by a Texas family. He took down the information I gave him and he took me to an immigration office situated at the entrance of the building. We waited in line. Many others like me wanted information about their cases. We waited; it was getting close to lunchtime. I grew concerned that the office would close during lunch, as it would in Italy, and I feared that it would be late afternoon before I could talk to any officers. It did not turn out that way. We saw an officer just after noon, and my friend spoke for me. He knew English much better than I did. The officer got hold of my file, and saw that an important document was missing: the financial statement all foreign students must have. It is a statement completed and signed by a bank officer indicating that either my family or I had a bank account large enough to guarantee the payment of my expenses while in the U.S., as well as the cost of my return ticket.

No one had ever advised me that such a financial statement was required. And it was a good thing—neither I nor my parents ever had a bank account. I had still been living with my parents, and I gave my pay to them. If at the end of the month they had some money left (it was always very little), my mother would hide it in one of the drawers of the bedroom dresser, underneath some clothes. There would have been no way for us to provide such a statement. My sponsors in Texas would have been able to do so, but I do not think I would have asked them. It was a good thing I did not know, because if I did, I probably would never have come to the U.S.

"What am I supposed to do now?" I asked. My Italian friend answered: your sponsor can post a $500 bond to guarantee that they will cover your expenses while you are here. "Five hundred dollars," I said, "that is a huge amount of money." They had already sent me fifty dollars to buy the train ticket to Texas. How could I ask them to post a $500 bond? I did not have a choice. With the help of my friend, I sent a telegram to Mrs. Bea Stone. I told her that I was in Ellis Island and I could not leave the island until she posted the bond. After that I went to lunch. I could not eat anything. I could not help but think of that bond.

I spent most of the afternoon sitting at the so-called "Italian table" worrying about that bond. Would my sponsors post it? And if so, how long would it take? I did not have the slightest idea what it would entail. My Italian helper and translator gave me words of encouragement. He was sure that my sponsors would post the bond.

Every half hour or so, he walked to the office and inquired about the bond. "It takes time," he told me. "Your sponsors may not have received the telegram right away; they may have been away from home. I am sure they will post the bond and you will get out of here soon." I do not know why I never asked him why he was there, how long he had been there, and when he was hoping to get out. I was so caught up with my problem that it did not occur to me to ask those questions of him, and for that matter of anyone else there. I feel sorry now that I did not.

At five o'clock that afternoon I learned that the bond had been posted, and I was free to go. It was too late to get my papers, my bags, the boat, and to get to the New York Grand Central Station. I did not want to spend the night at a New York hotel or the railroad station. I decided to stay there for the night and leave in the morning on the first boat available. I had some boiled rice and a few pieces of carrot for dinner. I spent the rest of the evening in the garden just walking, sitting, walking more, and thinking. "Finally," I said, "I am in the U.S." The morning after, I gathered all my belongings, said good-bye and many thanks to my Italian friend, and walked to the island port and onto a boat. It was June 7, 1951, nine in the morning. A group of others from the island got on the same boat. The engines started, and in not much time we reached the Port of New York. The *Vulcania* was still there, getting ready to sail back to Italy. I left the Ellis Island boat and took a taxi to Grand Central Station. I did not pay much attention to the area of New York I was crossing. I saw high-rise buildings, and many stores and restaurants, but what struck me the most were the hundreds of black people filling the street that morning. I did not know that there were so many black people outside of Africa. Until then, the only black people I had seen were those pictured in Italian newspapers during the 1935 Italian occupation of Abissinia (now Ethiopia).

Soon the taxi driver informed me that we had arrived at Grand Central Station. I paid the driver and walked to the entrance of the building. It was a beautiful, almost majestic structure, covered with marble all over, and with many statues. I did not recognize any of the people represented in the sculptures. One of the statues was moving; it turned half around the back. Its name was Grand Dad. The name did not mean a thing to me, but I later learned that Grand Dad was a whiskey brand. The large entrance room was full of people, some coming, some going, some standing, and many directed to a large curvilinear marble staircase leading to the floor below. There, the trains were lined up waiting for passengers to take them across the great U.S.A.

One of those trains, I thought, will take me to Chicago. Another train from there will take me to Saint Louis, and another train will drop me off at the Wichita Falls train station. I did not know where the cities were. I did not know how long it was going to take, but I felt sure that I was going to get there.

After my extended look at the station, I went to the ticket office and bought the ticket to Wichita Falls. It was somewhat less than fifty dollars. I removed from my billfold the fifty dollars sent to me by Mrs. Bea and paid the train fare. For the first time since I left the *Vulcania*, I felt a sense of great relief. I felt tired but I felt great.

While I waited for the train to depart, I sat on a bench in the waiting hall. My mind was soon contemplating the vastness of the U.S. and the large state of Texas. Texas was still far away, but I knew I would get there. Sitting there alone, I started regretting not my decision to come, but to come without some time to study even the rudiments of U.S. history, U.S. geography, and the U.S. political system. Why didn't the U.S. Consulate General office give me a book, even a short one, about the U.S.A. with my visa? I was young, I grew up under Fascism, and they taught us very little about America—almost nothing at all. I told myself that my first priority would be to learn as much as I could about the U.S. and its people.

The wait at Grand Central Station was longer than I expected, but finally the time arrived for the train to depart. I got up from the bench, gathered my things, walked to the train, stepped into a passenger car, and selected an empty seat next to a window. I wanted to see as much of the U.S. as that window would allow.

The train left New York early that evening, but soon night came upon us. I bought a sandwich and a Coke for my evening meal. I ate, and lulled by the sound of the train wheels on the track, I fell asleep. I woke up as the train slowly entered the Chicago railroad station. I took my two heavy bags and the little one and prepared to descend. As the train came to a full stop, I got off and dragged myself and my baggage into the station's huge waiting room. It was full of people, many more than at Grand Central Station. All of them, it seemed, were asking questions: "Where do I find this or that train? What time is the train coming? What time is it leaving? What is the best way to get here or there?" A group of ladies from a charitable travel organization provided answers to most questioners. They helped immigrants to get on the right train, and they could speak foreign languages. I approached one of them and showed her my ticket. She looked at a map, and said, "Take the train to Saint Louis, and from there take the Missouri-Kansas-Texas train, or Katy for short. It will take you to Wichita Falls." The train for Saint Louis was already boarding passengers and I decided to get on. I selected a window seat and sat there waiting for the train to depart. A kind lady who sat next to me went back to the waiting room for a cup of coffee, and she brought a cup for me as well. I did not like it that much, but I did not want to disappoint such a generous person. I drank all of it, slowly. At the scheduled time, just before nine o'clock, the train took off. Soon it picked up speed. Chicago and all its tall and not so tall buildings slowly disappeared. Agricultural land, new cities, new factories, and new fields were appearing and disappearing until we reached a vast expanse of cultivated land. Golden colored wheat, ready to harvest, and green corn, just beginning to form its tassels and its ears, dotted the landscape as far as the eyes could see. I saw more land, wheat, and corn passing the train window, for hours and hours. Once in a while there appeared pastures, cows, a small grove of trees, a few houses, or a church to break the monotony of the landscape. From that train window, I saw American richness, American progress, and American power. A country that can produce that much wheat and corn, I thought, will never fail.

Chicago, St. Louis, Kansas City, Oklahoma City, and finally, Wichita Falls, the city of my sponsors. The train was in Texas. I was in Texas. The landscape had changed. It was totally different now. No more wheat or cornfields. Ranches and cows were all I could see. The train stopped. I gathered my belongings and carefully stepped down from the train onto the concrete walk below. I was finally on Texas soil.

A New Cowboy is Born, Almost

I arrived in Wichita Falls, the place I had dreamed of for so long, on the evening of June 10, 1951. I had called Mrs. Bea from St. Louis, and she was at the railroad station waiting for me, driving a white Cadillac. It was the biggest car I had ever seen. I greeted her enthusiastically, loaded my two big suitcases in the trunk of the car, and sat in the front seat. She started the car and drove off. The railroad station was not far from downtown. It was not, however, what I expected. It was an old, run-down building, with a bus terminal next to it, and a cattle yard. It also had a small coffee shop. It must have served the local ranches well, but I felt that more cattle than people were moving through there.

We crossed the center of the city. It had a few tall buildings, a few stores, a few restaurants, a few churches, and a movie house—nothing spectacular and nothing worth writing home about. After a short drive, we reached an upper-class neighborhood. The streets were lined with trees, the lawns well maintained, and the houses quite large, each one different from the next. The car stopped in front of a house painted in white and trimmed in blue. It was the Stone family house. It was not the most beautiful house on the block. It did not have as much brick work as most of the other houses did, and it seemed smaller than most of the houses on that street.

Mr. Jerome Stone came out and introduced himself. I greeted him and thanked him for allowing me to be a guest in his home. He did not show much enthusiasm in his welcome. He was in his fifties, round in the face and belly. He was wearing boots and appeared to be a true Texan, like the ones shown in Western movies.

It was only a two-bedroom, two-bath home. It had a small kitchen, a living room, and a dining room. It also had a family room, probably added after the home was built. This last room had a sofa bed and its own bathroom. This was the room, I was told, that Robert and Kathy would occupy when visiting Bea, and it was the room temporarily assigned to me. Bea and Jerome slept separately, each occupying one of the bedrooms. It was not the best accommodation I could have expected, but given my lengthy journey the family room appeared comfortable enough. I brought my suitcases inside the room, and a few minutes later had dinner with the Stones. I answered all the questions about my trip—the ship, Ellis Island, the trains, etc. I gave my first impression of the part of Texas I had seen, and thanked them profusely for their kindness and efforts to get me to Wichita Falls. Then I excused myself and went to bed. I was very tired, very confused, and very sleepy. For the first time in my life I had a modern bathroom all to myself. I should have taken a bath after avoiding one at Ellis Island, and after such a long train trip. I was too tired and postponed that luxury to the next morning.

I spent the next day at the house. I took a shower, ate breakfast, and put some of my things away. In the afternoon, Mrs. Bea introduced me to a few of her friends, and later I took a walk in the neighborhood. When I returned, Mrs. Bea had left the house and Mr. Stone was still at the office. I decided to start preparing dinner for the three of us. I cooked some spaghetti, made a sauce with some butter and tomatoes from the refrigerator, set the dining room table for three, and when my hosts came home they were delighted to see that dinner was ready. They sat at the table and enthusiastically ate the food I had prepared. I happily joined them. After dinner, I cleaned up and went to my room and studied my English book. That evening I went to bed without learning what kind of work I was going to do. During the day I learned that Mr. Stone had an office downtown. He had various real estate investments and speculated profitably on the commodity futures market. Even though Mr. Stone had not impressed me positively, I thought that working in his office downtown would be a good start. In Italy, I worked in commercial agriculture, keeping books, doing personnel matters, and dealing with renters of both buildings and land. Working in Mr. Stone's office was something I thought I could do in spite of my very poor English. However, that was not the job in store for me.

The morning after, I was told to wear work clothes—we were going to the ranch. We drove there in Mr. Stone's new black Buick. Soon after taking off, we left the city and entered a very desolate, dry, desert-like landscape. A few oak trees here and there provided some shade to a few tired cattle laying down to rest after long walks foraging dried grass and tough shrubs that the parched soil still offered. That was all I could see for miles and miles.

The road to the ranch was paved, with two lanes from Wichita Falls, extending to a few cities in northeast Texas and southwest Oklahoma. Mr. Stone was driving; I was in the backseat and could not see the speedometer. I felt the car was speeding, but there was very little traffic on the road, almost none. In no time at all, maybe thirty minutes, we passed the town of Ringgold. All I could see were a few houses on the left side, a small store, and a bar. It would have been very easy to pass through the town and not even see it. The ranch was a few miles from Ringgold, but it was part of the city as were other ranches in the area. The entrance to the ranch was similar to many other cattle ranches in Texas: two large posts and a wooden arch with three large letters, RBK (the Robert Kuteman cattle ranch and brand), hanging just below the center of the arch. Mr. Stone drove into the ranch, not stopping at the ranch house but continuing to drive around the eighteen-hundred-acre spread searching for the cattle herd and checking some of the fences. The Buick was jumping, hitting one bump after another, the same way a Jeep would have done. When I first met Mrs. Bea in Italy, she told me that many Texas ranchers looked after their cattle using automobiles. It was one of the things that stuck in my mind and drove me to ask Mrs. Bea for a job. After all, I never saw an Italian farmer using a car to keep track of his cattle.

Mr. Stone's car was bouncing wildly, but he did not care. Every year he bought a new Buick; that was his preferred car brand. He never thought or talked about any other cars. He loathed pickups, and had no use for them. Mrs. Bea, like many well-to-do women in Wichita Falls, drove a Cadillac. She also loved to ride horses. The picture in her home she loved best was the one of her on top of a horse wearing cowboy regalia and a lady's cowboy hat. It was the picture the local newspaper printed when she died at the age of one hundred six.

The ranch had a house, somewhat bigger than the one in Wichita Falls. The furniture inside looked old to me, and oddly placed. A fine dust covered most things inside the house. It looked exactly the way you would expect to see a house that was uninhabited most of the time and whose owners had very little interest in occupying it. We were met by the foreman, who greeted me with a look on his face that was not endearing. I did not know if he had been told that I was going to be one of his helpers—maybe not a very good one, but one who was willing to learn new things.

What the foreman needed and expected was another cowboy: someone who could mount a horse, move the cattle from one part of the ranch to another, build and mend fences, and do other ranch work. As he greeted me, he knew right away that I was not the person he expected. He did not, however, complain. I figured that some extra help was always appreciated, even if it was just good enough to keep the ranch house clean and the vegetable garden nearby watered and vegetables picked.

That day while Mr. Stone in his Buick crisscrossed the ranch looking at the herd, Mrs. Bea and I dusted the furniture, cleaned the floors, and made the bed in one of the upstairs bedrooms. In the afternoon we returned to Wichita Falls; I still did not know what was in store for me. That evening Mrs. Bea suggested that I spend a few weeks at the ranch. Mrs. Bea knew that I had been born on a farm and worked in agriculture for much of my youth. In all the correspondence we had before leaving Italy, no mention was ever made about working on a ranch. However, my interest in coming to the U.S. was so great that even if I had been told that I would have to work on a ranch, I would have still accepted the invitation. After all, a cowboy job had its own fascination.

The next morning, I packed my things and Mrs. Bea moved me to the ranch. The foreman was outside the ranch house on top of his horse. He dismounted, removed his Texas cowboy hat and greeted Mrs. Bea. He looked at me and nodded his head. I said "Good morning" and he replied with "Same to you." He seemed to have accepted my presence there and helped me move in. I feel sure that I was told his name but I have never remembered it, and I am sure he never knew mine.

At the ranch I was never told what I was supposed to do. I really did not know what I was doing there. I figured I could stay for a few weeks, learn something about ranching, and then return to Wichita Falls and work in the office. I put my mind at ease, put my things away and decided to learn how to be a cowboy. I never made it.

It was June 13, 1951. It was my first full day at the RBK ranch. After Mrs. Bea left, the foreman got on his horse (a nondescript animal), and also left.

I understood him to say: "I will see you later this afternoon." There I was, all by myself, in the ranch house. It was about noon, and nobody had mentioned anything about lunch or food for that matter. I remembered hearing Mrs. Bea the day before saying that there was food in the refrigerator. Indeed, the refrigerator was full of food. There was milk in a gallon container, there were various packages of meat, different kinds of cuts, all labeled, and there were vegetables. The freezer section was also full of packaged meat—everything produced on the ranch. Among the packages, buffalo meat seemed to predominate. I learned later that the ranch had about eight hundred head of cattle, as well as a herd of some thirty buffalo. I took out a package of meat, beef to be sure. I cut a slice and put it in a frying pan with some butter. I lit the stove and cooked it slowly. I found a loaf of American bread in the refrigerator, and sat down to eat. I did not feel like fixing salad or vegetables. I postponed preparing them for the evening dinner. I did not see any drinking water in the house so I drank cold milk. It was the first time I had cold milk with food. At home in Italy I always had hot milk for breakfast and no milk during the day. However, I found it, quite good, and it tasted much better than water.

After lunch I washed the dishes and went outside for my very first real look at the ranch. It was a very hot afternoon, a heat I had never experienced before. I ran back into the house; I could not take it. I decided to go out later in the afternoon. Inside the house the heat was bearable. In the entrance room, a combination of a family and living room, there was a large ceiling fan, which provided much relief, if one sat close enough to it. The house also had a water cooler, which could reduce the inside temperature by five degrees or so. Since I did not feel like doing anything else, I took out my English book and set out to learn a few more English words and phrases.

Later that afternoon, I picked up a cowboy hat from those hanging behind the entrance door, went outside, and walked around the house. It was still very hot. I came from a place near the mountains, with mild summer temperatures, and now I was in a flat land with temperatures far above what I had known. I was not doing a thing, yet I started sweating as if I was working very hard. The sweat ran from every pore of my face, arms, and body. I tried to wipe it from my face with a handkerchief, but as soon as I dried it out, new drops appeared. I let it flow, and let the drops fall to the ground.

Soon my shirt was all wet, as was my undershirt. I decided there was nothing I could do. I took my mind off of it and continued my exploration of the surroundings.

I saw that the vegetable garden needed water. The bean and squash leaves were wilting; I watered them. And I watered the tomatoes and okra. I picked a few green beans and a couple of squash, and took them inside the house. I washed them and put them in the refrigerator, and went out again. I saw a horse with a man riding it, followed by another horse. It was the foreman who came to see how I was doing. He was a very hardened cowboy, probably in his fifties. He and his wife lived in the small town of Henrietta just west of the ranch. I knew he was not too happy to see me at the ranch. He most likely felt, correctly, that I was going to be more of a hindrance than a helper. I sensed that from the first time he saw me, he figured that I was not going to last long at the ranch. When he saw me that late afternoon, he was convinced that my stay on the ranch would be a short one. That afternoon he was kind to me, as he was during the next few days. Maybe it was cowboy compassion.

The foreman jumped off his horse and asked how I had spent my first day on the ranch, what I felt about it, and if I needed anything. My English was still too poor to carry on much of a conversation with him. Moreover, his spoken English was not easy for me to understand. He seemed to show approval of me watering the garden. He took a look inside and outside the house. He did not give me any instruction for the next day. He encouraged me to ride the extra horse he brought with him and left. His working day was over. The extra horse didn't have a name, or not one that I was told. He was tied up lightly at one of the trees next to the house. He was not a great horse, looking old, worn-out, and tired of ranch life, but he seemed docile and impervious to what next he would be asked to do. I brought him some water in a pan. He drank it. I caressed him. He remained impassive. I decided to call him Nino; it was the only name that came to my mind. It was evening by now. A huge, reddish-yellow sunset had appeared on the horizon. The air was cooling down, not much, but the outdoors was becoming more livable. I did not think Nino was interested in taking a ride that evening, and I totally agreed with him. I sat on the bench next to the horse and let my thoughts return to the beauty of the land I had left. This part of Texas did not, absolutely not, measure up to it. I loved my mountains. Many weekends I spent mountain climbing in the summer and skiing in winter. I loved the lakes and the beautiful green colors of our mountains and plains. Did I exchange all of that for a dusty, dry place in the middle of nowhere? And with almost no one to talk to? I did not want to answer those questions, at least not yet. The sunset was greater, more colorful, and even more spectacular than any I had seen in Italy. I stayed outside until it had completely disappeared. Inside, I prepared supper. Another slice of beef, a few beans, some bread, and a cold glass of milk. It was all I wanted. I washed the dishes and went to bed.

The morning came. I got up, shaved, showered, and ate a bowl of cereal. It was the first time in my life eating cold cereal. It tasted rather good and did not require much preparation. I felt that my breakfast problem was solved. I put a cowboy hat on and went out to look for Nino, the horse I was going to ride that morning before the temperature reached 110 degrees. He was no longer where I left him the night before. He was munching some hay near a small barn not far from the house. He still had the saddle on his back, and for all practical purposes he was ready to go. He did look better than the night before, or so it appeared to me.

I had never ridden a horse before. I did not know even the most rudimentary riding steps. I took the horse next to the bench, jumped on the bench, and from there mounted the horse. I did not have cowboy boots. I wore a pair of regular walking shoes. I managed to put them inside the stirrups and I commanded Nino to go. The poor horse did not know where to move or where to go. I repeated, in a somewhat louder voice, the same command. Nothing doing. I pulled the reins, and gave a little kick with my shoes. He finally moved, straight ahead. I let the reins fall on one side and Nino started moving in circles, as if he did not want to venture out in the ranch with an idiot like me riding him. I pulled the reins again and he stopped. A good thing to know, I thought. I relaxed the reins and he moved again. He kept going straight ahead. All of a sudden, I don't know what I did but he started a slow trot. I felt very uncomfortable right away. My weight was all on the saddle. I wasn't using my legs to help my body soften the horse's movements on my back. My body was jumping up and down on the saddle. I tried to stop the horse, but Nino would not understand my commands. I felt like I was going to fall off the horse; I expected it to happen at any moment. Fortunately, one of the ranch cowboys who was working on a nearby fence saw me, jumped on his horse, and stopped Nino. I jumped off the horse and heartily greeted the cowboy, who was aware of my arrival at the ranch but had not met me before then. He was in his thirties, married, and also lived in Henrietta. From his facial expression, it seemed like we each had the same thought about the other: "What are you doing here?"

"How do you do? My name is Mario. I arrived from Italy five days ago. It is very hot here. I don't think I was born to be a cowboy." That was all I could say. I walked Nino back to the house. I left him outside the barn and went inside the house. I sat underneath the moving fan. I was beginning to feel lost. I had worked so hard and for so long to come to the U.S., and things were not working out the way I expected, the way everyone had told me it would be. First there was the unpleasant experience at Ellis Island, and now the heat and the frustration at the Ringgold ranch.

I spent a few more days at the ranch doing very little work. I watered the garden, picked some vegetables, cooked my meals, drank a lot of milk, read my English book, and took long walks around the ranch. I saw the many head of cattle, which kept the land free of any green grass or shrubs. I met and soon ran away from the herd of buffalo, who absolutely did not like me. I even decided, at the suggestion of the cowboy I met mending the fence, to visit the town of Henrietta with him.

That evening he came and picked me up at the ranch house in his old, dusty pickup truck. He drove across much of the ranch onto a paved road, and a few minutes later we were in Henrietta. It was a typical small cowboy town one saw in many Western movies. All I could see from the road were a few shops, a bar, some houses, a small church, and a small school building. We stopped at the town bar, sat down, and had a beer. Inside, I saw only cowboys, or at least they were dressed as cowboys do. I did not see any girls like you would see in Western movies. My host introduced me to a few of his friends, emphasizing the fact that I had just arrived from Italy and I was staying at the RBK ranch. They did not laugh at me, but I felt certain that none of them thought I would become one of them.

After my visit to the town of Henrietta, I knew for sure that life on the ranch was not for me. I was absolutely convinced of that. Remaining there I would starve—not necessarily of food, but of everything else I was brought up with and which I loved. The morning of the sixth day of my ranch life, Mrs. Bea arrived in her white Cadillac. She told me that life on the ranch was not good for me and that I should pack my things. We were going back to Wichita Falls. I figured that the foreman had told her that much. On the way back to Wichita Falls, we passed the town of Ringgold, the town Mrs. Bea's father had originally built. We did not stop there, and while I stayed at the RBK ranch I had never visited it. I should have not only because it meant so much to Mrs. Bea and her son Robert, but also because I would have learned more about ranch life in north Texas at the time. Now it is too late. The big 2006 Oklahoma fire traveled far enough south of the border into Texas to destroy much of Ringgold and the RBK ranch house, the place of my short experience as a Texas cowboy.

That evening, back at home in Wichita Falls, Mrs. Bea told me that in a few days she was going to Aspen, Colorado, to spend the rest of the summer. She said she owned three houses there. Two were rented and the third one she occupied herself. Would I like to go there with her? I knew nothing about Aspen or the rest of the state. That day, I felt that any place would be better than Ringgold or Henrietta. I answered her as enthusiastically as I could that I would be happy to go to Aspen.

During the next few days, I cooked the evening dinner for the three of us. I had spent a lot of time in my uncle's restaurant kitchen and had learned to cook spaghetti, meat, and vegetables. I could make salads. My cooking was appreciated. I also washed the dishes, vacuumed the floors, picked up the newspapers on the floor of the bedrooms, and mowed the lawn in front and back. I did everything I saw that needed to be done. I wanted to be sure Mrs. Bea would not change her mind. I did not think Mr. Stone had anything in store for me. As the departure day arrived, I loaded some of my things and Mrs. Bea's suitcases in the trunk of the Cadillac and left Wichita Falls for Aspen, Colorado, with a short stay along the way at Rancho de Taos in New Mexico.

Taos, New Mexico

As Mrs. Bea drove to Aspen, we passed Amarillo and Tucumcary, stopping at Taos, New Mexico, the home of the Pueblo Indians. She had a good friend in Wichita Falls, Mrs. Griffin, who owned a spacious summer home in Taos. Mrs. Griffin lived alone with Theresa, her helper and cook. She invited us to stay with her for a few days. We stayed four days that turned out to be most interesting and rewarding.

Mrs. Griffin knew many of the Taos regulars, the ones living there year-round and those like her spending the summers there. Taos was then an artists' colony—not a Bohemian one, but mainly artists who had made somewhat of a name for themselves. They were painters and writers who found a place far from the urban areas, in a desert setting, framed by small hills and tall mountains, providing a quiet, relaxing atmosphere. Many of its inhabitants, having reached a certain amount of artistic fame, had been able to purchase a ranch or a house surrounded by a good number of acres. They did not do much ranching, but they did socialize with each other—a lot, I discovered. Afternoon tea at the house of one. A dinner at the house of another. An evening of talking and drinking at the place of a third. Mrs. Griffin was invited to many of these gatherings. She was reasonably wealthy and purchased a painting or two during a summer, but she also attended concerts, poetry readings, and other cultural activities in town. She went to as many of these events as she could.

During our four-day stay, Mrs. Griffin took Mrs. Bea and I with her to a few of these gatherings. I was twenty-four, handsome, polite, and Italian. I kissed the ladies' hands when introduced. Mrs. Griffin felt very comfortable taking me to visit her Taos acquaintances and friends, even if my English was poor; I was a good conversation piece.

During the first day in Taos, we visited the nearby Pueblo village. I could not believe such dwellings existed any place in the world. The village looked like something not of this world. Built with mud and straw bricks, the houses were perched one on top of another. External ladders climbed from the first house to a second and a third one, with communal baking ovens on the ground. The houses I had seen during the trip from Texas were unremarkable, but the Pueblo houses were different. They no doubt lacked modern comforts compared to those I had seen earlier, but were very different and worthy of a picture for the folks at home to see.

It was my first encounter with American Indians. I did not have any knowledge of them, their diversity, culture, or history. In fact, I did not know much about America herself. I knew that the U.S. had won the war, liberated us from Fascism, and helped us rebuild our lives. We knew American people were good, generous and prosperous. We knew that many Italians had come to America. Many of them had done very well. At home people said, "You are going to America? You are the luckiest person in the world." That was it. America's history was not part of my immigrant knowledge.

I stood for a time looking at that conglomerate of houses, with men and women going up and down those ladders. Men and women worked at making carpets and tourist trinkets; they did not seem to care about our presence. They quietly did what they had done for many years before that day. This first contact with American Indians made a deep impression, and never left my mind.

On my second afternoon at Taos we visited Frieda Richthofen, D.H. Lawrence's widow, at her ranch house. Mrs. Griffin had arranged for the three of us to have tea at Frieda's home. Before coming to the U.S., while I was waiting for my visa, I read many books including D.H. Lawrence's *Sons and Lovers* and *Lady Chatterly's Lover*. That afternoon I learned that D.H. Lawrence was Frieda's second husband, and that his ashes were buried in a mausoleum on his Taos ranch.

Frieda, as everyone called her, received us at the entrance of her ranch-style home. She had short white hair, lucid eyes, but had borne some of the ravages of time. She was sixty-nine and still showed her nobility. I was introduced to her as Mario, a student from Italy. She offered me her hand and I kissed it while at the same time bowing and expressing my great pleasure to meet her.

We sat in the veranda at a table already prepared for the occasion. The tea was brought and served by a handsome man in his early sixties who was introduced only as Angelo, and one could easily assume that he was her *maggiordomo* (butler). As the tea was served, Frieda began asking me questions which I would be asked many times again and again. Where did I come from in Italy? Why did I decide to come to the U.S.? What were my future plans? And the like. Except for having read two of his books, I knew very little about D.H. Lawrence and I asked her why he decided to move to Taos, New Mexico, a place so far away from a European writer's stomping ground? "D.H.," she said, "was sick, and he needed sun and quiet. He found both here, and he seemed happy here." She gently excused herself and returned with a small photo album she handed to me. The photos were few. They were pictures of her and D.H. in various parts of the ranch and of the ranch itself when D.H. was alive.

The pictures were not unusual, possibly taken by some of their local friends. What struck me the most was the realization that D.H. was so much taller than Frieda. He had a beard, not very well kept. He looked very skinny, emaciated, and very weak. Looking at those photos, one could almost have guessed that D.H. was very sick, his spirit spent or not much alive. The disease, whatever it was, must have been slowly eating his body away. Frieda, on the other hand, looked full of life. She had short hair (perhaps her favored cut), a full, almost round face, and a well-shaped body. Overall, in the photos she looked very attractive. Now at sixty-nine she had lost the extra weight and a little more, but she had lost none of her warmth and vitality.

Mrs. Griffin, Mrs. Bea, and Frieda talked for more than an hour. I listened to their conversation for a while, but I could not understand much of it. I asked to be excused and walked to the flower garden in the front of the house. Angelo, who had not participated in the ladies' conversation, joined me in the garden. He spoke Italian and showed a genuine surprise to see another Italian in a place where he had seen very few, especially visiting Frieda Lawrence. We exchanged pleasantries; he wanted to know more about myself and how I knew Mrs. Griffin. I gave him a brief account of my journey to the U.S., and how Mrs. Bea and I were in Taos as guests of Mrs. Griffin. He appeared very interested in my story, and invited me to join him that evening at the Hotel La Fonda, where he said we could listen to a live band and even dance if enough single ladies showed up. I was very happy, in fact, very enthusiastic to go with him to what would be my first evening at a bar listening to my first American band, and my first chance to dance with an American lady—a young one, I hoped. "Angelo, I am a guest here, I do not know if I can leave the house. I do not even have the house keys to get back if it gets late. Please ask Mrs. Griffin and Mrs. Bea if it is possible for me to come with you to the La Fonda Hotel tonight."

I went back to the veranda as tea time was coming to an end. The ladies got up. On our way out, Frieda showed us a batch of letters from D.H. and friends she was organizing for possible publication (I do not know if they were ever published). She also showed us the flowers she loved. We said goodbye to Frieda and Angelo, who had just joined us. We got into Mrs. Bea's Cadillac and headed home. I was very disappointed that Angelo did not ask Mrs. Griffin for permission to go out with him that evening.

Mrs. Griffin's home at Rancho de Taos had a big courtyard closed from the outside by a tall adobe wall. For security reasons, pieces of heavy glass of various colors were cemented into the top of the wall. When the sun hit them, their color changed, and each piece sparkled as is it was not made of glass but of diamond, ruby, amethyst, topaz, or sapphire. The courtyard below was full of flowers and of flowering plants. As we arrived home from our visit to Frieda, I walked slowly along the brick paths of the large patio, stopping, bending, observing and trying to identify the many flower plants that graced the paths, admiring the work and the competence of the gardener. Then I heard the telephone ring in the kitchen. Theresa answered it and called Mrs. Griffin. It was Angelo asking permission to pick me up after dinner for an evening at the La Fonda Hotel. Mrs. Griffin informed Mrs. Bea of the call, and both decided it would be good for me to spend a few hours in Angelo's company, the first real Italian I met since I left Ellis Island. They concluded we could have a lot to talk about.

After a very good dinner, the best food I had since entering the U.S., all prepared by Theresa, Angelo came and the two of us drove to the La Fonda Hotel. It was a good excuse for him to leave the house. Frieda was not going to object to Angelo spending the evening with a fellow Italian, a very rare occasion in Taos. My hosts felt the same way.

We arrived at the hotel just before eight. As we entered the hotel, the entertainment had not yet started. We sat at one table in the bar. The bartender was at work behind the semi-circled bar, and a young lady, scantily dressed but not scandalously so, came to take our order. Two beers, Angelo asked. Two Coors. My first beer in the U.S. It was very cold, greatly refreshing, and different from the Italian beer I was used to.

I knew nothing about Angelo. This was my first chance to ask him questions, find out how he came to the U.S., and why he came to Taos, New Mexico. What job or jobs had he worked while in the U.S.? How is the life of an immigrant here? Is America like Italians imagine? The way I expected it to be? What chances would I have to do well and where? All of these questions came to my mind in a sort of fury. I first answered a few of his questions. They were quite common ones. He knew Bergamo and seemed very pleased to meet me and talk to me in Italian. Then he spent most of the next thirty minutes or so talking about himself as he would have talked to a friend rather than a new acquaintance.

Angelo Ravagli was sixty-one, born in a small town in the Emilia-Romagna region of north-central Italy. At twenty he joined the Italian army. He attended officer school and a few years later was appointed captain of the *Bersaglieri* (a division of the Italian army that distinguished itself with great courage and fought with valor in both World Wars). At twenty-eight he married. Soon thereafter, he bought a modest three-story villa surrounded by a small park in the city of Spotorno on the Italian Riviera.

In 1926, he rented part of the villa to D.H. Lawrence and his wife Frieda. Lawrence, he said, "was sick, something was eating at his lungs. He had left Germany in search of more sunshine and quiet, and had brief stays in different Italian cities before arriving in Spotorno. I was thirty-four at that time, Lawrence was forty, and Frieda a little bit older at forty-two. One day I met Frieda in the garden. We met again and again. We walked, talked, and became close friends. I was young, handsome, and I loved women. Frieda was attractive, full of life, and still in her prime. We became attracted to each other.

"D.H.," he continued, "became aware of Frieda's extra friendship. His health was not improving, if anything, it was deteriorating. He felt his body weakening. He distrusted me, and one day, he decided to get away, far away from Spotorno. He and Frieda visited a few places and eventually moved to Taos. Mrs. Mable Dodge gave them two hundred acres of land. In one corner of the ranch, the closest to Taos, they built their home, a ranch-style home.

Taos's sun and dry air, however, did not cure him. His disease continued to eat at him. In 1930, on a voyage to France, he died in Vence, near Marseille in southern France. He was buried there. He was forty-six."

The bar was beginning to show some life—mainly local people, with jeans and cowboy hats. A few ladies talked and laughed, but no band or music yet.

"I learned of D.H.'s death from an Italian newspaper," continued Angelo. "I wrote a letter to Frieda. I expressed my condolences and invited her to come to Spotorno. She did. I was in love with her. I promised my wife I would send her some money every month for her and the two daughters, and I left for Taos with Frieda. I obtained a divorce in New Mexico and we married."

Angelo had not finished his story but I felt he did not have much more to add. The small band, four musicians in all, was getting ready to play. Angelo was eager to dance, but the single ladies were still in short supply. Angelo ordered two more beers and finished what more he wanted to tell me. "Tomorrow, if we can get together, I would like to show you the mausoleum I built, all of it with my hands. I personally picked up D.H.'s ashes in Marseille, and built a small sarcophagus for him. I used cement. To be sure that he would stay there, I mixed his ashes in the cement. Poor D.H. He was an excellent writer, and people will remember him. What a pity that his strong mind was in such a weak body." He lifted his glass full of beer in a salute to D.H. Lawrence. I followed suit.

The band was now playing, and a few couples were dancing. Angelo introduced me to one of the young ladies seated at the bar. He asked her if she would dance with me, and she agreed. He asked another lady to dance with him. The four of us reached the dance floor. He started dancing, and at first I just watched. What strong and fine dancer he was. At sixty-one he was clearly beating a very young man on the dance floor. He would turn, swirl, bend, and turn the young lady around again and again. He was having fun, and knew some of the people there. I joined the dance. The music I knew was not what they were playing at the La Fonda Hotel in Taos. I was not a good dancer, and have never been one—but I have never refused to dance when the occasion presented itself, as on that evening. So I danced or, at least moved around following the music as best as I could. I apologized profusely to the young lady who was dancing with me for not fitting the Italian mold, but I did enjoy myself. It was my first decent bar in the U.S., my first American girl, first American music, and first U.S. dance. After Ellis Island and Ringgold, Taos looked so much better. At eleven o'clock Angelo drove me to Mrs. Griffin's home. Theresa was up waiting for me. Ten minutes later I was sound asleep.

I never did see D.H.'s mausoleum. Angelo called the next morning but the ladies had already made different plans for the day. In the morning we visited a studio. There were paintings all over the place, large, medium, and small. Almost all depicted Western landscapes: beautiful sunsets, horses mounted by colorful cowboys and Indians, vast deserts with sage brush, and barely a tree. I was introduced to the painter—Russell, I think, was his name. Mrs. Griffin had two of his paintings in her living room. (On the way to Taos from Wichita Falls, Mrs. Bea stopped at a college, I think Canyon College, just outside Amarillo, to visit the college museum; similar landscapes, I believe from the same painter, covered much of one wall). The ladies greeted the painter, introduced me, and asked to see some of his latest works. They did not buy; we left.

That evening we were invited to the home of Mable Dodge. I was told that Mable was the heir to the Dodge automobile fortune, that Mr. Dodge had died, and she had decided to spend most of her time at their home in Taos. I was also told she had remarried and that her new husband, her fourth, was named Tony Luhan. She had a cook, chauffeur, and gardener, and was well known in the town where she had founded a literary colony and had given many cocktail and dinner parties.

The Mable Dodge house was one of the largest I had seen since my arrival in the U.S. It had a large garden with a swimming pool, and a park with abundant trees and flowers. Much of the property was protected by an adobe wall.

As we entered the house, Mable greeted us with enthusiasm and a fairly loud voice. Again I was introduced in the usual way and I kissed her hand as I was getting accustomed to do. She then took us around the big living room and introduced us to various guests who had already arrived. There was the painter we had seen earlier that day, and a lady friend of the painter who was talking with another painter, who in turn was introduced to me as Georgia O'Keefe. Georgia did not impress me at all at the time, even though Mrs. Griffin had one of her paintings in the dining room, and later when

I returned to Wichita Falls from Aspen, I saw one of her paintings in Mrs. Bea's home. Georgia O'Keefe, Mrs. Griffin told me later, was a well known American painter and lived in a small ranch-style home in a hilly and rocky part of the desert not far from Taos, and was often a guest of Mable Dodge. As guests were mingling around, and new ones were arriving, I was left alone and I walked around introducing myself to various persons, whose names I totally lost right after were told to me. I was hoping to see Angelo and Frieda at the party, but they never arrived. I joined Mrs. Bea, talking to Tony, Mable's husband. He was bigger than any of the other men in the room; his Indian features set him apart. Mrs. Bea introduced me to him, and told me that before his marriage to Mable Dodge he had been the head of the Taos Pueblo Indians. She then left me for another guest. I did not know what to say to Tony or what to ask of him. He must have felt the same way. "Hi Tony," the guests would tell him when they came through the door, "How are you today?" He would answer: "Hi, I am fine. How are you?" He was certainly not the center of attention at the party. I felt at the moment that he was just like me. Out of place in that crowd. We were not fitting in at all. The centers of attention were Mable, who was greeting people and giving orders to the help, and Georgia O'Keefe, who had come to the party with a lady friend. The landscape painter was the loudest of the bunch, but I could not make heads or tails of what he was talking about.

I don't know what the occasion was for the party—whose birthday, anniversary, accomplishment, or new summer arrival. I was happy to be among the invited guests. It was my first party in the U.S., my first hard drink, my first encounter with American artists, and my first glimpse at American success. I did not fit in with the crowd, but was not bored or disappointed. I just wished my English had not been so poor so that I could have conversed with Mable, Georgia, Tony, and other guests.

Dinner was served, buffet style. Afterwards, coffee was served, but I did not take any. I just could not drink American coffee—not yet. A little later we said our thanks and goodbyes, and returned to Mrs. Griffin's home.

The next morning we had coffee at the home of Giselle, another friend of Mrs. Griffin. Giselle was also a painter, and lived in Taos year-round. I had seen her the evening before at Mable's party but had not talked with her. She wanted to know my name again, and asked where I came from in Italy, and why the U.S.? She said she had been in Italy, but had not visited Bergamo. I told her that she missed the best city in the country.

Giselle, as she signed her paintings, was different from the rest of Taos art colony. She was dressed in Mexican attire, Indian jewelry, and homemade slippers. She served coffee and then showed us some of her works. Most of her paintings were postcard size—children, animals, flowers, prairies, and houses and the like. She painted the originals and sold them to greeting-card companies. She also had some regular-size paintings, all featuring the same subjects she used for the cards. I do not know if she ever made it big, but I thought she had great talent. Mrs. Griffin knew art. She had a good collection, including some of Giselle's original works.

That afternoon, Bea and I packed our suitcases, loaded them into the Cadillac, and early the next morning left Taos for Aspen, Colorado. Years later I returned twice to Taos, but I was not able to see Angelo again. I was told that Frieda died, Angelo buried her next to D.H. in the mausoleum he had built, and then he returned to Italy.

Aspen, Colorado

From Rancho de Taos, Mrs. Bea drove the Cadillac through Colorado Springs, Pueblo, Grand Junction, Glenwood Springs, and finally to Aspen. Aspen was my kind of place: cool air, green meadows, spectacular mountains, and thousands of aspen trees. It was a delightful place to be in the summer of 1951. The city of Aspen, an old silver-mining town, was at the start of its transformation into a summer resort town and winter wonderland.

As we arrived in Aspen, Mrs. Bea stopped in front of a fairly modest house. It had only two bedrooms, one for Mrs. Bea, and one with two bunk beds— one to be used by myself and the other by Mrs. Bea's granddaughter, Kathy, when she came visiting. The house had a kitchen, living-dining room, and one bathroom for everyone to share. It was not ideal, but comfortable. For me, Aspen was a paradise when compared to Ringgold's RBK ranch. I chose the lower bunk bed and put my things in the closet. After that I took a walk in town.

At the time, Aspen had only one hotel: the Jerome Hotel, built during the silver-mining boom. It was a brick building, similar to other buildings in town. It closed for a time when the silver mines in the area failed, but it was later refurbished and reopened as Aspen began to attract tourists. Besides the Jerome Hotel restaurant, Aspen had three other reputable restaurants. They were the Red Onion, the Mario Italian Restaurant, and the Kopper Kettle. Aspen also had the Pickwick County Bank, the City Hall, a few shops lined up along the city's two main streets, and a railroad station with train service from Aspen to Glenwood Springs, possibly left over from the mining era. Aspen also had a bar—a piano bar, with ragtime music pouring into the street. Standing in front of the Jerome Hotel and looking up toward the mountains, I saw the Aspen ski lift, built some years earlier. Mrs. Bea's son Robert was one of the Aspen Ski Company founders, and he had a small apartment in town.

Besides the ski lift, two notable organizations had been founded not long before my visit to Aspen: the Aspen Summer Music School and Music Festival, and the Aspen Institute. Each of these were instrumental in putting Aspen back on the map.

The Aspen Institute was sponsored and partly founded by Walter Pepky, the CEO and chairman of the board of the Continental Can Company, as well as owner of the newly restructured Jerome Hotel. That summer, the institute organized a series of evening lectures delivered by some of the best U.S. minds. The lectures, according to Mrs. Bea, were well attended and of great interest. The Aspen Institute is still alive today and has expanded to other cities including New York and Venice, Italy.

The Aspen Music School attracted many U.S. and foreign music teachers and performers, as well as a large number of talented college students who came to Aspen from throughout the country to improve their music skills. On Wednesday nights and Sunday afternoons, the school provided the community and tourists with great symphonic concerts. They were held under a big tent in a large meadow in the southwest part of the city. The performances that summer were always sold out. I could not attend the institute's lectures because I worked at night, but I did enjoy going to the Sunday afternoon concerts. Mrs. Bea took me with her and paid for my ticket.

Soon after arriving in Aspen and settling down at Mrs. Bea's house, I started worrying about a job. I walked the town, saw most of its buildings, stores, bank, and restaurants, and I concluded that there was no job for me in Aspen that would even come close to what I was trained to do. I did not have any money except for what you may call a small allowance once in a while from Mrs. Bea. However, it was very embarrassing at twenty-four years of age to take money from her. I needed a job. Even one with little pay would do.

Mrs. Bea's house was across the street on the left side of the Jerome Hotel. I decided to try there first. I walked in the back of the building. A man dressed in white was sitting outside the back door of the hotel kitchen. He was the pastry cook, a German. I asked him if there was a job available. He brought me to the chef, Arnold, who came from Switzerland and spoke English, French, German, and some Italian. He offered me a job as a kitchen helper—twenty-five dollars a week. I accepted. I did not have a social security number and was unaware that a student visa did not allow me to work. He hired me anyway. My pay was entered in the books of the hotel as the cost of a box of vegetables, or some trout or shrimp.

The job was physically hard and tiring. I washed pots and pans when the two cooks had finished with them. I made mashed potatoes and mayonnaise, cleaned shrimp and trout, and did a few other things, including washing the dishes when the dishwasher did not show up. I was punctual. I did everything I was told to do. I never complained and I did not mind the job at all. On my days off I joined some of the students who worked at the hotel to go mountain climbing or just to sit around and talk. I learned more English in my two months in Aspen than I had ever thought I would.

At the end of the summer we returned to Wichita Falls. There I spent a few weeks working as a stock boy at a Safeway store. I helped unload trucks of fruit and vegetables, and kept the produce section well stocked. I also worked for a week or so in a Mexican restaurant making tortillas, enchiladas, and tamales. I quit that job because I did not like the food, and I had a hard time getting along with one of the cooks.

None of these jobs in the U.S. had been very satisfactory, but they kept me occupied and I earned a few dollars. The time had arrived for me to start attending the university. I had a student visa and was told that if I did not attend the university, the immigration office would send me back to Italy. Returning to Italy, after what I had experienced since my arrival, did not seem that bad. What I would not be able to stomach, however, was the reaction I would have received from my Italian friends and relatives. All the promises, expectations, and dreams I had, and which they shared for me, would have been crushed. I did not think I could have talked or looked at them, at least not for a while. I decided to give the university a try.

Midwestern University, Wichita Falls

As required by my student visa, I enrolled in the School of Business at Midwestern University. Mrs. Bea paid for my tuition, fees, and textbooks. The university gave me nineteen units of credit for the work I did in Italy. To my surprise, I passed the English proficiency test so I did not have to take the bonehead English course. I continued to live with the Stones, walked to school, and passed all my first year exams with good grades. After two months at the university, I was able to find an afternoon job with a small firm selling construction material. I mainly did accounting work, two hours a day. The salary paid my extra expenses.

During the spring semester, I started looking for a full-time job. Mr. Stone's office was basically a one-person place. The town did not have much to offer, and my English was still too poor for an office job. I decided to ask for a job at Testa Italian Restaurant. Arthur Testa, a Sicilian, was the owner. Isabel, his wife, was the hostess and cashier. It was located on Tenth Street, not far from downtown.

I had two good reasons for working in a restaurant. First, I had some cooking experience. I learned to do some cooking at the Jerome Hotel in Aspen, and I had helped my mother many times when she was cooking at my uncle's restaurant in Seriate. Second, and more important, by working at a restaurant I could go to school in the morning and work in the afternoon and evening. Besides, while working I could eat as much as I wanted and be less of a burden to my sponsors.

Mario, Do You Know How to Make Pizza?

When I talked to Mr. Testa about a job, he did not have an opening at the time, but he asked for my phone number in the event that one day he would. Fifteen days later, he called. He asked, "Mario, do you know how to make pizza? My pizza man had to take off for a while and go to Dallas to take care of his sick mother. I need to replace him." I had never made pizza pies. In fact, I had never seen one. It was not a dish we ate in our part of northern Italy at that time. I knew it was something southern Italians enjoyed, and I learned soon that many Americans did too. However I did not want to lose this opportunity. I felt that making pizzas could be an easy thing and could be learned fast. I answered that I should not have much trouble replacing his pizza man, even for a short time. He was delighted and asked me to be at the restaurant the next day at four. The hours were from four in the afternoon to eleven o'clock every evening except Monday.

The next day, I arrived by bus at the restaurant at ten minutes before four. I did not have any classes after two o'clock. I was introduced to all the workers in the restaurant and then directed into the kitchen. It had a ceiling fan but it was quite warm. The pizzas were prepared on a working table next to a big, stand-alone gas oven. On the table I found a kitchen scale, cans of flour and cornmeal, a large pair of scissors, a stainless steel spatula, a bottle of olive oil, a bowl of grated Parmesan cheese, a small container with oregano, a garlic salt shaker, a large round wooden board with a foot long handle, and a large rolling pin. Next to the table there was a three-gallon bucket full of leavened pizza dough. The other ingredients necessary to make a pizza—to-mato sauce, mozzarella and provolone cheese, pepperoni, sausages, ancho-vies, and hamburger meat—were kept in a refrigerator on the right side of the working table. The oven was on the left side.

The restaurant menu offered a small variety of pizzas. Customers could choose one of the meats or other toppings, or they could order a combina-tion pizza with two or more ingredients. Pizzas could be small or large; the small required half a pound of dough, and the large one a full pound.

After a short orientation, it was time for questions. My first question was both a statement and a question. I said, "There are many ways of mak-ing pizzas, how do you do it here?" Mr. Testa, the owner and chief cook, proceeded to show me how to make a large hamburger pizza. He dug both hands in the bucket and came up with a blob of dough. He weighed it on the scale, added a little more dough to reach a pound, and worked the dough with his hands for a few seconds to create a round blob. Then he spread some flour in the middle of the table using three fingers, put the dough in the middle of the circle of flour, took the rolling pin, and passed it with some force three or four times in an up and down direction. He turned the elongated dough ninety degrees, sprinkled white flour on it, and passed the rolling pin over the dough again, up and down, producing a large piece of dough (sixteen-inch diameter), round and fairly thin. Then he sprinkled some cornmeal on the wooden board and transferred the dough to the board. Using the first two fingers on each hand he pinched the edges of the dough to create something like a small wall to keep the sauce from spilling off. He covered the pie with tomato sauce and mozzarella cheese, and then sprinkled it with Parmesan cheese, garlic salt, and a bit of oregano. He picked up a bowl of ground beef mixed with raw egg and parsley, and used two fingers of his right hand to deposit small portions of ground beef on the pizza, until a good amount of meat covered it. Last, he poured some olive oil in circles.

The pizza took no more than two minutes to prepare, and was then ready to bake. The oven was kept at a temperature of 550 degrees. Inside the oven was a hot, thick steel sheet, big enough to cook two large pizzas at a time, or one large and two small. The pizza cooked directly on the steel sheet.

Mr. Testa opened the oven, took the pizza board by the handle with both hands, approached the oven, and with a small jerk of his hands landed the pizza on top of the hot steel plate; the cornmeal helped the pizza slide off smoothly from the board. Seven minutes later it was ready to eat. He opened the oven, took the pizza out with the spatula, put the pizza on an aluminum plate, cut it in eight slices using the large scissors, and offered it to the restaurant workers. I ate a slice; it was very good.

Four o'clock had arrived, and the restaurant opened. After observing Mr. Testa making the pizza, I thought the operation looked relatively easy. Of course, I was very apprehensive but felt I should give it a try. Maybe it was going to be my first and last day making pizzas.

My first order was for a large hamburger pizza, just like the one Mr. Testa had just made. The first thing I did was to put both hands in the bucket to grab a glob of dough. As I pulled my hands up, the whole bucket of dough came up. The dough stuck to my hands like glue, and it took quite a while to get the proper amount of dough. Next I sprinkled some white flour in the middle of the table, worked the dough with my hands as I had seen Mr.

Testa doing, and deposited the resulting blob in the middle of the table. I took the rolling pin and went up and down over the dough to make a round base. It turned out more oblong than round. Moreover, it was very thin in some parts and thick in others. I thought it was an acceptable shape. I then sprinkled cornmeal on the pizza board and transferred the not-so-round, thick and thin piece of flat dough onto the board. It took what seemed like a long time to make the border, pinching the outer edges a small piece at a time. With a large spoon, I spread tomato sauce and mozzarella cheese on the pie, and sprinkled some Parmesan, garlic salt, and oregano over the sauce. I put two fingers of my right hand in the hamburger meat bowl, and tried to take small pieces out of it. Everything is not easy when you don't know the proper way to do it. The ground meat stuck to my fingers, just like the dough. Eventually I covered the pie with hamburger meat, but the pieces were not uniform. Some were smaller than the proper size, and some too large. At the end of the operation, I picked up the bottle of olive oil and poured it over the pizza in a few circles.

The pizza was now ready to bake. I opened the oven, picked up the board, gave it a jerk as I had seen Mr. Testa do, but the pizza landed on the hot steel sheet upside down. As the sauce hit the hot steel, a cloud of dark smoke came out of the oven. I took an empty bucket and cleaned the oven with the spatula. I did not look around. I did not want to see the reaction of the other restaurant workers, and especially of Mr. Testa, who was very busy preparing spaghetti, scaloppine, and other Italian dishes. It was payday at Shepperd Air Force Base, located just outside of town. That day it seemed like everyone stationed there was coming to eat Italian food, especially pizza. I kept the embarrassment I felt all to myself. I put my head down and started making another large hamburger pizza.

This second try produced a not-so-round large pizza. It took me less time than the first one, and it looked acceptable. I opened the oven, gave a jerk to the board, much more smoothly than the first time, and the pizza landed almost the proper way on the hot steel plate. Some tomato sauce spilled at one side of the pizza, and smoke rose in the oven, but it was limited and died down soon. I started my third large pizza.

It was a large cheese pizza. I repeated all the same steps as with the first two. The mozzarella cheese was precut in cubes. When the finished pizza was cut, each slice was covered with melted cheese. It was going faster, but still very slow—too slow to satisfy the airmen's demand. They were becoming impatient, and Mr. Testa told the four waitresses to advise customers who wanted a pizza that they had to wait two hours. That meant the pizza business for that day was practically over. I was not informed of this, and continued with my work. I finished my third pizza and opened the oven door. To my great dismay, my second hamburger pizza had burnt. It could not be saved. I put it in the garbage can, and put my third pizza in the oven. It landed on the hot steel plate the proper way, no sauce spilled.

I started making my fourth pizza, a pepperoni one. I was told that the person who ordered the hamburger pizza had changed his mind. He had switched to spaghetti and meatballs.

As I worked the dough for my fourth pizza and assembled all the required ingredients, I began to sweat—partly because it was hot in the kitchen, but also because of the emotional trauma I was feeling. It was as if all the pores in my body had opened at once. Drops of sweat poured profusely down my face, and I could not stop it. I had a white rag that I used to wipe off my hands from flour, sauce, sticky hamburger meat, and other things, and I used it over and over on my face, but the flow would not stop. Helplessly, I saw drops of my sweat mixing with the pizza ingredients. I tried hard not to be noticed, and felt that if any of my germs had contaminated the pizza, the 550-degree oven would kill them.

That day I worked my seven-hour shift, and probably made ten pizzas in all. Mr. Testa did not fire me. Either he realized that I was trying very hard to learn the job, or he could not find another pizza maker in the town of Wichita Falls. Maybe it was both. He asked me to return the next day. My total pay was thirty dollars a week.

I continued working there. Mr. Testa decided to stop cooking, and hired a chef, but he helped cook when we had a crowd. By then I had really learned to make pizza pie. I made the dough, sauce, and hamburger meat. I cut the cheese and prepared all the other ingredients. I even tried, with some success, to improve upon Mr. Testa's recipe. I improved the taste of the dough by adding a few spoons of olive oil to the flour and yeast. I also spread a tablespoon of olive oil over the dough before distributing the other ingredients, which enhanced the overall flavor of the pizza.

I never mentioned my cooking activities to my parents or my Italian friends, except very late in life. I was embarrassed. It was something that I felt my parents and friends would not understand or appreciate. "My son went to America, to the university, and worked as a cook? He could have stayed at home. He had a good job here as a *ragioniere*, a professional accountant. He could have worked in our restaurant if he wanted to be a cook." I knew that many U.S. university students worked at jobs even worse than mine. Nobody looked down on them, neither friends, family, nor teachers. I realized that this was something good about America, which Italians needed to learn.

In the fall of 1952, I returned to the university to continue my study. I chose to major in accounting. I had a good background for it because of my work and studies in Italy, and it did not require a vast knowledge of the English language to follow the class material and complete the homework assignments. Moreover, I had a young professor, probably not much older than I was, who was an excellent accounting teacher. As I continued my university studies, I also continued to work at Testa's restaurant, as well as a few hours a week at the construction supply firm. My academic performance remained good.

In the spring semester of 1953, the music department at the university asked if I could help the voice professor (a Hungarian opera singer at one time) teach students how to pronounce the words from Italian opera arias. Of course, I was happy to do so. I met with the students one hour a week and read them the arias the professor had selected. Most of the arias I knew by heart, because I had seen or heard many opera performances in Italy. I enjoyed the work. I introduced new arias of my own choosing, and even wrote a few pages explaining basic rules of Italian pronunciation. It was a small teaching assignment but the students appreciated my efforts, and it was an opportunity to make new friends and acquaintances.

During my years at Midwestern University I met a number of female students, all interested in Italian mores and culture, it seemed. A few times, I was invited to their houses to teach them or their mothers to make a good spaghetti sauce. Some had seen me on the local television station, where I appeared a couple of times showing the audience how to make a pizza and a good Italian pasta dish. Dating any of them turned out to be very difficult for me, mostly because of my busy schedule, but partly because my first try at dating was not very successful. One day I asked a young lady for a date; we had met in a political science course taught by Prof. John Tower (later U.S. Senator Tower), and she was very interested in learning about Italy. I thought we could talk about Italy while having dinner at a restaurant downtown, and maybe go to a movie after that. She agreed to go out with me on my day off from work. I arrived at her sorority house, rang the bell, and was ushered in to wait. After a few minutes she greeted me enthusiastically, and introduced me to a sorority sister who was probably waiting for her date. As we walked out the door, the first thing she asked was, "Where are you parked?" I told her I did not have a car, but I had carefully studied the bus routes (one ran from the university to downtown) and if she did not have a car and did not mind, we could go by bus.

She was disappointed, I think. It never crossed her mind that I would not have a car. At the same time, she probably felt that she could not cancel the date at that point. We walked to the bus stop, waited a few minutes, then rode the bus downtown. We had dinner and talked for some time about Italy and how she would enjoy visiting the country. We saw a movie and returned by bus to the university. I walked her to the sorority house and said good night and goodbye. She was very pleasant and courteous all evening. She said she enjoyed the evening and said goodbye, smiling as she entered the house. I thought I had made a good impression and that perhaps we could go out again. A few days later I called her for another date, but she refused politely. I don't know why she did not want to go out with me a second time. Maybe she learned all she wanted about Italy, maybe there were other reasons. Was the fact that I did not have a car the major obstacle? Perhaps, because no young ladies from the university accepted my subsequent invitations for dates.

This experience shows how expectations are conditioned by one's society. In Italy I did not have a car, but I did not have any problem dating a girl. The bus, streetcar, or even a bicycle provided our transportation. In the U.S. I realized that without a car, in a town like Wichita Falls, it would not be easy to date any of the young ladies I would have asked. Therefore, I put dating out of my mind and devoted all of my time after class to study, work, and keeping my sponsors from getting tired of me.

In late 1953, I moved from the Stone's house to stay with Mrs. Griffin. She had a bigger house, Spanish style, with a guest room attached to the garage.

She also had a cook and housekeeper, Theresa. It was a move arranged by Mrs. Bea, and it was a very good move for me. Mrs. Griffin, whom I had met for the first time in Taos, New Mexico, was living alone with Theresa. Having me in the guesthouse gave her added security. She had known me for over two years, but to my great surprise she showed sincere happiness in having me as a guest. The best thing for me was that I was not expected to do a thing in or around the house. Theresa took care of the cooking, cleaning, and even the driving, as well as looking after the little Chihuahua dog, and a gardener tended the yard.

After moving in I tried to help Theresa as much as possible, especially in cooking. She appreciated everything I did and always treated me very kindly, almost as a newfound son. She never married and spent all of her adult life taking care of Mrs. Griffin. She followed her to Taos, New Mexico, during the summer, and to Brownsville, Texas, during the winter, where Mrs. Griffin owned another home. The rest of the year she spent in Wichita Falls. Mrs. Griffin's home was furnished with very tasteful, well-maintained antique furniture. Each piece was always in its proper place and formed an integral part of the room's decoration. All the food was prepared in the kitchen, but the meals were served in the large and beautiful dining room. Mrs. Griffin never talked about money in my presence, and I never asked where her fortune came from. That question never occurred to me, and even today I do not know the source of her wealth. I was just happy to share her home, the beautiful garden, and the peacefulness of her very well-to-do street.

From Mrs. Griffin's place, I could walk to the university. After classes, I spent as much time as I could studying and doing homework in the library. At three thirty in the afternoon I took the bus to the restaurant for my evening job. I still did not have a social security number. I did not realize I could easily have obtained one with a student visa. None of my employers ever asked me for one, so I did not feel I needed it.

At the beginning of 1954, when the recently hired chef left, Mr. Testa promoted me to "chef." Mr. Testa continued to supervise the kitchen, and I became the second in command. In my new position I prepared all kinds of pasta dishes with whatever sauce the customers requested—tomato sauce, meat sauce, anchovy sauce, sauce with meat balls, or with Italian sausages. I fixed T-bone steaks, New York cuts, filet mignons, and all kinds of veal scallopini—with Marsala, white wine, lemon, or capers. I also cooked veal parmigiana and melanzane parmigiana. Those were all the dishes featured on the restaurant's menu. Each meat dish was served with a side-order of spaghetti and sauce. The waitresses prepared salad if the customers asked for it.

Of course the restaurant was still making and selling pizza, but I was no longer working in that section of the restaurant. Before moving me to the main counter, Mr. Testa had hired a pizza man. He gave me the responsibility to teach him how to make pizza the way I did it. I had become very good and very fast at making them. On one payday I made 192 pizzas, including preparing dough and sauce, and cutting cheese. My pay had slowly increased to thirty-five dollars a week. On the days I made over a hundred pizzas I received a case of beer as a bonus, which I shared with the rest of the restaurant workers. I spent almost a week showing the new person how to make pizza. He eventually did well, but on some rare occasions when special customers came to eat pizza, I would take time and make it myself.

In June 1954 I obtained my bachelor's degree in business. I did not celebrate the occasion, and did not go to the graduation ceremony. I had to work. In Italy we do not have graduation ceremonies at any educational level, and I did not consider it necessary to go. None of my sponsors could participate. I was happy, however, that I had received a degree from a U.S. university. The question that I faced at the time was what am I going to do now?

My experiences in the U.S. up to that point seemed still very incomplete. I was not yet ready to go back home and give up on the U.S. With a student visa I knew I could not get a challenging job. However, things were beginning to improve. I enjoyed attending university courses, I was living in a beautiful home, I was beginning to make American friends, and I had a full-time job that allowed me to go to school, eat as much as I wanted, and earn some money, most of which I saved.

I continued my cooking job during the summer, and then I decided to continue to attend the university to study for a master's degree in accounting. Because of a professor's illness that fall, I was invited to teach a lower division statistics course. I was happy to do it. It did not interfere with my studies or with my job. Not only did I enjoy teaching the course, but also I realized for the first time that a teaching career could be worth considering, either in Italy or the U.S.

The opportunity for a teaching career came sooner than I expected. From a flyer posted on the business school bulletin board, I learned that the University of Texas at Austin was looking for teaching assistants in economics. Even though I was studying for a master's degree in accounting, I used elective courses to take economics classes. I liked the subject very much. In fact, my master's thesis had a lot more to do with economics than with accounting.

Because economics was my newly acquired interest, I applied for admission and a teaching assistantship at the Graduate School of Arts and Sciences at the University of Texas. My new goal was to obtain a Ph.D. in economics. In February 1955, I was notified that I had been accepted, and was offered a three-year teaching assistantship paying $125 a month plus free tuition. Happily, I accepted.

In June 1955 I completed my master's degree in accounting. I used my savings to purchase my first car, a 1946 Pontiac convertible. I bought it from a student, Leon Russell, who had become a good friend. He was planning to buy a newer car and sold it to me for $325. It turned out that the car was in good mechanical order, and was a very good buy.

I gave Mr. Testa fifteen days' notice, and quit the cooking job. I had already lost the accounting job a few months earlier. The construction supply store had closed down; it could not compete with the new bigger, cheaper, and better-organized ones. I loaded the few possessions I had accumulated into the back of the convertible, thanked and bid farewell to Mrs. Griffin, Theresa, and Mrs. Bea, and took off for California. I decided to visit Rose in Oakland, and while there spend some time doing reading and research at U.C. Berkeley. I planned to go from Oakland directly to Austin, Texas.

The Engagement

I had not seen Rose since we left the *Vulcania*. Four years had passed since that goodbye—an uncertain goodbye, without a real kiss or a promise—more of a farewell than a see-you-again. The fact that something was missing or not right with my entry visa had almost totally frozen my enthusiasm and my thinking. As Rose left the bridge of the *Vulcania*, she looked back at me, waved, and smiled. She wanted to let me know that everything would turn out all right for me. I smiled at her as she disappeared.

During those four long years we kept in touch. Once in a while (not that often), we exchanged letters telling each other what progress we were making. She was now twenty years old, and I was almost twenty-eight. She had just completed her second year at the University of California, Berkeley. She had decided to major in microbiology, and I had completed my bachelor's degree in business and a master's degree in accounting. Our letters were always very informative, but were not the kind of letters that lovers sent. There were some flashes and tentative words of love here and there, without much fire. Once or twice we included some photos, but they did not produce any real spark. In those four years I had lost a lot of hair, perhaps because of the change in diet or for other reasons, and my photos showed that in the worst possible way. Her photos revealed a young and attractive woman, but one still very much tied to a village on the Ligurian coast. However, I wanted to see her, talk to her, and spend some time together. If each of us could generate that spark for the other, we could even get engaged. I wrote to her of my planned visit to Oakland. I told her that I wanted to see her, and that I felt very close to her. I asked if she kindly could find a room to rent in the vicinity of Berkeley for a month's stay. She answered that she would love to see me, and that a room would be available when I arrived.

The 1946 Pontiac convertible

I left Wichita Falls on July 15. I drove through the Texas Panhandle and spent my first night in a motel in Tucumcari, New Mexico. The next day I continued toward California, stopping a few times to admire the expansive landscape—miles and miles and miles of it. It seemed you could see forever. The road was Highway 66, a two-lane road that cut the landscape in the middle. It went on forever, disappearing from sight when it reached the top of a hill, returning again and again as the car passed over one hill and then the next. Much of the land was desert, and rather barren. There were a few green shoots here and there, a few bushes, thirsty oaks, and the dried stumps of dead trees. Once in a while I saw a few skinny and sad-looking cows or a horse or two. No humans were ever in sight, except when passing through scattered small towns. It was hot in the morning and even more so in the afternoon. The vast expanse of land and small towns seemed all at rest, perhaps created to remain that way forever. The evening sky in contrast was very alive. It made up for what the land could not give, offering travelers spectacularly glorious sunsets. As the evening approached and the western sky began to change from blue-gray into a myriad of new colors, I stopped, got out of the car, and marveled at the triumphant colors of the western sky, constantly changing, constantly moving in the vast, open expanse. It was a delightful experience that I will never forget.

I do not remember stopping anywhere to eat. I am sure I did, but I do not remember at all where and what I ate. The whole trip was like a dream.

As I was driving, many thoughts were going through my mind. How would I appear to Rose and she to me? What about her parents? How was I going to do at the University of Texas? Would my students like or abhor my heavy Italian accent? Would they understand me? Did I know enough economics to teach them anything? I did well studying for my master's degree. Would I be capable of persevering to complete a Ph.D.? The next stop was Flagstaff, Arizona, at another motel with a swimming pool. It was a very warm night but I could not swim; I never learned how. So I took a shower and went to bed, tired enough to sleep the whole night.

The following day I started early. I filled the tank of the Pontiac and headed toward Bakersfield, the best and shortest route into California and on to Oakland. Flagstaff was surrounded by mountains and hills, and the air was much cooler than what I had experienced since leaving Texas. The morning air was crisp and pleasant, and I enjoyed it after two days of driving in such hot weather. The Pontiac was not air-conditioned. As I left Flagstaff, its hills and greenery quickly disappeared, and the desert returned to accompany me with sagebrush and scrub pines along the way to Bakersfield. I stopped there for a few minutes, grabbed a sandwich, filled the gas tank, and headed north following the map to Oakland. It was a vast agricultural area from Bakersfield to Fresno, Modesto, and Oakland. Tomatoes, cotton, almonds, figs, peaches, grapes, corn, and cattle for milk or meat filled large fields, whose size I had never seen. What abundance and delight. California was the bountiful America that everyone in Italy talked about.

Finally I arrived in Oakland. Rose and her family lived on Galindo Street off Fruitvale Avenue. It was late in the evening, and I stopped at a motel near the Oakland Coliseum, under construction at the time. I settled in and then called Rose. When she answered the phone I was delighted to hear her voice, and she seemed excited to hear mine. She offered to come and see me at the motel, but I was too tired, poorly dressed, unshaven, and in great need of a shower. I told her this, and we agreed that she would pick me up in the morning to drive me to her place.

She seemed very happy that I had arrived, and invited me to spend the month or so that I planned to stay in the area as a guest of her family. They had an extra bedroom that I could use. Since I was short of money, the invitation seemed very good, and I accepted.

The next morning, Rose arrived with her father's car. We greeted each other joyfully and kissed. We were very happy to see each other after four years. She was now close to her twentieth birthday. I left her at the port of New York as a teenager full of enthusiasm and a strong drive to do well. I found her as a mature young woman who had easily absorbed a new culture, learned a new language, and was now attending one of the world's greatest universities.

After greeting each other, we got in our cars and I followed her lead as we drove to her place. That part of Oakland was not so attractive, as we passed small stores, some dilapidated buildings, and many wood-framed small homes. Some front yards were neat and clean with flowers, and others were untended and full of weeds. Some yards were cultivated for vegetable gardens.

In ten minutes or so we arrived at Rose's home, and I parked the Pontiac in front of the house. It was a sizable two-story home in a cul-de-sac with well-maintained homes and yards. It was mid-morning, and Rose's parents were at work. Rose took me to a bedroom on the second floor of the house and helped me put away the few clothes I had brought. When we finished we felt the urge to kiss again, this time with more passion than during our first kiss in the parking lot of the motel.

During the next thirty days, Rose and I spent much time together. We went to the university together; while she attended a summer class, I waited for her at the library. We had lunch together in one of Berkeley's many coffee shops. We visited the campus, went to movies, and had dinner at home with her parents. One Sunday, the four of us went to visit Rose's uncle, Vincent, who had just built a summer house in Boulder Creek, near the city of Santa Cruz. On the way to Boulder Creek we stopped in downtown Santa Clara on Franklin Street and bought a cake at the old Wilson's Bakery to bring to Uncle Vincent's family. We also passed in front of Santa Clara College, a small college with a beautiful campus. We stopped a few minutes at the entrance of the college, and then continued our drive to Boulder Creek. It was a chance for me to meet some of Rose's relatives. She had many cousins in Oakland and surrounding cities, from both sides of her family. They were sons and daughters of aunts and uncles who had immigrated from Italy in

Rose at Bay Farm Island, age twenty-one, left; undated, right

earlier times. All of her cousins were born in the U.S., and all received good educations and were doing well. They all admired their new cousin from Italy, were proud of her accomplishments, and loved her.

When we returned home that evening, I realized that my time in Oakland was soon coming to an end. By now I was securely in love with Rose, and I was sure she was in love with me. I felt it was time for me to tell her how much I loved her, and to ask her to marry me. The next day, as we returned home from Berkeley, I asked her if she would consider marrying me. She did not hesitate a moment. She answered, "Yes, I love you very much." That evening as dinner came to an end, I asked her parents for permission to marry their daughter. They said yes. It was now official—we were engaged to get married. We did not set a date for the wedding. Rose had to complete her studies at Berkeley and I had to study for my Ph.D. in economics at the University of Texas. No official announcement of our engagement was made, and no dinner party was planned. I did not think it was necessary. Besides, I did not have any money and could not have bought an engagement ring at that time. Rose and I were happy with the way things turned out. No festivities would add any greater joy to what we already shared.

Too soon my time in Oakland came to an end. I gathered my belongings and put them in the trunk of the Pontiac. I gave a big hug and a big kiss to Rose. I promised that I would write to her often, and would return to marry her as soon as I felt settled in my new undertaking. I said goodbye to her mother, Carmela. Her father Giacomo was at work and I had said goodbye to him the night before. After a final farewell, I jumped into the car, waved my hands, and left. Three days later I was in Austin, Texas.

This time I followed the southern route, Interstate 10, through San Bernardino to Blythe, where I stopped for the night. It was a dusty place with many tall, skinny palm trees, planted to produce dates. I stopped at the first motel I found, next to the road. I washed the dust off my hair and face, and ate a few dates and some cookies Rose had prepared for my return trip. I drank a bottle of cold beer, and asked the motel clerk to wake me up at six thirty in the morning. I slept soundly until someone knocked at my door. It was a clear day, with the sun beginning to show itself beneath a light red sky. I knew the day would be very hot and decided to get on the road while the temperature was still mild. The land and sky soon became monotonous, with desert and more desert, and a blue-gray sky as far as one could see. I turned on the radio, louder than usual, following the music and moving my body and head in time with it. I could not sing the words because I did not know or understand any of them. After passing Phoenix, Arizona, I reached Lordsburg, New Mexico, and stopped to fill the tank. I checked the oil and added a quart to replenish what had been lost. I checked the air in the tires and took off for El Paso. Approaching El Paso, the landscape changed from flat land and small hills to taller hills and rocky mountains. I stopped at a motel in El Paso, nicer than the one in Blythe. I put a few of my things in the room, cleaned up, and went into town for dinner. I had not had a decent meal since I left Rose. Mexican restaurants were abundant, but I had not yet learned to like Mexican food. I settled for a steak house, eating a T-bone steak with a bottle of beer, returned to the motel and went to sleep.

The next morning I took off for Austin before seven o'clock. Even though it was early in the morning as I crossed El Paso, I saw a number of people in the streets. Many of them had darker skin than mine, and wore colorful shirts and hats, which I had not seen in such numbers in Wichita Falls, Aspen, or Oakland. I realized that they were natives of Mexico who had settled in that part of Texas. Looking at them, I felt that they demonstrated what is good in the U.S. The blacks of New York, the Italians in the San Francisco Bay Area, the Mexicans in El Paso, the Pueblo Indians in Taos, and all the other races seemed to be living peacefully together. I wrote about this perception of the U.S. in letters to Mrs. Murri and my Italian friends.

I left El Paso with many thoughts in my mind, especially concerns about my job at the University of Texas. I wanted to do well and complete my studies for a Ph.D. as quickly as possible. The road I drove on was good, and I traveled at the speed that the road signs said was legal. After many miles, I reached San Antonio, where I saw a lot more Mexican people, and Mexican restaurants all around. I did not stop; I wanted to get to Austin. An hour and a half later I was there.

Austin, the capital of Texas, was then a rather small city, a university town. There was one main street with a hotel, movie house, department store, restaurant, bar, a few small specialty stores, and little else. At the west end of the main street, the Texas Capitol and two government buildings towered over the rest of the city. Not far from the downtown was the campus, at that time the only campus for the University of Texas. A twenty-two story tower dominated the campus.

I did not know a soul in Austin, and felt it was too late in the evening to move into the room I had reserved in one of the university dorms. I found a motel with the vacancy sign lit, and spent the night there. In the morning I shaved, showered, and drank a horrible cup of coffee, courtesy of the motel management. I drove to the university and found my room, double occupancy, in a graduate dorm. My roommate, whoever he was, had not arrived yet. Classes did not start for another week. I put all of my belongings in one of the closets and went to lunch in the student cafeteria. I planned to use the time before classes started to get acquainted with the professors in the economics department, prepare a syllabus for my two classes, study the textbook for the principle courses, and familiarize myself with the university library.

The University of Texas, Austin

The University of Texas campus was much bigger than I expected. Tall cranes overhead indicated that the campus was still growing. The department of economics was on the second floor of Garrison Hall. The professors' offices were large, well-lighted, and very comfortable with plenty of room for the professor and visiting students. The offices of the teaching assistants were on the upper floor of the university tower. I was assigned an office on the nineteenth floor. It was all my own, large enough for me and students when they wanted to ask a question or complain about a grade.

My office had a large window. From there, I could see much of Austin and beyond. I could see the students talking, walking, and running. They all looked small. There were no cell phones, iPhones, or iPads. The students entered and exited the buildings of higher learning. I could see small cars passing, stopping, and honking, afraid of hurting little men crossing the street. I saw many wood-frame houses—not really houses; they were homes. Their walls hid many emotions: the hope of the young, the tribulation of the old, the joy of lovers, the pain of the sick, the satisfaction of the rich, the worries of the poor, and much more.

Late in the evening I would look at the sky. It seemed much closer from the nineteenth floor. The stars were brighter, the moon seemed bigger, and the whole universe looked more vast. Red, yellow, and green lights, fluorescent, incandescent, and neon lights from the town below illuminated the sky above. The air was clear, the lights shone bright. Looking at the myriad stars in the sky and the thousands of colors on earth relaxed me. My mind cleared, and I went back to reading and studying more. I wanted—I needed—to succeed.

When I finished studying for the evening, I wrote to Rose, often telling her about the view from my office on the nineteenth floor of the tower.

My first year at the University of Texas passed quickly. I enjoyed teaching and I worked hard to stay two or three chapters ahead of the students in my two economic principles courses. I also progressed well with my Ph.D. courses. I received good grades on research papers and on exams, and at the end of the year my teaching assistantship was confirmed for the whole three years. My Italian accent did not seem to be a major hurdle for my students, even though I realized that I could not pronounce some words properly and had to repeat them, sometimes more than once.

In June 1956, at the end of my first academic year in Austin, I decided to make some money during the summer and not go to Oakland, to the chagrin of Rose and all her relatives. With two other foreign students—Orio Giarini from Trieste, Italy, and Rasto Klopčïc from Belgrade, Yugoslavia—I drove to Aspen, Colorado, where we were offered the opportunity to work at Mario's Restaurant. I was a cook, and the other two were waiters. We agreed to split the tips equally three ways. I had found the jobs, and we drove there with my Pontiac.

Mario's Italian Restaurant was unique in a town that was beginning to become a popular winter and summer resort. Mario, the owner, had a good tenor voice. His brother Tish had a decent baritone voice. They hired a soprano and a pianist from Dallas. Each evening during dinner, the three singers walked around the tables and sang opera arias, accompanied by the pianist. The place was always full. I was cooking with two other people. The food we prepared, not a large variety, was well received. It was good.

Working at Mario's was also fun. Quite a few times each evening we heard the musical signal to gather around the piano and sing the chorus of whichever opera piece the trio was performing at the moment—me in my cooking outfit, plus the two waiters and two waitresses. We always got tremendous applause from the audience. The *brindisi* of Verdi's *Traviata* was always a favorite with the customers, and helped sell more wine. At the end of the summer, we returned to Austin to continue our studies.

At the beginning of my second year at the University of Texas, my roommate and I rented a small one-bedroom apartment within walking distance from the university. It was not in very good condition, but at forty-five dollars a month it was cheaper than the room in the dorm. My roommate Alvin Cohen, from Washington, D.C., was also a teaching assistant in economics, and a very orderly and disciplined fellow. In many respects, I admired him, but in other ways I found it very difficult to share the apartment with him. Every morning, even on weekends, he awoke at six thirty, showered, shaved, and dressed. He always looked very neat in a blue or dark suit, white shirt, and tie. He put his coat on after breakfast—the same breakfast every morning (cereal that his mother shipped to him from D.C.). After breakfast he washed his dishes, opened the closet, put on his coat, picked up his briefcase, and walked to school. At noon he ate a sandwich at the student cafeteria, and then returned to his office on the seventeenth floor of the tower. At five thirty in the afternoon he returned home, fixed dinner, ate, cleaned up, returned to school, and went to the library, which occupied the first twelve floors of the tower. At nine thirty he returned home, put his coat and briefcase in the closet, checked the mail, and registered all of the day's expenses, no matter how small, in a special notebook. At ten o'clock he went to bed after neatly folding his clothes. He followed this routine day after day after day, until the semester was over. Then he returned to Washington, D.C.

I had never been that disciplined, and at times it pained me to watch Alvin perform his daily routine. He did not have a minute of recreation or relaxation. Maybe his routine brought him relaxation. I never saw him at a sports event or with a girl. I was quite different. My first class was at eight in the morning. I got up at seven fifteen or later, and rushed to arrive on time. I ate lunch and dinner at the cafeteria, except for Sundays, or went out with other teaching assistants. At night, I almost always came home after midnight. I spent a great deal of time at the library and at my office, studying and doing research. I went home when I had completed the work I had set out to do. I became friends with five or six other teaching assistants. Many weekend nights we gathered at one or the other's home, discussing the political and economic problems of the day. We were all pretty liberal at the time. We focused on recessions, inflation, the Bretton Woods agreement, the gold standard, Keynesian economic policy, socialism, communism, and the like. There were hours of discussion, and zero accomplishment. When Alvin's path crossed mine, which was not too often, he told me that I was irresponsible. At the very least, he told me that I should come home earlier at night and get up earlier in the morning. I never did. He finished his course work earlier than most of us, and later took a teaching job at Lehigh University. After he left Texas, I saw him once more at an economics association convention. He was married and doing well. I was happy for him.

At the end of 1956, after I had completed my third semester of teaching, I resolved to enter the teaching profession, teaching economics at an American university. I had not informed my parents or any of my Italian friends of this decision, not even Mrs. Bea or Mrs. Griffin. I had talked to Rose about it during my visit in the summer of 1955. At that time, however, it was only a possible alternative. I had not yet started teaching at the University of Texas and I did not know if I would be any good at it. I did, however, inform Mrs. Murri of my decision. Mrs. Murri sent me frequent letters to keep up with her grandson, Robert, and with Mrs. Bea. On December 18, I wrote the following letter to Mrs. Murri:

Dear Mrs. Murri,

From your last letter I learned that you had not felt well lately. I hope you are now completely recovered and that our good Lord will keep you in good health for many years to come.

I agree with the sentiments you expressed in your last letter. Many ugly things exist today in the world: massacres, civil unrests, famines, and a lot of poor people. As a member of the world community, one feels so upset about all the suffering, and even more so when, on one hand there are men that try to build, to create, to give the world a better life, and on the other hand there are other men that destroy what the first had tried to build. However, in spite of all the terrible things one reads every day in newspapers, men want to live, want to believe, want to fight, want to hope, and want to achieve.

My dear Mrs. Murri, I think of you very often. I hope to see you and all my relatives and friends when I have completed my studies. I cannot believe that so much time has passed since I left Italy. I am doing well and my course grades are good. At times, I feel discouraged, but then I think of all I have already done, and I find the will to continue. The more I study, the more books I read, the more I realize how little I know.

I am very happy with my teaching. The students give me very good evaluations. I really like these American kids. Many of them are not well prepared to take classes at the university level. At times, it is difficult to make them understand some of the very important economic concepts, but at the end they turn out well, and become good business and community leaders.

I have decided to pursue a career teaching economics at one of the many U.S. universities. I am aware that university salaries in the U.S. (as is the case in Italy) are not as good as the ones in industry or commerce. University teaching, however, offers such great psychological and intellectual benefits that outweigh the financial rewards. Teaching is continuous learning. By teaching at a university you are constantly in touch with young minds that respect you for your knowledge, and you are surrounded by colleagues in many disciplines that you can question and from whom you can learn new things.

I hope to visit Mrs. Bea at the end of this month. At present, she is in Philadelphia with Mary. Robert is still in Loveland Pass, Colorado. His new ski lift is fully working. The place is beautiful and I feel sure many skiers will take advantage of it.

I enjoy your letters very much. They are always full of great suggestions. They offer me a feeling of joy and give me encouragement. Please continue to write. Please give my best to everyone at the Pradello, but especially to Dr. Zavaritt, whom I always remember and whose values I will try to follow.

With much affection,
Mario

By March 1957 I had completed much of the course work required in the economic fields I had selected to follow—public finance, international economics, monetary theory and policy, and economic development. I had also completed one of the two language exams that all arts and sciences Ph.D. students were required to take. I easily passed the French exam because I had studied that language in Italy both in middle and high school. For the second language I could not use Italian or English, since neither were considered a foreign language for me. I also could not use another romance language, such as Spanish, because the rule allowed only one romance language. Therefore I chose Russian as my second Ph.D. language. The requirement was to be able to translate one article of my choice from a Russian economic journal. I took two semesters of Russian, and selected an article from *Voprosi Economiki*

(Economic Questions) to translate into English. I decided, however, to postpone the exam to my third year.

At the end of the month, I felt that things were very much under control. I also had decided that my future career was going to be teaching economics at the university level. I enjoyed studying and teaching economics, and many teaching jobs were available. I had also decided that I would stay in the U.S. My future here looked good. The time had come for Rose and me to get married.

The Wedding

Since our engagement in the summer of 1955, Rose and I kept in touch frequently. We wrote each other a letter every week. In spring 1957 I bought engagement and wedding rings from an Austin jewelry store. I paid the $200 price on an installment basis, twenty dollars a month, and mailed the engagement ring to her. In early May that year, I asked her to arrange the wedding. She set the wedding date for June 8, 1957. The ceremony was to take place at Saint Elizabeth Church, her parish in Oakland. It was the same month that Rose would complete her bachelor's degree in microbiology at Berkeley, and she already had a part-time job at the Sutro Laboratory in Oakland. It was also a good time for her to get married.

As May ended and my university work was done, I packed a few things, jumped into the Pontiac, and drove to Oakland on the southern route. I arrived six days before the wedding. Most of those days I spent with Rose, and at night I slept at her uncle Vincent's home. I could not help much with the wedding preparations. Rose did most of it, and her father paid for everything, including renting my wedding suit, and Rose's corsage. At the wedding ceremony, Rose had 150 guests, and Mario had none. My Italian parents and relatives were too poor to afford the voyage. My graduate-student friends either did not have money to travel or had summer jobs. However, they heard me talking about Rose and were happy that the two of us would marry. I was the most happy of all.

After the wedding reception, dinner, dancing, cake, and throwing of the garter, Rose and I changed into casual clothes and took off for our honeymoon. We took Rose's father's car, a 1953 Pontiac sedan. We counted the money we received that day as wedding gifts, and headed for a week at Lake Tahoe. It was late in the afternoon, and we decided to spend our first night together in Sacramento. The next day we reached Lake Tahoe and stayed in a cabin at the Caesar Motel, just south of Tahoe City. We spent time at the beach, went to a few movies, drove to the Nevada state line, played slot machines, heard Ella Fitzgerald at the Harvey Casino, drove to Reno, and made love. We had fun and had time to catch up with our lives and to make some plans for our future. Besides my decision to teach at a university, which was still a few years away, we did not know what lay ahead for us. However, we were very optimistic that with our education and willingness to work, our future was going to be bright.

The seven peaceful and beautiful days at Tahoe came to an end. It was time to return to Oakland. We counted the money we had left, put aside a couple of dimes just in case we had to make a phone call, filled up the gasoline tank, and with the money left (less than one dollar) had breakfast. We left the lake and never stopped until we arrived at Rose's home in Oakland.

We still had about two months before we had to get back to Austin. I did not have a penny left, but Rose had a savings account with about $600. We did not want to touch that money. The next day Rose went back to work at the Sutro lab, on Oakland's Pill Hill. I needed a job. A few days later I found a job at the Flinkote Paper Company in Hayward, a fifteen-minute drive from Oakland. I was hired to work in the factory laboratory. My job was to check and report every hour the pH (acidity or alkalinity) of the paper pulp in a huge holding tank in one corner of the factory, sourced mostly from old newspapers. The pulp from the tank was channeled into a huge paper machine that had a number of different-sized steel cylinders. It looked to me like a giant pasta machine. The machine ran twenty-four hours every day. As the pulp rolled through the machine, hot cylinders slowly dried it until it became paperboard. As it reached the end of the machine, the finished paperboard rolled up into a large, heavy bundle. As the roll grew to the proper size, it was cut off from the rest of the paper, sent to a different section of the plant, and made into cardboard boxes of all shapes and sizes. When one roll was cut from the giant machine, a new roll was formed and cut, and then another, and another. It seemed endless. Besides measuring the pH of the paper pulp, my job also required that I measure the weight, strength, and capacity to absorb water from a sample of cardboard that I would cut from each roll before it was moved.

My job at Flinkote Corp. was not heavy or difficult. However, I had to work shifts, including the night shift, which was the most difficult for me.

Moreover, in order to get the job I was required to join the Teamsters Union. This gave me a chance to learn how unions worked at the factory level. I never saw the union representative on the floor of the factory interfere with the workers, manager, or my work. In fact, during the two months I spent there, he never approached me or asked me any questions. It was a closed shop, but for the first three months of work I was not required to pay union dues. I joined the Teamsters, but actually I never became a member of the union.

The Ph.D.

At the end of August, we loaded all the wedding gifts (pots, pans, glassware, dishes, bedding and tableware) in the Pontiac, and headed for Texas. A few miles south of Monterey, in King City, the differential broke, either because of age or because of the weight on the car. The owner of a garage nearby towed the car to his shop, called around to find the parts he needed, and two hours later the car was ready to go. That evening we stopped at Blythe, close to the Nevada border. The next night we stopped at El Paso, Texas, and the night after we arrived in Austin. The night we arrived, Austin was literally taken over by crickets. They were all over. They blackened the store windows, and laid by the thousands on the sidewalks for people to step over. They were on the floor inside grocery stores. Chuck, chuck, chuck—you could hear the sound everywhere as people walked over them. Rose was horrified by the sight. It was not what she had heard about Austin or had expected to see.

We did not have a place to stay yet. A graduate student and his wife, Peter and Shirley McLoughlin, took us in for the night. We remained with them for over a week until we rented a house on Red River Street. It had a bedroom, kitchen, living room, bathroom, and dining area. The living room had a water cooler. It was semi-furnished for seventy-five dollars a month.

Soon after we settled in our new home, Rose found a job as a medical technologist at the university student hospital. Her salary, at $180 per month, was higher than mine, which had increased to $150. With our two salaries, we became the most affluent of our graduate student friends. Our house became open to all of them, and sometimes even professors would show up at our parties.

At our very first dinner party we had ten guests. We asked them to bring a few chairs and some dishes. We were celebrating the birthday of one of the students. We promised a homemade spaghetti and steak dinner. As guests arrived, the oven of our electric stove burned out. The steaks had to be cooked two at a time in a skillet on top of the stove. While waiting and drinking, our guests came into the small kitchen to greet Rose, as she experienced her first major frustration as a host. One of the guests sat on the small kitchen table, still covered with the white flour that Rose had used to make noodles. The same guest then sat on the green couch in the living room, transferring the white flour from his pants to the couch. At coffee time, one of the ladies put her cup full of coffee on the floor (we did not have a coffee table), and another lady stepped into it, splattering coffee all over the living room carpet. Bits of the birthday cake also landed on the carpet. At midnight the party was over. Everyone had a lot of fun. It was a joyous evening. When everyone left, Rose cried. She felt that her first attempt at entertainment had been a disaster. I explained to her that everyone had a very good time. They all enjoyed the food and company. They did not expect perfection. She did not have to be sorry, but happy. She felt better, and from that evening on we had an open door for all of our friends. Rose enjoyed feeding and talking to them. Most of them had less than we did. Graduate school turned out to be hard work, but also fun for all of us. Food and drink were always accompanied by great arguments. Politics, economics and history were our preferred subjects. Marx, Veblen, Shumpeter, and C.E. Ayres were some of our preferred thinkers. How liberal, even downright socialist, we had all become. How easy it was, even for graduate economics students, to overlook the benefits of economic freedom.

The last two years at the University of Texas passed quickly and without major difficulties. By the end of June 1958, I had completed all the required course work, had passed all the Ph.D. exams, and had completed all the language requirements. I still needed to complete the dissertation. That summer, I was offered a teaching job at a Texas university. I did not take it. I wanted to complete my Ph.D. dissertation before leaving Austin. I learned that many graduate students who left the University never did complete it, or finished after many years. My teaching assistantship had ended, but Rose still had her job. On July 2, 1958, our son Paul was born. We used a large part of our savings to pay for doctors and the hospital. Shortly thereafter, Rose returned to her job and I was able to obtain a one-year teaching assistantship in the university accounting department.

Rose and Paul

In November 1958, I started looking for a permanent teaching job. Rose and I had agreed that it would be best if possible to get a job on the West Coast, or as close to it as possible. Her parents did not speak English and needed her help. I sent out ten letters to various economic departments applying for a teaching job. The University of Arizona answered that they could not hire me because I was not an American citizen (I was a permanent resident with a green card). The University of Nevada at Reno offered me a job, but I turned it down because the state legislature still needed to approve the financing. I turned down San Jose State University because the job required supervising students who planned to become high school teachers. Long Beach State offered me a job; I had never been in Long Beach and did not know anything about the town or university, but the name made it sound quite attractive, and it was in California. As March 1959 arrived, Santa Clara University had not answered my November letter addressed to Fr. King, S.J., the dean of the college of arts and sciences. The time was getting short and Rose and I decided that I should take the Long Beach job. I had less than a week to answer their offer. The day after we made that decision, the phone rang. It was Dr. Pagani, the associate dean of the college of business and chair of the economics department at Santa Clara, inquiring if I was still interested in a position there. I said yes. He invited me to visit the campus for an interview with the dean of the college of business and the academic vice president. I had visited the campus with Rose the summer we married. It was close to Oakland, in a beautiful valley, and relatively small. It was ideal.

The next day, I hopped on a Braniff plane to Dallas and then an American Airlines plane to San Francisco. The following day, I was at the Santa Clara campus. I answered all the questions they asked, and at the end of the day Dean Dirksen offered me a job. I called Rose and I accepted it. It paid $6,000 a year. It was $500 more than Long Beach State offered me, and the courses I would teach were more in line with my interests.

By June 1959, I had completed my Ph.D. dissertation. Prof. Everett E. Hale, who supervised my writing and research, approved it but asked for some minor changes. The other two members of the supervising committee agreed with Prof. Hale. I made the changes I was asked, and was awarded the degree in 1960. The deadline had passed to petition for the 1959 graduation.

My studies and teaching at the University of Texas were now over. Almost four years had passed from my first day there. I had now completed my Ph.D. work, and had a full-time teaching job. I was ready to move on to a new life, new experiences, and a new state, California. I felt I had arrived. In a few months, I was to become a university professor.

The University of Texas at Austin turned out to be a great choice for me. I met and worked with very talented faculty: Prof. Everett E. Hale taught me macroeconomics; Prof. Murray Polokoff, monetary theory and policy; Prof. Clarence E. Ayers, institutions, technology, and economic progress; Prof. Walter P. Webb, the great frontier thesis; Prof. Eric Zimmerman, world resources and industries, and many others. You could not fail to learn from these superb teachers and scholars because they were so passionate in their teaching, so convincing in the exposition, and so attached to their work.

I liked all of my professors at the University of Texas. They were all kind, helpful, and available when I needed help. I became particularly fond of Prof. Clarence E. Ayers. He was the prototype of the southern gentleman. He had a Ph.D. in philosophy, and had written many books and articles on institutional economics among other subjects. During the academic year he taught three courses; I took all three. The basic subject covered was the same for each course, but the major differences were the examples, historical perspective, sources of his inspiration, philosophical foundations, and relevance of the subject to economic policy. His first and last lectures focused on Veblen institutions and technological change. Everything in between was covered by his own books and articles. His students learned the importance of the institutional structure of a country in defining, designing, and carrying out any economic policy. His lessons turned out to be very useful in carrying out my consulting work in developing countries.

It was at the University of Texas that I saw my first football game, on Thanksgiving Day, 1955, Texas vs. Texas A&M. I did not know any rules of the game, but I admired the hitting, strength, and size of the players. I felt sorry for those that got hurt. I enjoyed the bands, cheerleaders, and crowd enthusiasm. The game ended the way it started. I don't know which team won and lost. It did not matter; I won. What a difference between the soccer I grew up with and football. It was Europe vs. the U.S. One was fast, played with a force that was almost elegant and artistic. The other was slow and played with a force that was almost brutal. Attending a football game was a new experience for me, one worthy of writing home about.

It was in Austin, on Red River Street, that I learned to eat Mexican food: tamales, enchiladas, tacos, refried beans, tortillas, and guacamole sauce. They were all good—I liked them all. The Mexican restaurants in Austin knew how to make good Mexican food. Nowhere else, even in Mexico, could imitate them.

In Austin I also discovered that I was allergic to shellfish, including all the crustaceans Texans like to serve their dinner guests. I never had such food in Italy. They were too expensive, and we never had a refrigerator to store them. At one faculty party, I ate some. I liked them very much, so I ate a few more. Two hours later, I felt sick to my stomach. Everything I ate at the party came back up. I blamed the wine, for I had drunk my share of it and probably more. At the next party, I ate another helping of shellfish, oysters this time. I liked them. Two hours later, everything I ate that evening came back up. This time I did not drink much. The culprit was the shellfish. From that day on, I stopped eating shellfish. Since then, my stomach has been fine with the food I eat.

Rose and her Family

Rose is an extraordinary wife. She practically raised the children without much help from me. She drove them to school, piano lessons, and after-school activities. She organized birthday parties for them, and drove them to their friends' parties. She taught them how to cook, dress properly, prepare their own school lunches, and behave at the dinner table. She also taught them Italian. She did all of this while she was working. Besides taking care of the children, she has always been a very gracious host. She cooked for student graduation parties—about forty-nine years so far. She cooked for faculty members, administrators, and their wives who I invited home, as well as for friends in the Saratoga-Los Gatos area, and for strangers visiting the Department of Economics whom I brought home for dinner. The time that most revealed her patience and willingness to be helpful occurred one day in the summer of 1962 when I called her from the University of California at Berkeley, where I was participating in a fifteen-day economic seminar, and told her that I had invited twenty-five other seminar participants (economic professors from different parts of the country) to come to our house for a barbecue dinner. The dinner was ten days later, on a Saturday. At the time, Rose was working, she was pregnant with Julie, and the house was being remodeled. Her only question to my phone call was, "What do you want me to fix?" She felt it was good for me to associate with other professors in an informal setting. One of the professors who came to the barbecue was Franco Modigliani of MIT. Later I visited him at his home in Cambridge, Massachusetts. Rose has always worked hard to prepare the food and to insure that each party would be successful. She used only ceramic plates and regular tableware and glasses, not minding the extra cleaning time after the party was over.

Rose's work did not end with the children and with cooking and cleaning; she also took care of the family finances. As my work at the university intensified, she agreed to handle the family checkbook. My paycheck went directly to Bank of America, and she paid all the bills and purchased whatever was necessary to run our household. I never interfered, and never asked what she was doing or buying with the money. There was no need to. She provided me with whatever cash I needed for my weekly expenses, and I always kept a blank check and a credit card in my billfold just in case I needed to get some extra funds. By handling the finances this way, we avoided the many fights when a husband tells the wife that she spends too much, and the wife argues that he does not give her enough money. Besides handling the family finances, Rose also continued to help her parents with their bills and bank accounts.

Rose was also very helpful to my mother during the last few months of her life. Twice she flew to Italy by herself to be sure that my mother had the proper care. She wanted her to feel comfortable. It was something I could not do.

Now we have seven grandchildren—Emma, Gregory, Cristina, Vincent, Kate, Sophia, and Lauren—and Rose is devoting much of her time to them, probably as much as she devoted to our three children. She does all the cooking for all fifteen of us when we gather together as a family for Easter Sunday, Thanksgiving, and Christmas. For her, Christmas dinner is not complete without her homemade ravioli. All the rest of us, especially the grandchildren, appreciate her efforts and greatly enjoy her ravioli and all of her cooking.

Rose loves to cook. She taught our three children to cook using many of the recipes she brought from her Ligurian kitchen and many others she acquired in the U.S. The children learned well from her, and all shared her interest in cooking. One of them, Claudia, has even written a cookbook (*Cooking Dinner*), and Paul, besides cooking at home, puts together a dinner menu once a month for an Italian club he helped establish in Santa Clara County.

Rose loves her family and everyone in the family loves her. Many years she organizes a family vacation somewhere so that the children and grandchildren can play together, sit at a table, and have fun. She believes that if there is no family love, there is no happiness and no future.

Rose Came From a Solid Italian Stock

Rose's real name was Maria Rosa. She changed it to Rose when she came to the U.S. Many members of her extended family had emigrated to the U.S.

long before she did. As Rose tells the story, her maternal grandfather came to San Francisco toward the end of the nineteenth century. He worked as a cook in the town of Stella where he was born, and was offered a cooking job in a logging camp in the Santa Cruz Mountains. He accepted the job and planned to remain in the U.S. for ten years, and then return home to live with his two sisters. After ten years had passed, he decided to stay longer. He did not know how to read and write, and did not communicate his decision to his sisters back home. One of the sisters, concerned about his health and whereabouts, contacted the Italian consulate in San Francisco to inquire about him. The consul inserted an ad in the *Voce d'Italia* (the Voice of Italy), the local Italian newspaper, asking for information about Giuseppe Martino. The wife of the logging camp supervisor saw the ad and informed her husband, who in turn informed Mr. Martino that his sister was trying to contact him. Not knowing what his sister wanted, he decided to return to Italy. He was somewhat disappointed when he learned that his sister only wanted to know about his health and his whereabouts. While in Italy he married, and after his first child was born he returned to the U.S., then returned home again two years later. He fathered a second child and returned to the U.S. for a third time. A few years later he returned home, and spent the rest of his life working the family's land. He had a total of eight children; three of them, including Rose's mother, emigrated to the U.S. and settled in the San Francisco Bay Area.

Giuseppe Martino's return did not discourage others in Rose's extended family from emigrating to the U.S. In 1919 Rose's aunt, Antonietta, reached the city of Alameda, near Oakland. Her boyfriend had shot at her the year before, because she had innocently kissed a boy from her town who was leaving the village to join the army. The wound was superficial; the boyfriend was arrested and tried, but the judge considered his action a nonpunishable crime of passion. He was freed and continued to stalk her until she feared for her life. A town acquaintance who had moved to Alameda offered to hire her as a babysitter and to pay for her way to the New World. She accepted the offer. She was nineteen, did not know a word of English, and did not know where she was going, what to expect at her destination, or what kind of life was ahead for her. She left her town by train and reached Naples. There she boarded a ship that took her to New York. She was cleared to enter the U.S.

at Ellis Island. A train took her to Oakland, where she met the person who offered her a job.

After a few years of babysitting and housekeeping, Antonietta married a local farmer, also an Italian immigrant from her area, who owned a small farm on Alameda Island. They produced vegetables to sell at local markets. They did well, and like most immigrants saved as much as they could. When her husband died, she sold the farm and bought a house close to the center of the city, where she died in her eighties. She raised two children. One, Thomas, received a bachelor's degree from Santa Clara University and became a lawyer, and the other, Carlo, invested in the local real estate market and became a partner in the Oakland Scavenger Company.

Lalla Antonietta, as she was called by her relatives, was the oldest of eight children born into the Rusca family in the small Italian town of Stella, in the province of Savona. The people in the town made a living cultivating plots of land, making charcoal, and gathering chestnuts from the surrounding mountains. As the population of the town increased and the land was divided up among heirs, the plots became smaller and geographically dispersed, until they became too small to sustain a family. Consequently, as in other parts of the world where subsistence agriculture prevails, many people were forced to find jobs in large urban areas or to emigrate. A number of the people from Antonietta's area in Liguria emigrated to the U.S. and especially to the San Francisco Bay Area, where the climate and agriculture production were very similar to home.

As people from Stella and surrounding towns immigrated to California, it became easier for others to follow. Relatives and acquaintances provided help to the newcomers. The fear of the long, arduous voyage soon disappeared as so many emigrants made it to their destination. Even though many of them were subject to bondage (paying off the borrowed cost of the trip), it did not worry them because they learned from friends or relatives that such bondage would soon be paid off. Many left Liguria, Piedmont, and Tuscany in search of a new life in a prosperous country, and with their hard work they helped transform the Santa Clara, Napa, and Sonoma valleys into some of the most beautiful and productive agricultural centers the world had ever known.

After Antonietta's marriage, it became easier for the Rusca clan to immigrate to the Bay Area. One day Antonietta showed a photo of one of her

Antonietta and her husband at Bay Farm Island, 1955

sisters, Caterina, to a neighboring farmer, also an Italian immigrant from her area. The man was impressed by her sister's good looks and told Antonietta that if her sister would come to the U.S. and marry him, he would be glad to pay all of her trip expenses. Antonietta wrote her sister with as much information as she could about the man who wanted to marry her. Caterina decided not to leave home, but passed the information to her sister Eugenia, who was willing to marry him if he would take her as his wife. He did, and Eugenia soon reached Alameda Island and wed the neighbor.

After the sister arrived and settled on Bay Farm Island, Antonietta sponsored her sixteen-year-old brother Vincenzo (Vincent), helping him to come to the United States. He settled in Oakland, worked hard, and soon was able to purchase a partnership in the Oakland Scavenger Company. The company was strictly controlled by Italians for many years, as were other scavenger companies in the Bay Area. All the partners were Italian, mostly immigrants from northern Italy or their descendants. They bought the partnership from the company, and sold it back when they retired. If approved they could pay for much of the partnership on installments. Because of the good profits, the value of each share would increase year after year, providing each partner a nice supplement to his social security pension at retirement time.

After World War II Vincent Rusca sponsored his brother Giacomo (Rose's father) to come to the U.S. He arrived in Oakland in 1950 and lived in his brother's home, sharing it with him, his wife, and four children. Soon Vincent helped him get a job as a truck driver with the scavenger company. A few years later he purchased a partnership in the company. The job started at four thirty in the morning and ended after eleven o'clock. He would go home, eat lunch, and take a nap. A few afternoons each week he walked the streets to collect monthly fees from the customers he served early in the morning. The fee when he started was $1.29 a month for a single home.

Giacomo Rusca was a typical Italian immigrant in the Bay Area. He worked hard at his job and saved most of what he made. He grew up in the town of Stella, the youngest of the Rusca children, and spent most of his youth working the family land: four small plots, only one of them good enough to grow grapes, corn, vegetables, and potatoes. The other three plots were located on mountainous terrain and were good only to produce wood, charcoal, fodder, hazelnuts, and chestnuts. In 1932, at age twenty-two, he married Carmela, a young lady from the same town, and in 1934 Rose was born.

Several years later he moved his family to the city of Savona, where he had found a job as an electrician with the local utility company. During World War II, he was drafted and sent with the Third Alpine Division to fight in Yugoslavia against the advancing Allied troops. When the Italian armistice was signed in September 1943, he and many fellow soldiers walked home using back roads and sleeping in agricultural fields, to avoid being captured or forced to join the German army.

After the war was over, he returned to work with the town electric utility, until coming to the U.S. in 1950 with a permanent immigrant visa. Rose and Carmela joined him in June 1951, and for a few months they also shared Vincent's home with his family.

Four months after Rose and Carmela arrived, Giacomo bought a house in east Oakland, with help from his brother, sister, and brother-in-law. It was a two-story house with a partial basement and a small backyard. After moving in, he devoted much of his spare time to remodeling it. When he finished with the house, he started enlarging the basement, one shovel of dirt at a

Rose with her parents

time. After excavating he reinforced the foundation, and used two-thirds of it to build an apartment, which he rented, and in the other third he built a wine cellar and storage area. He did all the work himself, except for the plumbing because of the city building code requirements. Every fall he made wine. He would buy a half ton of red grapes at the Oakland produce market, crush it, let it ferment for a few days, press it, and store the wine in forty-gallon barrels. He did not age it; when he ran out of the previous year's wine, he started with the new. He had a passion for it, like many Italian and Portuguese immigrants in the Bay Area. At home in Italy the family made wine from its own grapes. In the U.S. he continued that tradition. Jack, as he was called in the U.S., enjoyed drinking his wine; he would open a bottle after he returned home from work. Sometimes he drank half a glass as he worked at home, and finished the bottle before going to bed at night. He loved his wine but he never over used it, and never got drunk. Besides making wine, he enjoyed cultivating a vegetable garden. The backyard was not that large, but it was always intensively cultivated. There were vegetables of one kind or another all year-round.

Jack never did learn much English. He tried adult education a couple of times, but he dropped out. He learned the words he needed for his job, and like many other Italian immigrants in the Bay Area, he Italianized many everyday English words. Thus car became carro, block became blocco, check became checco, cake became checca, truck became trocco, and so on. English was very difficult for him. He only had a second grade education, and even though in Italy he had worked as an electrician, plumber, and carpenter, he never learned the Italian language well. Without a good foundations in one's own language, it is that much more difficult to learn another one, especially after middle age.

Jack was able to survive and do well without learning much English. Most of his coworkers either understood or spoke Italian, or spoke the Ligurian dialect. His friends and relatives were Italian. The DMV issued his driver's license by providing questions in Italian. The Ligure Club, Alpicella Club, Toscana Club, and other Italian organizations that dotted the Bay Area provided abundant recreation, festivities, dancing, and other cultural activities. The Oakland Ligure Club was his favorite. One of Jack's great disappointments in life was not to have learned enough English to pass the exam required to become a U.S. citizen. However, he and most Italian immigrants pushed their children not only to learn English, but also to get a good education. Many failed to teach their children even the rudiments of their own language. They wanted the children to learn and speak English well.

Carmela, Giacomo's wife, was a few years older than her husband; she was a rather shy person and had no knowledge of English. At the beginning of her life in the New World, she found herself somewhat lost. Oakland was becoming a busy city, but she could not participate in much city life. For the most part she stayed home to cook, clean, mend clothes, help in the garden, and take care of the family needs. During the food canning season, she worked full time at the Del Monte cannery on Fourteenth Street in Oakland.

She walked several blocks to work, and did not need to learn English to work at the cannery. Many employees and some supervisors at the plant were Italian or Portuguese, and she could do her job well without speaking English. She never tried to learn the new language. The few words she knew were the Italianized ones. Besides a few acquaintances from the cannery and her relatives in the area, she never showed much interest in meeting or socializing with other people. She did not drive. A few times a year Rose drove her to visit her sister Caterina in San Francisco, and her brother Jimmy in Alameda. Her parish, St. Elizabeth Church in Oakland, provided a Mass in Italian every Sunday. After the Mass she would meet some of the people she knew. That more or less rounded out her life.

Neither Giacomo nor Carmela ever went to see a movie, a play, or a musical. English was a major barrier for them. They enjoyed watching the Lawrence Welk and Ed Sullivan shows on TV on Sunday evenings, especially Giacomo. The music and singing overcame the language. They always lived modestly, and saved everything they could. In a few years they paid off the debt incurred when they purchased the partnership and the home. They sent their daughter Rose to the University of California at Berkley, and they were able to provide us with a down payment to purchase our home in Saratoga when Rose and I got married and moved from Austin, Texas, to Santa Clara, California. When both of them retired from work, they sold the home in Oakland and bought one in Saratoga, not very far from our home. In Saratoga they did not know a soul. Even the Mass in Italian was not available. They had only us and our three young children, and they spent a lot of time with us. Rose continued to take care of their checking accounts, bank deposits, bills, and whatever needed to be done when English was involved. When Giacomo arrived in Saratoga, he took a look at our backyard, one and a quarter acres of mostly bare land, and he started planting trees and a number of grape vines. When the vines matured, the whole family picked the grapes, crushed and pressed them, and put the red wine in forty-gallon barrels he brought down from Oakland. This operation is continuing on a somewhat smaller scale today, to the delight of the grandchildren who enjoy crushing the grapes with their feet. Jack died peacefully in our Saratoga home, his body wasted by a malignant tumor. He was seventy-four. Carmela died at ninety-six due to old age.

Our First Return Trip to Italy

In July 1959 we packed and shipped all of our possessions from Austin to Oakland and sold the Pontiac for twenty-five dollars (a drunk, unlicensed driver had demolished the left side). Rose and I boarded a Braniff airplane to Houston with Paul, our one-year-old son. We transferred to a Continental flight to New York, and then a TWA plane to Milano, Italy. We spent most of the summer in Seriate and visited friends and relatives of both sides of the family. It was the first time back in Italy for both of us. Everyone greeted us warmly, and they showered Paul with thousands of kisses. Italy was still enjoying the "economic miracle" that had started a few years earlier, and all of our cousins had jobs. Many were married with children. They all seemed happy about their jobs and their lives, and were happy to see us. They were surprised and wondered how I could have possibly become a university professor, and Rose a medical laboratory technologist. All seemed to say: you have done well. We enjoyed meeting all of them, and I was especially delighted to see my two best friends—Pino Farina and Virgilio Carbonari—with whom I had shared much of my youth.

Pino had completed his studies at Catholic University in Milano. He taught Italian and Latin literature at secondary schools in the city of Bergamo, where he was successful and loved by his students and colleagues. We wrote to each other frequently. I kept him apprised of my progress in the United States, university studies, decision to teach and remain in the U.S., and engagement and marriage to Rose. His letters kept me in touch with him, his family, the city of Bergamo, and the country of Italy we both loved. Without any doubt, if it had been possible, he would have been the best man at my wedding. We have continued to be close friends. Now during our summers in Italy, we spend a week together with our spouses Rose and Marina, and visit the best in art and culture that Italy has to offer. Pino (an Italian nickname for Giuseppe) knows all the times, dates, historic persons, great

Pino Farina, Mario, and Virgilio Carbonari in 1959

artists, writers, and their works that we discover throughout the country. He possesses a monumental knowledge of everything Italian.

Virgilio, after the fifth grade, took a job with a small firm producing wooden clogs. In his spare time, he drew pictures using charcoal, the cheapest of the design materials. Countess Ambiveri saw some of his works and sent him to study at the Carrara Art Academy in Bergamo where he learned to paint from some of the most talented artists of the time. One day he started singing while painting in the garden of the academy. A professor heard and suggested that he take voice lessons, so he did. His voice teacher was Mrs. Dolci, the wife of a renowned tenor. He learned to sing, and for many years he performed opera parts at La Scala in Milano. When the opera season was over, he spent time painting in his Seriate studio. During the summer he would spend a month painting delightful scenes from the island of Burano in the Venetian Lagoon. He died at the age of sixty—far too young to die. A few of his paintings still decorate our home.

As penniless young men, the three of us spent much time together; we wandered the area during school vacations, attended soccer games by climbing the wall of the stadium, and frequented the Donizetti Opera House in Bergamo, waiting outside until the music started, and then sneaking in to climb up the stairs to the last balcony. On Sunday afternoons when no opera was offered at the Donizetti theater, and no soccer game was playing, the three of us gathered at my apartment and listened to music on the radio, eating boiled or roasted chestnuts that my mother was always willing to prepare. My preferred forms of entertainment are still going to the opera and watching a soccer or football game on TV.

While in Seriate during our summer visit, we lived in my parents' small apartment with a red brick floor. By this time it had a sink and running water—only cold water. It still lacked an inside bathroom. Everyone still used the little concrete box with the hole in the middle, located at the end of the small terrace, still shared with the family next door.

My father and mother were the happiest people in the world to see us after so many years, and especially to see Paul, their first grandchild. They were at a loss to try to figure out what to do for us. Their son was a university professor, one of the world's best professions. They were full of joy. My father, Lorenzo, had retired from the Breda Works at age sixty. After retirement, he continued to work at my uncle's restaurant. His dream throughout his life was to purchase his own apartment or to build his own house. A few years before retirement, he used all of his savings to purchase a building lot of about ten thousand square feet. He enjoyed cultivating it. He grew tomatoes, onions, and cabbage, all of which he sold to the restaurant. He was very proud of his produce, not because of the little money he made, but for its quality. Chicken manure was his favorite fertilizer. However, he did not have any money to build a house and achieve his dream.

After our vacation was over, we boarded a TWA flight to New York and on to San Francisco. Rose's father drove us to his house where we spent the

Mario and his parents with baby Claudia, 1961

next few weeks. During this time, we traveled to Santa Clara almost every day. I got acquainted with the university where I had been hired, and Rose found a job at a San Jose medical laboratory on Park Avenue, owned by Yosh Uchida. One week before school started, we bought a house in Saratoga, a quiet suburb about fourteen miles south of the university and about twelve miles from Rose's workplace. Rose's parents helped with the down payment, and also gave us their 1953 Pontiac. By now all of our savings were gone, and I think it was the same for Rose's parents. However, we did have a house, a car, a child, two good jobs, and great determination to do well.

My Father, Lorenzo

My father was the second oldest of the Belotti brothers. He was born in 1894 in the same village where his father and his son were born. At age four, as he was playing with some pieces of wood in front of the blazing fireplace, trying to keep warm, he accidentally hit a pail of hot water hanging at the end of the chimney iron chain. The water was close to boiling, and much of it landed on his head. He passed out from the pain, and almost half of his head was scalded. He was taken to the doctor in the next village, who applied some cream to soothe the pain and save the skin. The damage turned out to be not as serious as feared. However, he was badly scarred, and carried that scar all of his life. No hair ever grew on the front of his head. He always tried to hide the scar by covering it with the hair from the part of his head that the hot water had not touched.

At age six, he started first grade, and at age eight he completed the second grade. I don't know why, but after the second grade he stopped going to school. He could read and write, although not very well. I remember that he was good at numbers. He always haggled on prices, and looked to buy things at a bargain. He knew how to add, subtract, divide, and multiply in his head. I always thought he could have successfully completed the third grade, but I suspect that my grandparents did not push him to continue school. I don't think my grandfather ever went to school. I remember he had a hard time signing his name, and I never saw him read or write. I don't know anything about my grandmother's education, but I never saw her read or write either.

When my father was eight years old, his parents sent him to live and work with another family in the village. His pay was a place to sleep and food to eat. I am sure his parents loved him as we love our children today, but by the time my father was eight, there were four other children, little money, and even less to eat. Sending him out to another family meant one less mouth to feed, and also guaranteed that Lorenzo himself had enough to eat. This form of child indenture was common at the time; nobody thought it morally wrong or inappropriate. The priest of the town would not consider it wrong, either for the parents or for those taking the child.

Such children working and living with host families were called *bagaï* in our dialect. I do not know the word in Italian or English. They may or may not have completed the third grade; children were required to complete the third grade, but no government agency ever checked or did anything to enforce the rules. The *bagaï* system occurred mainly in rural areas. The children came from peasant households, and they were farmed out, so to speak, to other peasant households. They helped their host families to feed the chickens, rabbits, and pigs, pasture the cows, clean the courtyard, bring food and water to the workers in the field, and many other small chores. Some were treated very well, like a member of the family; some were not so fortunate. When things got rough, they escaped back to their families. There were no contractual obligations, so the family could take the child back home at any time.

Child indenture in many variations still happens in poor countries today. According to recent newspaper reports, in Ivory Coast children as young as eight and ten were brought in from surrounding countries to help harvest cocoa. Children of that age are of great help to farm families in some poor countries today, and were of great help in the developed countries until higher standards of living brought most of this practice to a halt. (Charles Dickens masterfully portrayed the work of young children serving very unscrupulous men and women.)

I don't know when my father returned to his family, what other jobs he may have had, or at what age he returned. He never talked much about his past, and I never asked him to tell his story. When a person grows up in such poor circumstances, he or she does not want to look back, and does not want to dwell on the past. They want to look forward, and hope that the future may be a little better for them and their families. The only thing they will say is that they worked all they could, doing various things—what and for whom was not important.

Because of his head wound, my father was excused from military duty in World War I. After the war, he joined the Italian Socialist Party, the party of

Mussolini before he founded the Fascist Party, and the party of many intellectuals of the time. However, he was never active in the party, or in any political activity. He never talked about it, and probably left the party after he married.

One day in 1920, he was hired by the owner of the town's wine bar to transport three barrels of wine from the Frizzoni cellar in Torre de Roveri. The cellar was located in the back of my mother's house, and while the wine was being loaded into the barrels on the cart and Nino was resting, he met Rosa, Chino's daughter, and fell in love with her. She also fell in love with him, and in 1921 they married. Rosa was close to nineteen, and Lorenzo was eight years older.

After two of his brothers left the family, Lorenzo worked hard to keep the farm going. The loss of two sisters-in-law made him abandon raising silkworms; he could not accept the increased burden on my mother. It was the family's main cash crop. He and his two remaining brothers kept the farm producing well enough to satisfy the sharecropping agreement. Family life, however, was not improving. My mother was now alone to take care of most household chores, and was not happy. He was aware of it, and suffered for her pain. I was in school, but all my cousins had left and I did not have anyone to play with. The Sarzilla kids next door had also left, as their family was breaking up.

The sale of our horse, Nino, was the last straw. It convinced my father that it was time for us to leave the family, even though he realized it meant that what remained of the Patam family would not survive for long. Our move to Torre de Roveri, then to Seriate shortly thereafter, and especially getting a job at Breda Works, brought him happiness and hope that he could see a much better future than was possible to obtain on a sharecropping farm.

My father did not have great expectations about his future. He worked hard to provide us with basic necessities, but he never talked about wanting a car, refrigerator, radio, or any of the new consumer goods that became available after World War II. His only dream was to be able to purchase an apartment or build a house. He had always lived in someone else's place and wanted his own. He purchased the small piece of land, but he did not have money to build a house, and mortgage loans were impossible to get. His dream had to wait.

My father's expectations were modest, but his situation demonstrated the principle that people's aspirations for a higher standard of living usually grow faster than the country can reasonably provide. I have always believed that this is a prime cause for much of the turmoil, civil strife, and social and economic discontent in the world. In other words, people's expectations grow faster than even an efficient, well-organized economic system can satisfy.

Economic theory tells us that the standard of living of a nation increases because of growth in productivity, due to more efficient workers, better managers, better production processes, more efficient tools and machines, more research, and so on. Improvements in productivity, however, tend to be limited. A measure of productivity published by the U.S. Labor Department (output per hour of work in the private, non-farm sector, or labor productivity) shows that it has been increasing at about 2.3 percent per year in the U.S. on average over many years.

This rate of increase in labor productivity has two major implications. One, it tells us that the national output (real GDP) can expand at this rate without employing any extra workers (or without increasing the number of hours of work). Second, yearly increases in productivity of this rate imply that there is only 2.3 percent of extra income every year to distribute to everyone who participates in the production process. In general, when someone in the economy gets more than that amount, someone else will *have* to get less or the economy will generate inflation.

There are three crucial aspects of this last statement. One is that the distribution of this extra yearly income, in our society and all others, is not a simple task. Generally, the economically·(or politically) stronger groups get the lion's share, and the weaker groups get less or none at all. A progressive income tax, designed in such a way that it does not reduce economic incentives or create tax shelters, is the best way for democratic governments to effectively reduce this problem.

The second aspect of the statement is mainly social. People's expectations for improvement in their standard of living run faster than the growth in national productivity. They usually want more than the economy can give at any one time—sometimes, much more. My experience working in many countries tells me that this phenomenon is worldwide, and it is becoming more pronounced. The radio, TV, and internet are pushing the so-called "demonstration effect" to all corners of the world, creating greater expectations, more wants, and increased civil unrest.

The third aspect of the statement is political. Politicians worldwide promise voters much more than the country can reasonably give in order to get elected. Even if the government appropriates all the income generated by increases in productivity (an unwise economic policy), the increased revenues may still not satisfy what has been promised. Because of the limits imposed on government revenues by the increases in productivity, the newly-elected government cannot keep all its promises, and to avoid defeat it finances part of what was promised through deficit spending. If the deficit is financed by creating new money, it will give rise to inflation. Eventually the country's central bank will increase interest rates to curb inflation. In both cases, the economic losses from inflation and higher interest rates will hurt the lower income classes. Most of the time, those who get hurt are probably the same people the politicians expected to help. Inflation is a form of taxation. The ones who pay are those whose income fails to keep up, mainly the poor and the lower-income people. On the other hand, high interest rates do curb inflation, but they cause a drop in economic activity, decrease in income, and an increase in unemployment, again hurting the lower classes.

Distributive or commutative justice requires that everyone participating in the production process, no matter how important or how humble the job might be, should receive a share of the extra income generated by increases in productivity. This sharing is justified also by the fact that increases in productivity (mostly technological change) are not due to a particular person or group, but to industrial progress and the overall culture of the whole society. One example will clarify this concept. Some fifty years ago, Food Machinery Corporation (now FMC), then headquartered in Santa Clara, introduced a tomato-picking machine. The machine revolutionized the tomato industry in California, and was responsible for very large increases in the industry's productivity. Who should have benefitted from the increases in productivity?

Certainly some benefits should have gone to FMC and its workers who produced the machine. Some benefits should have gone to the tomato growers who purchased the machines, and who had to prepare the soil and plants in the right way for the crop to be picked by machine. The farm workers running the machines should also have received some benefits because their task had now become more precise and difficult. Some of the benefits should also have accrued to the professor at the University of California at Davis who designed the machine, and even more so to the other Davis professor who created a tomato plant with fruit that all ripened at about the same time, and with skin hard enough to be picked by machine without breaking. This is just a simple example of how the benefits of productivity derive from the industrial art of the society, and how benefits should be distributed to everyone who participates in the production process.

My Parents' New Home

When Rose and I first returned to Italy to visit my parents in the summer of 1959, we contacted a *geometra*, a professional who designed houses. In Italy such people followed a five-year program after the eighth grade, at an institute specializing in this profession, without the need to attend university. He was not an architect, and his professional activity was restricted in scope, but he could design single homes, obtain required city permits, and follow the construction work. He knew the building codes and all the property laws, and he was much cheaper than an architect. This profession is still active today.

The *geometra*, Mr. Conelli, listened to our ideas and designed a nice two-bedroom home with one modern bathroom, central heating, a combination living/dining room, and a kitchen, which turned out to be the only American-style one in the area. The expected cost: about $6,000. We promised to send the money from the U.S. as soon as we were settled in our new jobs.

When we returned home, settled down, and purchased our house in Saratoga, we realized we did not have any money left. The savings we had been able to accumulate in Texas were all spent on that summer trip to Italy. The house in Italy had to be built—we had promised to send my father the money. We decided to borrow $3,000 from Bank of America. The manager of the Santa Clara branch, Mr. Souza, was a friend of the university. When he learned I was teaching there, he gave us the money. I just needed to sign a promissory note, no questions asked about the reason. We sent the $3,000 to my father, and the contractor started building. We sent the rest of the money in small amounts as needed, from our earnings and from some extra courses I taught. By the summer of 1960, the house was finished, and my parents moved in. My father's dream had become reality. He was proud and happy about his new home, but he did not enjoy it for long. On September 11, 1961, about a year after moving in, he died. Stomach cancer killed him, at age sixty-seven.

The Purchase of our Saratoga Home and the Birth of our Two Daughters

Buying a house was quite a difficult undertaking for me. In Italy, after we left the farmhouse we always rented an apartment. My uncles, aunts, cousins, and most friends never owned homes. Rose and I hired a real estate agent, and within a few days we saw six homes for sale. We did not like much about any of them. They were too expensive, or too old, or had very small yards. We liked the last one we saw, despite the fact that it was not very attractive, and that its price of $25,000 was more than we wanted to spend. However, it was in Saratoga, and it included one and a quarter acres of land. It had two bedrooms, a living room, dining area, small kitchen, small family room, two baths, and large detached garage. It was $10,000 more than a similarly sized home would have cost near the university, but I wanted a large backyard. I had studied agronomy, and had worked in agriculture, and I wanted a place to plant grass, flowers, vegetables, and fruit trees. This place was just right.

We decided to purchase the house. After the down payment, we borrowed the rest of the money from the local Hibernia Bank. The interest on the mortgage was 6.75 percent. We prepared the needed documentation, signed all the papers, and the property at 19401 San Marcos Road was ours. We could not move into the house for another thirty days, so we continued to commute from Oakland. We were very lucky to purchase the house we did, because of the location in the city of Saratoga. We could have bought a larger, more modern, and lower-priced house in Santa Clara, Campbell, or San Jose, but after a few years Saratoga became one of the most preferred cities to live in the San Francisco Bay Area, and property values increased manyfold.

We bought the house without knowing anything about termites. Our homes in Italy were made of stone and brick, and termites could not eat into

The original house in Saratoga

them. The house we bought was all made of wood, and termites were feasting on it. At that time sellers did not have to disclose any termite damage, or any other damage for that matter. Even the lender did not ask for a termite inspection. So a few years later when we started remodeling and adding to the house (refinancing the mortgage and borrowing more money), we had to tent it for fumigation. We tented again on a second remodeling. We did not tent, but termites were seen again on a third addition. From two bathrooms we went to four. We may not use all of them now, but it was probably an overreaction to the fact that at twenty-four years of age I did not have an inside bathroom with tub or shower or washbasin. Today, only two small walls of the old house remain, but I feel sure that some termites may still be in there.

Another thing we did not know was that the house had septic tanks. I had lived with septic tanks all my life in Italy, but that was different. Our new house had leaching lines on the property, which I did not know. I discovered the whole mess when the lines did not do their job, and the whole backyard began to smell. The septic tank needed to be cleaned out, and new lines installed. Fortunately, a few years later the local sanitation department decided to cover that part of Saratoga with sewage lines, and the problem disappeared.

We also did not know about city zoning, and did not inquire. We bought the property principally because of the size of the lot. We reasoned that if at some time in the future we needed money, we could sell at least half of the land that we owned. Later we discovered that we could not sell off any part of it because the property was located in a one-acre building zone.

We also did not know about the gopher population. As we started planting vegetables, grapes, and fruit trees, the gophers feasted on them. We used traps, poisoned grains, gas bombs, flooding, and other techniques suggested by neighbors and by the state agriculture department, but we have never been able to eliminate the problem. Every year a few of them still appear, and Rose continues to fight the pesky creatures.

If we had known all of those things, we may not have bought the property. Ignorance paid off. Buying in that location turned out to be one of our most important financial rewards. Moreover, when you have space you can add rooms, build a new garage, remove a wall, and build a terrace or patio with a barbeque and other amenities. Besides two extra bathrooms, we enlarged the living room, built a new kitchen and family room, and added a formal dining room, study, new master bedroom, guest room, wine cellar, and small apartment for out-of-town visitors. The yard is now covered with lawns, various flowering plants, fruit trees, vegetables, and grape vines. We can harvest fruits, vegetables, and flowers all year-round.

On the morning of Sunday, April 23, 1961, Paul and I drove Rose to O'Connor Hospital. She was ready to deliver our second child. We waited in the corridor of the maternity ward for what seemed like an eternity. It was noon, and the baby had not been born yet. Paul wanted something to eat, so we left the hospital, ate a hamburger at a nearby café, and returned. To our surprise, the baby had arrived, a little girl we named Claudia. Mother and daughter were both doing well, and Paul and I returned home. Paul was very excited to have a sister and I was happy to have a daughter.

In the summer of 1961, we took the whole family to Italy. Claudia was only nine weeks old. Before leaving, we shipped all the baby food and diapers she would need during our stay. Upon arriving in Seriate, we decided to spend all our time with my parents. My father was sick, and my mother could use Rose's help to cook lunch and dinner, and take care of the children. We settled in the new house, which turned out much better than I expected. We took advantage of my father's vegetable garden and my mother's cooking. We had a lot of visitors among relatives and friends, and in mid-August we returned home. My father was sick but jovial, and did not want us to see his sickness, especially Paul. We were all glad that we were able to see him happy in his new home.

On December 14, 1962, Rose gave birth to our second daughter, Julie. That morning Rose was at work and I was at the university. She felt it was time to go to the hospital. She called her doctor and drove herself to O'Connor Hospital. She was not able to contact me because I was teaching and she did not have much time to wait. After my lecture, the doctor called telling me that I was the father of a beautiful new girl. I drove to the hospital and visited Rose and the just-arrived baby Julie. I was delighted, and both of them were doing well. I returned to school, completed a few administrative chores, told everyone around about Julie, and drove home, remembering to pick up Paul and Claudia at the babysitter. Two days later, Rose came home with little Julie, and five days later she returned to work. The babysitter could not handle all three kids, so Rose took Julie with her. She kept her in one of the laboratory patient rooms. At times her boss, Mr. Uchida, helped feed her. After a few months, we decided to hire a full-time babysitter. Things did not work out well. The children were allowed to do whatever they wanted. The day Paul painted part of a wall with red paint the babysitter was let go, and Rose temporarily quit her job. A few years later, as Paul entered kindergarten, Rose returned to work. Her boss insisted he wanted her back. He had acquired a number of medical laboratories, and offered Rose the directorship of the one in Los Gatos, just three miles from home. Rose found a new babysitter for the two girls and took the job.

In the summer of 1964, we all returned to Italy. Julie was one and a half years old, and we realized that my mother was not going to be of much help with the kids, so we took a babysitter with us. She had just graduated from Santa Clara University, and had a strong desire to see Italy. We stayed at my mother's place. Rose, the children, and the babysitter traveled to Rome and other parts of Italy, and I mostly stayed at home with my mother, friends, and many relatives. At that time, my mother was still spending most of her

Mario's mother Rosa

days at my uncle's restaurant. *Ristorante La Faraona* had become very popular, and my uncle could always use my mother's help. Most nights she slept there. She was treated as part of the family, and she enjoyed being with people. Everyone, including the customers, called her *zia Rosa*, Aunt Rose.

Three years had passed since my father's death. I was happy to learn that my mother had adjusted well to her new life. She was not feeling alone any longer. However, that summer she mentioned to me a few times that she would like to work less and spend more time at home, but she felt uncomfortable living there alone. At the same time she could not stomach the idea of having someone else living with her. She was still strong and capable of caring for herself, and she could still work at the restaurant.

Before returning home that summer, we decided to build an apartment on top of the existing home. We had just learned that the family of my mother's sister, Vittoria, had to move from the apartment they rented. We felt they could occupy the new apartment, help my mother, and also take care of the garden. Everyone agreed to the idea, and I contacted a local architect and a contractor. The cost was estimated at about $6,000, the same as the original home. The construction started in 1965 and ended in 1966. The apartment had three bedrooms, one bath, a living room, and kitchen. It was just right for my aunt, her husband, and their three children. They moved in early in 1967. This time we did not borrow any money. We sent the money slowly, as needed.

Adding a second-story apartment to the existing home turned out to be a very good move, because no matter how hard and how often I asked my mother to join us in California, I was not able to convince her. She was terribly afraid of flying, and she wanted to die in her home. As time passed, aunt Vittoria's family, especially my cousin Teresina, stepped forward to be very helpful to her. They took care of her when she could not take complete care of herself. They took care of the garden and shared vegetables with my mother when she was home, and with us when we came to visit. It also turned out to be a good investment.

Santa Clara University

On September 22, 1959, I started teaching at Santa Clara University, then called the University of Santa Clara. It was founded by the Jesuits in 1851—the oldest institution of higher learning in California. The campus was small but beautiful. Flowering rose trees of all colors lined the walking paths that led from one building to another. Flower beds, changing color from season to season, surrounded the manicured lawns that kept the campus green all year round. Cedar, olive, and palm trees that had been planted many years earlier dotted the landscape and provided one of the most beautiful backgrounds anywhere for graduation or convocation ceremonies. An army of workers from the local Portuguese community kept the campus clean and colorful for everyone to see and enjoy. The university chapel was the historic mission church, the symbol of the university, and it satisfied the students' spiritual needs. Many returned to be married there after graduation.

Santa Clara University was founded and grew in the middle of the Santa Clara Valley, a vast expanse of land reaching from the Santa Cruz Mountains to the San Francisco Bay. With its temperate climate and productive soil, the valley was home to thousands of farmers growing vegetables, fruits, and grapes. It was the best place in the United States I could have landed. The house we bought was surrounded by apricot and prune orchards. Saratoga Avenue was my highway almost directly to the university campus. It crossed orchards on the left and right. My route passed a small shopping center at the intersection with Payne Street, and there was only one traffic light, a portable one, at the crossing with Stevens Creek Road. The traffic light was attached to a cable. At four o'clock each workday afternoon, a highway officer took the pole with the signal lights from the corner of the street to the middle of the intersection. Two hours later at six o'clock the same officer took the pole back to the corner. In 1959 Santa Clara Valley was a picture of peacefulness, solid farm work, and old family values. Santa Clara University was an oasis of learning that reinforced those values.

When I arrived, Santa Clara enrolled about nine hundred male students. They were distributed in four colleges: arts and sciences, engineering, law, and commerce. The Department of Economics was academically located in the College of Arts and Sciences. Its students received a bachelor's degree in science. The chair of the department was John Pagani, who was also associate dean of the College of Commerce and a professor of accounting. The College of Commerce at the time did not have departments, but functioned as one department. It only had seventeen full-time and part-time faculty members, four of them teaching a few courses in economics, among other subjects. The dean of the college, Charles Dirksen, himself a professor of marketing, made all the appointments, assigned faculty offices—usually a desk with a chair in a large room with other professors—and made all the teaching assignments according to the academic or professional background of each faculty member, including those teaching economics. Thus, for all practical and administrative purposes, the economic faculty belonged to the College of Commerce. The college program was accredited by the Association of Collegiate Schools of Business, of which Dean Dirksen was a member of the accrediting committee. The dean had a personal secretary, and one other secretary took care of the needs of the seventeen college faculty. The teaching load for full-time faculty members was four courses per semester. For my first semester, I was assigned to teach two sessions of an economic principles course, one course in business finance, and one course in accounting principles. All four courses were well suited to my academic background.

In the fall of 1959, the College of Commerce started an MBA program for working professionals, a program which turned out to be of great importance for the college itself and also for the university as well as the future of Santa Clara Valley. Seventy-five students enrolled in the first year. Courses were offered from five thirty to ten in the evening. I was not asked to teach MBA classes during my first year of teaching. The required macroeconomic course was taught by a newly hired part-time professor, Joe Kelly, who had just retired as dean of the School of Business at Golden Gate University in San Francisco. The microeconomic course was taught by Clarence Ham, one of our full-time faculty members and a Ph.D. student at U.C. Berkeley.

Jesuit universities have always been concerned about educating the whole person, and Santa Clara was no different. When I started teaching, a large part of the curriculum was devoted to this purpose. Besides the required courses in English, history, math, and science, all undergraduate students were required to take six courses in philosophy and eight courses in theology. Engineering majors took only six theology courses. Almost all these courses were taught by Jesuits, including the president of the university, Fr. Donahoe, S.J., who taught a course in philosophy. No courses in theology or philosophy were required for MBA students.

My first year of teaching at Santa Clara was hard on Paul, Rose, and me. At seven o'clock every working morning, all three of us climbed into the Pontiac. Rose first dropped Paul off at his babysitter, who was the wife of a Santa Clara GI Bill student, then she drove me to the university, and finally drove herself to her job in San Jose, which started at eight o'clock. At five in the evening or later, she picked up Paul, then me, and drove home. At home she took care of Paul, prepared dinner, and took care of what else needed to be done. I worked in the garden, and after dinner I worked on preparations for the next day's lectures.

By the end of my first year of teaching, our life quieted down. Rose, Paul, and I had adjusted to our daily routine. Rose loved her job as a medical technologist. She got along very well with her co-workers, patients, and especially with her boss, Yosh Uchida. He was a leader of the local Japanese community, a professor at San Jose State University, and a national judo coach. Paul loved his babysitter and was happy at her home. I enjoyed teaching, talking with my students before and after class, and sharing ideas with other faculty members and administrators.

In the fall of 1961, at the very beginning of the semester, Prof. Joe Kelly, who was teaching economics in our MBA program, died suddenly. I was asked to teach his course instead of one of my undergraduate courses. By that time, the program had grown to over three hundred students. Much of the growth was due to the efforts of Dean Dirksen, John Pagani, and other members of the faculty, including myself, to convince the six largest firms in the area at the time (Lockheed, General Electric, IBM, Food Machinery Corporation, Hewlett-Packard, and Continental Can Company) to pay tuition for their employees who were qualified and willing to spend their evenings pur-

In the classroom, early 1960s

suing an MBA degree. As the MBA program grew, more faculty were added to the school, and the quality greatly improved. The MBA program at Santa Clara was accredited by the Association of the Collegiate Schools of Business as part of the first batch of MBA programs approved nationwide. This status helped ensure that local large employers continued to pay tuition for their employees. The employee tuition benefit has continued throughout the many years of the program, and has been adopted by many new firms in the valley.

In the fall of 1961, the university administration opened admission to women, and many enrolled. They were from the same families as the male students: American, Italian, Irish, Portuguese, Yugoslavian, and others whose parents or grandparents had settled on the West Coast. Their presence not only increased the number of students in the undergraduate program, but also improved the quality of the student body as well as overall student behavior in and out of the classroom.

In 1961, the name of the college was changed to the School of Business and Administration. In 1962, four new professors were added, and four academic departments were established: management, accounting, marketing, and finance. The economics department continued to be housed in the School of Business. It provided all the required economics courses in the new School of Business, as well as courses for the School of Arts and Sciences major in economics. The department increased by two new faculty positions, and I was appointed chair, a position that I maintained for twenty-two consecutive years. From that year on I limited my teaching to economics.

One day in the spring of 1962, as I was walking on the lawn between Kenna and Walsh Hall, I encountered Fr. Aloysius May, S.J., the university academic vice president. He asked how I was doing, and how I enjoyed my work at Santa Clara. I answered that I was happy with my teaching, and that I had made a good choice to take a job here. He inquired, "How long have you been here?" "About three years," I replied. "In that case," he said, "I will promote you to associate professor. I cannot give you tenure until next year, because the faculty handbook specifies a minimum of four years at the university." The next day, I received a letter from him announcing that I was promoted to associate professor. I was delighted with the promotion because it indicated that my job at the university was appreciated and was becoming secure. One year later, I received tenure.

In the spring of 1965, Rose and I organized the first dinner party in honor of the graduating economics seniors. Students, faculty, and their spouses were invited to our house to celebrate the occasion. Rose did all the cooking—lasagna, chicken teriyaki, and bean salad. We served beer, soft drinks, and our own wine to drink at dinner, plus ice cream for dessert. I cleaned the backyard and set all the tables, chairs, tablecloths, silverware, and whatever else was needed to make the place attractive and festive. The party was a great success. The students formed a greater bond with each other and with their professors, whom they were about to leave. The professors, maybe for the first time, recognized that the students were happy with what they had learned from each of them. The economics seniors' party at our home has become a tradition. Every spring since 1965, with two exceptions due to sabbatical leaves, Rose and I have continued to host the party. Once in a while the menu has changed, but the rest has remained the same.

In the spring of 1968, I was promoted to full professor, the highest university faculty rank, and the best of all academic jobs. As I received the letter an-

Leon Panetta with Mario at a 1990s economic forecast

nouncing my promotion, I felt that it had all paid off: all my work and effort to come to the U.S., all my study to obtain a Ph.D., my decision to enter the teaching profession, and my choice to teach at Santa Clara University. At that point in my life, I had an enjoyable and secure job. I had a terrific wife, three lovable children, and a comfortable house large enough for all of us to share.

In the fall of the same year, spurred by a group of MBA alumni who had attended my classes, I started an economic forecasting program. Each year at the beginning of January, I spoke before alumni and members of the business community to present my expectations for U.S. economic performance in the year ahead. The program was well received and well attended, and lasted thirty-six consecutive years. At the last presentation, the participants contributed an extra $100,000 to the School of Business. The income from the donation has been used to provide yearly prizes, called "the Belotti Prize," for the best MBA students. In subsequent years I have continued to give speeches about the economic outlook in a more informal way, as well as writing newspaper articles on various issues and problems affecting U.S. economic performance.

In 1970, I asked and received a leave of absence for the spring semester. A colleague of mine, Peter McLoughlin, was working on a project sponsored by

An economic forecast for a group of San Jose business people

the Ford Foundation and carried out by the East African Development Bank, and asked if I could join the project as a macroeconomic consultant. Peter was an associate professor at Santa Clara and an expert in economic development, with an especially good knowledge of Sub-Saharan Africa's economy and culture (he spoke Swahili). I spent the next six months working on long-term gross national product estimates for the countries of Uganda, Kenya, and Tanzania, which at the time formed the core of the East African Community common market. Zambia, Rwanda, and Burundi were expected to join at a later date. I worked hard, traveling from one country to another. I visited the rural and urban areas, and the newly established industrial zones. With the help of two interpreters, I talked to hundreds of people in government, commerce, and industry, and also to many ordinary people. I asked about their country, their work, their most urgent economic problems, and their economic expectations. I talked to many young people about their aspirations, their families, and their future plans. During the day, I observed, listened, and gathered as much information from government offices as I could. In the evening and into the night I put together what I felt were reasonable macroeconomic projections.

The East African Community project was my first consulting job on such a large scale. I admired the great beauty of the three countries: their mountains, rivers, lakes, wildlife, and parks, their plantations for coffee, tea, sisal, and pyrethrum, and their people. I felt the countries had good economic prospects. Some foreign help in the form of investment projects, a few good technicians, and a few capable and bright politicians could have created a long period of sustainable economic growth. It did not turn out that way. Shortly after I left, Uganda was taken over by Idi Amin, who mostly destroyed what good the country had accomplished instead of building on it. In Kenya, the government of Jomo Kenyatta, a member of the Kikuyu tribe, repressed members of the Luo tribe, causing major civil strife. In Tanzania, President Nyrere, a socialist at heart, nationalized the banks (mainly English and Indian institutions), causing a reduction in investment funds. He also forced many of his people to move from urban to rural areas to populate the Ujama villages he established in the countryside, thereby stirring discontent among the populace. Soon after all these changes took place, the East African Community common market broke up, and the countries did not achieve the economic progress that their people had wanted.

This first African project helped me to understand the problems, obstacles, and institutional difficulties that nations experience in the process of economic development. Not only did I learn a great deal from my participation in the project—knowledge that I have been able to use in the classroom—but also it encouraged me to continue to spend my summers working in developing countries. For twenty-two consecutive summers I worked in various countries in Latin America, Africa, Asia, and Eastern Europe. In most places, Rose joined me for a time, and the children as well on several trips. While I was busy with my work, Rose and the children spent their days visiting the churches, mosques, temples, museums, stores, and whatever else attracted their imagination. It was good to have my family join me for part of the summer, but it was even better for the children to learn about different people and different cultures at an early age.

While working in developing countries, I learned three important aspects of economic development. First, time is very important when considering how fast or slow a country is growing. When working and studying in Thailand in the late 1970s, I spent much time in the rural areas and discovered that most rural towns offered a sixth-grade education. By comparison, the town where I was born in Italy offered only a third-grade education. A small medical clinic was available in this town, and most houses had electricity, neither of which we had in Italy. Agricultural production, mainly rice and cassava, was still inefficient, and yields were low. That was also the case in our part of Italy when I was a child. From what I observed in rural and urban areas, I concluded that Thailand of the late 1970s was probably thirty years behind northern Italy in economic development. I also thought that Ecuador was about forty years behind northern Italy, Honduras was maybe fifty, and Sub-Saharan Africa was probably a few more years than that. Such time analysis gave me reason for optimism, because I felt that thirty, forty, or fifty years was a very short time in the history of mankind to wait for reaching sustainable development.

A second thing I learned during my summer work is that as a country's standard of living increases, the fertility rate falls. The decline in fertility rate eventually leads to a slowdown in population growth, which in turn makes it easier to improve the country's standard of living. This lesson is confirmed by statistics from the United Nations Population Division.

The third point I learned is that as a country begins the industrialization process, its agricultural practices show great improvement, and agricultural production increases faster than population growth (as shown by statistics from the UN Food and Agriculture Organization). During the last thirty years, many countries I visited grew faster than I had expected. Some of them, however, are still struggling to reach a sustainable level of economic growth.

In 1972, the School of Business received a substantial gift from Mr. Naumes, the head of a major Oregon agribusiness firm. He wanted the money to be used to establish a program that would prepare students to be effective managers of agribusiness enterprises, of which there were many in California and other parts of the West Coast. The dean of the school established a committee that he chaired, along with me, Prof. Stucky (chair of the marketing department), and one outside advisor, Mr. Rathjen (vice president of the Food Machinery Corporation), to design a program that would satisfy the donor's wishes and that would be of importance to the growing agribusiness industry in California. After many interviews and much research about courses and programs at other universities directed at satisfying the needs of the agribusiness communities, our committee decided (with the approval of the university) to establish the Agribusiness Institute, whose main objectives were to conduct research in food and agribusiness, hold conferences with speakers from academia and from agribusiness enterprises, and to offer MBA degrees in agribusiness to qualified students from the U.S. as well as developing countries. The committee felt that developing countries, most of them still rooted in agriculture, needed talented managers not only to improve agriculture production but especially to improve their marketing and financial management skills, and to make their products more competitive on international markets. The MBA program in agribusiness started in 1973 and graduated many U.S. and foreign students. The institute, which I directed from September 1988 to June 1996, is still functioning today under a somewhat different organizational structure. Today it provides an agribusiness specialization under the regular MBA program, but it has also expanded to provide a food and agribusiness minor in the university undergraduate program.

In the fall of 1975, Don Lucas, one of the earliest and most knowledgeable venture capitalists in what is now called Silicon Valley, came to the university together with the presidents of Memorex and Ampex. They asked the directors of our Executive Development Center if the center would be interested in establishing an economics program for business executives. They felt that many executives in the area did not know enough economics to understand the potential impact on their firms from national and international economic events.

Don Lucas agreed that if the program revenues did not meet the expenditures, he would make up the difference. The director of the center, Dr. Trickett, called me to participate in the discussion as chair of the economics department. The center agreed to create a program for their approval, and I was asked to develop and run the program. After going through different possibilities, I came up with the idea of an economic symposium with three one-day sessions a year: one each in the fall, winter, and spring quarters. For each session, I would invite two well-known national or international economists to present a formal paper in the morning on a topic of my choosing, and answer questions from participants in the afternoon. The program was accepted with two possible changes. One was to limit the participants to no more than thirty invited executives, to allow everyone to participate in the question-and-answer period. The other was to ask the invited economists to make a half-hour presentation on the day's topic to our students afterward. This last change was intended to offer our students a better understanding of the economic issues of the day, and also so that they could meet prominent economists responsible for writing books and articles assigned to them by their professors.

The first session of the Economic Symposium took place in January 1976. It was the year the Western world celebrated the two-hundred-year anniversary of the publication of Adam Smith's *The Wealth of Nations*. The first speakers at that symposium were Nobel Laureate Prof. Paul Samuelson of MIT, and Prof. Harold Demsets of UCLA. Prof. Milton Friedman and Prof. James Tobin followed in the second session in March of that year. After those initial sessions, top economists from all over the world, including most Nobel Laureates in economics, participated as speakers in the program. Many attendees frequented the program year after year, and eventually became very good friends of the university. After a total of thirty-two years and sixty-eight sessions, the participants and I decided to end the program.

Overall the Economic Symposium turned out to be very successful. The participants had enough time to ask speakers all the questions they wanted to raise. Moreover, discussion of the day's topics continued on a person-to-person basis during the evening cocktail hour and dinner. Students and some community members would fill a conference room for the evening lectures. They raised many questions on the economic issues of the day, and visited with speakers at the end of the session. Financially the program turned out to be self-sustaining. The small surplus that remained was used to pay one or more research assistants.

Even though the program did not directly generate extra revenue for the university, it helped to generate many friends who made major contributions of time and money to other university activities. Led by the fundraising work of Don Lucas, who participated in almost every one of the symposiums, many participants contributed to the establishment of an endowed professorship in my name. It is presently held by Prof. Hersh Shefrin, one of the very best authors of articles and books in the field of behavioral finance.

After the economic symposium program ended, Don Lucas joined the university's Board of Trustees and funded a large part of the new School of Business building. It is the best and most technologically advanced building

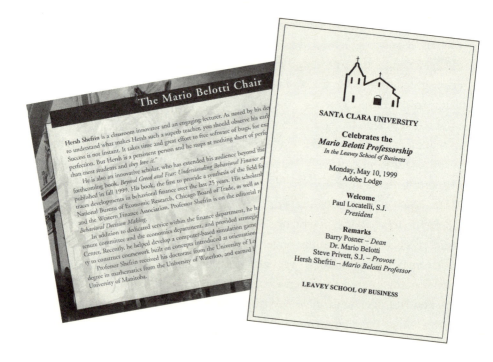

The Mario Belotti Chair

Hersh Shefrin is a classroom innovator and an engaging lecturer. As noted by his de... to understand what makes Hersh such a superb teacher, you should observe his earl... Success is not instant. It takes time and great effort to free software of bugs, for ex... perfection. But Hersh is a persistent person and he stops at nothing short of perfe... than most students and *they love it.*"

He is also an innovative scholar, who has extended his audience beyond the... forthcoming book, *Beyond Greed and Fear: Understanding Behavioral Finance* a... published in fall 1999. His book, the first to provide a synthesis of the field fo... traces developments in behavioral finance over the last 25 years. His scholars... National Bureau of Economic Research, Chicago Board of Trade, as well as... and the Western Finance Association. Professor Shefrin is on the editorial r... *Behavioral Decision Making.*

In addition to dedicated service within the finance department, he ha... tenure committee and the economics department, and provided strategi... Center. Recently, he helped develop a computer-based simulation game... ty to construct coursework built on concepts introduced at orientation...

Professor Shefrin received his doctorate from the University of Lo... degree in mathematics from the University of Waterloo, and earned... University of Manitoba.

SANTA CLARA UNIVERSITY

Celebrates the
Mario Belotti Professorship
In the Leavey School of Business

Monday, May 10, 1999
Adobe Lodge

Welcome
Paul Locatelli, S.J.
President

Remarks
Barry Posner – *Dean*
Dr. Mario Belotti
Steve Privett, S.J. – *Provost*
Hersh Shefrin – *Mario Belotti Professor*

LEAVEY SCHOOL OF BUSINESS

on campus, and is appropriately named Lucas Hall. Another participant, B.J. Cassin, provided the university with a very large sum of money for student scholarships. He is also a well-known venture capitalist in the area, as well as a founder and promoter of the Cristo Rey Network of high schools in urban communities with limited educational opportunities. A third participant, Jack Sullivan, donated a very up-to-date aquatic center. Other participants donated or helped raise funds for the new School of Business building.

Since joining Santa Clara University fifty-five years ago, I truly participated in her life by working on many committees, teaching many courses and many students, hiring, guiding, and helping new professors, and raising funds. Overall, however, the university gave me much more than I gave her. My children and their spouses all attended the university. They all received a good education and learned important life values. My life at the university has been enjoyable, peaceful, and greatly enriched by faculty colleagues from my department, my school, and the university as a whole. There are very few jobs in the world that provide the opportunity to enrich the mind as much as a university faculty position. I consider myself very lucky in landing such a job, and I recommend to many students that they consider university teaching as a future career.

After so many years, I still love teaching. I am still eager to enter the classroom, to lecture, listen to the students, look them in the eye, and see that they want to learn. I have always felt very uncomfortable missing a class. In my fifty-five years of teaching at Santa Clara I feel sure that I have not lost more than five lectures because of illness. Four times I went to the hospital for minor surgeries, but each time I waited for a vacation period. One of my great satisfactions is to hear at the beginning of each new class a few students saying, "My father (or, my mother) said to say hello."

Many things have changed at Santa Clara University during the last fifty-five years. The number of students has increased from less than nine hundred to over eight thousand. Many new programs and research institutes have been established. The faculty has increased both in quantity and quality. New buildings have appeared, and the university campus has expanded in all directions. The magazine *U.S. News and World Report* has for many years rated Santa Clara University the second best among comprehensive universities in the West. Students with Irish and Italian names are being slowly replaced by students with Mexican, Vietnamese, Chinese, and Indian names. The university's MBA program for many years has been ranked among the top twenty best programs for working professionals in the nation, according to *Business Week*. Two things, however, have not changed: the beauty of the campus and the university's mission. All throughout my fifty-five years, the basic mission of the university has been educating students to become good at the jobs they select, and to act honestly and be compassionate with those less fortunate. I have listened to five university presidents, who have brought Santa Clara University from a small college to an excellent midsize university, through hard work, patience, perseverance, and love. Each of them repeatedly said that the goal and reason for educating students at Santa Clara was to help them live good, honest, and compassionate lives. Many students leave the university determined to lead such lives.

From Poverty to Affluence, or, How I Joined the Top 1.0 Percent

This chapter has been the most difficult one for me to write. Going from poverty to affluence was not quick, but rather it was a long process. It happened slowly, one step at a time, one experience and one lucky choice after another, with much help from many people I met along the way.

The cost of the voyage to the U.S. must have wiped out all of my parents' savings. I had no savings when I left Italy, and none when I completed my master's degree in accounting—just enough to buy an old Pontiac convertible for traveling to Oakland, so that I could ask Rose to marry me. I did not have any money when I traveled to Oakland to marry Rose two years later. I did not have any money left after I completed my Ph.D. and paid the airfare to Italy, and I did not have any money left when we moved to Santa Clara and bought our home. I did not have any money, but I had a good wife and one of the best jobs in the world.

In the pages that follow, as I describe my investment results, I do not mean to express any superior investment ability or wisdom. I am just telling how things worked out.

As I wrote earlier, our first and probably best investment we ever made was the purchase of our house in Saratoga. The home was quite small, and in the summer of 1962 Rose and I decided to refinance our mortgage and increase the loan enough to add to our house an extra bedroom-study combination, a separate dining room, a guest room, and a basement, which later was turned into a wine cellar. The family was growing and we needed more space. We spent about $10,000 on the addition, and our monthly payments increased from $157 to $255.

In the fall of the same year, as the U.S. stock market was still recovering from a modest 1961 decline, I decided to open a brokerage account, in partnership with two other professors from the School of Business. I wanted to be able to answer student questions about stock market investments. Each of us contributed $2,000 to our investment fund; I borrowed the money from the local branch of Bank of America by signing a new promissory note. I had repaid my previous loan. Given the size of our fund, we limited our purchases to ten or at most twenty shares of a stock at any one time. I did not start with any particular stock market investment strategy, but to begin I followed the market with more of an academic interest than as a way to make money.

One of the partners, a professor of marketing, suggested we adopt a simple strategy he had read in one of the financial magazines. The strategy was to purchase this week the stocks that gained the most in the previous week. The strategy worked for some stocks but it did not work for others. It did not work for those stocks that did well because of a buyout offer or because of transitory good news. Following that strategy we did reasonably well. However, given the size of our portfolio and the broker commission, the results did not pay off for our time and efforts. In any case, the buying and selling of stocks was invaluable in familiarizing myself with the workings of the stock market.

On November 15, 1962, I was granted U.S. citizenship. The judge in charge of the proceedings knew I was a professor of economics and asked me to comment on Charles Beard's book, *The Economic Interpretation of the U.S. Constitution*. I had read the book a few years earlier, and I answered that I agreed with many of the things Beard said but that I was not quite in agreement with others. The question created a certain amount of panic in the large group of immigrants seeking U.S. citizenship on the same day. Fortunately, after my short answer, the judge did not go into details in his inquiries with other immigrants, and no one else was asked a similar question. In the process of becoming a U.S. citizen, I decided to change my first name from Lorenzo to Mario. Lorenzo was my father's name, and from the day I was born until the day I became a U.S. citizen, my parents, my Italian relatives and my friends always called me Mario. Changing citizenship gave me the opportunity to rectify a municipal clerk's mistake. Becoming a U.S. citizen made my life in the U.S. much easier.

In the spring of 1963, the university granted me tenure. My faculty position at Santa Clara University had become secure. By this time, Rose felt that her job as a medical technologist was also quite secure. The demand for her skills was increasing. More medical laboratories opened in the Santa Clara Valley as the population expanded. My parents' home in Italy was almost fully paid. Our home in Saratoga was now large enough to comfortably accommodate all of us. We had secure jobs, a good income, and a home in a beautiful residential area. Soon we were able to save some money.

In the summer of 1963, one of the partners in our investment fund left the university. We liquidated our portfolio, paid out his share, and with the remaining partner I opened up a new account and increased our contribution to the investment fund, bringing it to $12,000. The size of the new fund made it possible for us to purchase forty to fifty shares of a stock at a time, or up to a hundred if the price per share was very low. One of the first investments we made was to purchase one hundred shares each of Continental and Braniff airlines. By the end of the year their prices rose much above what we paid. This increase in the value of our portfolio made it possible for us to diversify, but also gave us the incentive to follow the market more closely.

At the end of the same year, Rose and I decided to remodel our old kitchen. Sears & Roebuck did the work. They installed all new cabinets, replaced a very old stove with a new, all-electric one, and installed a dishwasher, which we did not have. The total cost was $3,000. Sears suggested we pay the bill in twenty-four monthly installments. I decided instead to pay cash. We did so by selling some of the airline stocks we had bought earlier, with agreement from my partner. It turned out to be a really bad choice, because after the sale the prices of those stocks increased sharply.

Our first really good investment came about in May 1964, when we purchased four acres of land on Allendale Avenue in Saratoga. Rose and I regularly drove along Allendale Avenue to drop off our kids with one of our babysitters on Quito Road. One morning we saw a sale sign on a parcel of land that I had admired every day for its location, and for its potential as a site for building four beautiful houses. I called the number listed on the sign, and a real estate broker answered my call. He explained that Mrs. Barco, who owned the land had moved to Virginia, and that the property was listed for sale at $8,000 an acre. I offered the owner $7,000 an acre. She accepted the offer, and for tax purposes she required a down payment of 29%, or a total of $8,120. The rest was to be financed by Virginia Savings and Loan Association with a ten-year fixed mortgage at 5 percent. My father-in-law and Bank of America helped us with the down payment. After I signed the agreement at the title company, I felt really good. I liked that piece of land, and now Rose and I owned it. Eight months later, three gentlemen, members of the Mormon Church from Salt Lake City, came to my home. The church wanted to build a house of prayer and a recreation facility on the land we owned on Allendale Avenue. They offered $11,000 an acre in cash. That was $16,000 more than we had paid for the property, and it represented a return of about 100 percent on the cash we actually used. One hundred percent return in only eight months! We sold it and paid off all of our debts except for the mortgage on the house. From that day on I became more willing to take on some extra risk. The amount of risk I would take on at any one time, however, was never above what I could afford to lose without jeopardizing the family welfare.

In the summer of 1964, all five of us went to Italy on a charter flight. In Italy that summer we bought our first new car. It was a 1500 VW sedan "notchback." We ordered it from a VW dealer in San Jose, and Rose picked it up in Milano. We used it in Italy and shipped it home. The car cost $1,100, plus $350 for shipping, tax, and duty for delivery to the port of Oakland. We kept the car for about twenty years, and it became the family car. All three of our children learned to drive using that car. It was a great addition to our old Pontiac; finally, we had two cars. Rose could go to work without driving me to school, and so my teaching schedule became much more flexible, and my commute much easier.

In June of 1966, my investment partner was let go by the university. After seven years of effort, he was not able to complete his Ph.D. dissertation at U.C. Berkeley. A short time later, we liquidated our account and divided the remains equally. At the end of that summer, Rose and I opened a new account with the same broker, Marty Sammon, one of my earliest MBA students. This time, we decided to open a margin account, which increased our stock purchasing power. For the next several years, we maintained a very low margin exposure. The Federal Reserve kept the margin requirements at 70 to 90 percent of the stock price most of the time, and limited the number of stocks that could be purchased on margin. Also, the stock market during the late 1960s was weak and did not present many good investment opportunities. The stock market was suffering from the escalating war in Vietnam and from the beginning of an inflationary trend that would accelerate in the 1970s.

The 1970s was not a good decade for the U.S. economy and for the stock market. The period was marked by devaluation of the U.S. dollar, price and wage controls, high inflation, and years of high unemployment. Okun's "misery index" (unemployment plus inflation) reached an all-time high. The manufacturing belt of the U.S. was turning into the "rust belt." During this decade, however, the University of Santa Clara continued to grow in the number and quality of its students, in new facilities, and in new programs. Santa Clara Valley was transforming itself into Silicon Valley. New high-technology firms were emerging here, and more and more skilled workers found their way to the valley. Many of them enrolled in the university MBA program, which our School of Business established especially for working professionals. The program had started in 1959 with seventy-five students, and by the end of the 1970s it enrolled over one thousand students and was considered one of the best in the nation. The university and the valley were doing much better than the nation, and Rose and I were also doing well.

During the 1970s, I did not put any new money into the stock market. Our stock portfolio changed little. The dividends we received were more than enough to pay for the margin interest. I had some purchasing power in the account, but I decided not to purchase new stock until the economic situation improved. I did, however, engage in a few real estate deals. The valley's population was growing, and real estate values were increasing rapidly—fast enough for property taxes to jump by 10 percent or more a year, until California residents amended the California constitution in 1977 by passing Proposition 13. This restricted county assessors to increase property values by only 2 percent per year, beginning with the value from 1975. This valuation was to continue as long as the present owners and first offspring occupied the property.

In 1971, in partnership with a colleague, I bought a thirty-two-acre, run-down apricot farm in the east foothills of San Jose. The property had a house, a large storage facility, and an apricot-drying facility, all of which was rented to the family running the farm. We paid a total of $91,000, assuming the existing mortgage on the property plus a small ($10,000) down payment. The property was in an unincorporated area of the Santa Clara Valley, and could have been divided into nine or ten building lots. The size of each lot depended upon its slope and varied from one to five acres. Neither of us were in much hurry to sell the property, and we did not follow the county planning commission deliberations and proposed zoning changes. Consequently, we did not present a property development plan or subdivision map to the commission before they decided to temporarily limit the construction of homes in the hills by changing the zoning to require a minimum of twenty acres for each new home. Given the size of our land and the fact that we already had one house on the property, we could not subdivide the property at all. Five years had passed since our purchase, and we decided to wait until the planning commission made a final decision. Many more years passed and no final decision was ever made. In 1996, we remodeled the house on the property, added a new room and a new bath, and sold it the year after for a return on our investment of over 12 percent per year, a much smaller return than we would have received if we had presented a subdivision plan during the first few years of ownership.

In 1975, with another university colleague, I bought a four-unit rental building on Almaden and Blossom Hill Roads in San Jose. All four apartments were rented. We assumed the existing mortgage and paid cash for the rest of the purchase price. We had a small positive cash flow from the very first month that we owned the property. However, we did not have much time to devote to the proper management of the property. It was painful for both of us to ask a renter to leave the place if he or she were late in paying the rent. It was hard for us to call the sheriff for eviction until a number of months had passed.

After about four years we were tired of calls complaining about the plumbing, the electricity, the stove, the neighbor making too much noise, or the one growing marijuana, and we decided to sell the property. To our surprise, we were able to sell it at a much higher price than we had paid for it.

In the fall of 1978, our son, Paul, transferred from Santa Clara University to pursue a degree in architecture at U.C. Berkeley. In his freshman and sophomore years at Santa Clara University he took the courses that Berkeley's School of Architecture required as prerequisites. After a week or two of searching in Berkeley, he was not able to find a convenient place to rent. Two weeks before school started, Rose and I drove to Berkeley, and we found and purchased a two-bedroom, one-bath home on Grant Street within walking distance from the university. The house was empty, and Paul could move in right away. The three of us did some scrubbing, painting, fixing, and yard work. Paul moved in, and invited a high school friend who was studying at Berkeley to share the house with him. The friend's rent helped to pay the mortgage. In June of 1980, Paul completed his bachelor's degree in architecture. We kept the house for another two years, renting it to a couple of Paul's friends doing graduate work at the university. When they left, we decided to sell. Berkeley was too far for us to properly maintain and rent the property. Also, Berkeley's rent control and rental regulations had become so onerous and difficult to follow that selling the property was the best thing to do. After some alterations, an exterior paint job, and some garden and fence work, we were able to sell the property at about twice the price we paid for it.

In the summer of 1980, Paul decided to enroll at the University of Washington in Seattle to study for a master's degree in architecture. That summer I was working in Thailand. Rose and Paul flew to Seattle, took a look at the housing market around the university, and found a suitable apartment for sale. Rose called me in Bangkok with some details about the apartment and asked for my approval to purchase it, and I agreed. The price was reasonably low, and Paul would look for a roommate. Two years later, as Paul completed his work, Rose sold the apartment, not much above what we had originally paid.

In the summer of 1981, our daughter Claudia had just completed her sophomore year at Santa Clara University and wanted to move out of the university dorm during her junior and senior years. At that time a construction company had just completed a six-unit apartment building within walking distance from the university. Each apartment had two bedrooms and two baths, with a kitchen and a living-dining room combination. We obtained a mortgage from Bank of America and bought one of the apartments. Claudia moved into it with three student friends. The rent from Claudia's friends' was enough to pay for the mortgage and a small amount of maintenance. Two years later, as Claudia and her friends completed their degrees and vacated the apartment, our daughter Julie moved into the apartment for her last two years at Santa Clara, with three other students sharing the space once again. When they completed their degrees, we sold the apartment at a somewhat higher price than we paid for it. Both Rose and I were very busy at work and at home and did not want to be in the rental business. We were very satisfied with the results of these last three real estate purchases. Besides obtaining positive returns, our three children went through some years of their university education without having to pay rent. In this respect, I copied the example of a wealthy Filipino I knew a few years earlier. He bought two luxury apartments in Palo Alto, sent his three daughters to Santa Clara University, and when all of them graduated six years later, he sold the apartments. The profits he made turned out to be enough to cover all the tuition he paid plus all of their living expenses, with enough left over to purchase a Mercedes for each of them.

In 1981 and 1982, the U.S. economy experienced a deep recession, the most severe since the 1930s. The recession was engineered by the Federal Reserve to reduce the very high inflation the country experienced in the 1970s, which had reached a high of 15 percent in the first few months of 1981. To fight high inflation and the growing inflationary expectations, the Federal Reserve dramatically cut the growth of the money supply and allowed interest rates to rise, so that in April 1981 the prime interest rate (what banks charge their very best customers) reached what must have been a historic high of 21.5 percent. Mortgage rates and all other rates also soared upward. The economy fell into a major recession, the unemployment rate went up to 10.7 percent, and some of our major corporations were on the verge of bankruptcy. Because of the Fed's action, by June 1982 inflation had declined to about 7 percent. The U.S. economy, however, was still deep in recession and the Federal Reserve reversed course to an easier monetary policy. At the same time, President Reagan and the Democratic Congress cut personal income tax rates across the board by 25 percent, phased in over the next two years, and this all provided a great stimulus to the stock market to start rising, followed a few months later by a fast turnaround in the economy. Stock market prices had moved very little in the 1970s, and had fallen during the recession, but they increased quickly as the Fed reduced the margin requirements to 50 percent. Rose and I felt that it was time for us to return to the market.

The change in margin requirements had increased the purchasing power of our account, and we purchased as many shares of stock as our account limits allowed. As the value of our portfolio increased, we purchased more shares, running up our margin debt. At the end of 1982, for the first time our net holdings reached what at the time I considered the fabulous sum of $100,000.

In April 1983, I was invited to join a venture capital firm, Sand Hill Financial, that Don Lucas had established for family and friends. Don Lucas and Larry Gerdes (another Economic Symposium participant from Atlanta) were the general partners of the firm, and about twenty-five others, including me, participated as limited partners. My initial share in the company was 1 percent, later rising to 1.25 percent. The general partners kept the firm's operations simple. They read the requests for investments by startup companies, and decided which to fund and how much. After the decision, they sent a letter to the partners requesting a check in the amount of their participation for the firm's capital. It was agreed that if a partner did not send the check on time, his partnership would be dropped and offered to one or more of the other partners. Once a year the partners gathered to hear presentations from the chief executive officers of the companies we had financed. When a company in Sand Hill Financial's portfolio made an initial public offering (IPO), each partner received shares of the new public company equal to his percentage participation. After the established blackout period (generally three or six months), each partner would sell some or all of his shares. In my case, as the blackout time expired, I would sell a portion of the shares so that I could pay down my credit line at Bank of America, and have the line available to use in the next investment call.

Sand Hill Financial was then and is still now a small venture capital firm. However, it was one of the pioneer VC firms in the Silicon Valley. It helped many companies to get started, grow, innovate, and prosper. Moreover, because of the acumen, business knowledge, hard work, and rigorous investment approach of Don Lucas, who made most of the investment decisions, Sand Hill Financial's investors also did well.

During the rest of the 1980s and throughout the 1990s, we continued to be very active in the stock markets. We opened two new stock accounts with other full-commission brokerage firms. The two new financial advisors, Gerry Down and Paul Joas, were both symposium participants. In one new account we deposited the shares received from Sand Hill Financial after a company in the portfolio went public, and added other stocks as we purchased them. This account was also a margin account, but we borrowed only mod-

In the office, 1985

estly from it. The other new account we used to take advantage of the many initial public offerings occurring in the U.S., especially in the Silicon Valley at that time. Paul Joas's firm in Minneapolis was able to purchase shares in some of these new offerings for our account, and we paid for them in cash.

Why did we buy stocks on the margin? For a few simple reasons. First, as stock prices increased, which was mostly the case in the 1980s and 1990s, it made it possible for us to increase the size of the portfolio without adding new money. Second, the margin account allowed us to short a stock when it was profitable to do so. We used this strategy very few times, and mainly by shorting against the box (selling short a stock in our portfolio either for tax purposes in order to postpone a gain to the next year, or protecting a gain during long absences from home). Third, and most important, we used the margin account as a fast source of funds when we needed money for a venture capital call, for a trip, or for a home improvement. As long as the account had equity available, a call to the broker was enough to receive, the next day or the day after, a check in the mail without the need to file financial statements, tax reports, or sign any papers. Moreover, the interest we paid on margin borrowing has always been lower than what banks would have charged us on similarly sized loans. By the end of 1998, our margin debt had increased to about $400,000, supported by a portfolio more than six times as large.

In 1984 I was invited to join the board of directors of American Bank and Trust, a five-branch bank headquartered in downtown San Jose. As a professor teaching a course in money and banking, I felt it was important to learn first-hand about banking regulations, procedures, and administration. I joined the board and purchased five hundred shares as an initial investment in the bank. In 1993, the regulators wanted the bank to raise more capital or sell the bank. The major stockholders decided not to invest more money in the bank, so the branches were sold and the bank was closed. The bank's ratio of capital to assets was greatly reduced by the decision of the board, before I joined, to build a new headquarters in San Jose instead of renting or leasing space. This also reduced the lending ability of the bank. There were two major lawsuits involving the bank trust department that lasted for a very long time. On many occasions our lawyers told us that the bank was going to prevail, but ultimately the bank lost, and the damage turned out to be so severe that the bank was not able to recover. As a board member I was not able to make any significant contributions to save the bank, but I learned a lot about the internal workings of the bank as well as the supervising regulatory agencies.

In 1999, stock prices continued to climb, especially those of new technology companies listed on the NASDAQ stock exchange, and the value of our portfolio climbed with them. Our capital gains had soared, and by the end of the year we felt that it was time for us to diversify and reduce our stock exposure.

On December 16, 1999, Rose and I, with the approval of our three children, decided to establish a one million dollar remainder trust at Santa Clara University. We transferred to the university a million dollars worth of stocks in which we had large capital gains. Because of the transfer, we did not have to pay any capital gains taxes, and according to an Internal Revenue Service formula, we were given five years to deduct $435,000 of the value of the stocks we donated from our adjusted gross income. Establishing a remainder trust at the university was one of the best investments we ever made, and we recommend establishing such a trust to donors that can afford it. The trust agreement specified that the trust would pay us a fixed percentage of the trust's available funds every year of our lives, and after our death the accumulated balance will be used to provide scholarships for poor students.

Throughout the years, Rose and I spent much of each summer in Italy whenever we could, often joined by our children for shorter periods of time. However, the house in Seriate that we helped build in the 1960s had become too small for all of us. By 1990 it was surrounded by more houses, a grocery store, pizza restaurant, and coffee shop. The place had become crowded, noisy, and was no longer suitable for us. By 1995 Rose and I had already started looking for a new place in Italy. We wanted to continue to visit our many friends and relatives, but even more so we loved Italy, and our children spoke Italian and enjoyed visiting with us.

We decided that if we ever purchased a vacation home, it would be in Italy. We found several places we liked, but as long as my mother and aunt Vittoria were alive, it was difficult to move from Seriate. After my mother's death, my cousin Teresina bought the apartment upstairs, and we sold the one downstairs. We spent part of the summer of 1997 looking for a new place at one of the northern Italian lakes. After weeks of searching we found what we wanted, an apartment in Villa Sourour in the town of Lesa on Lago Maggiore—the second largest, and in my opinion the best lake in Italy.

We sold more stocks to purchase this beautiful apartment, one of six created in a large villa overlooking the lake. The villa was originally built in 1914 by an Italian industrialist from Milano. In 1994, a talented female architect had directed work to divide the villa into modern apartments. The villa is surrounded by a large garden with many trees and an abundant display of azaleas, camellias, and rhododendrons.

We signed the purchase papers in December of that year, and moved in during the summer of 1998. The apartment was new and had no furnishings or built-in facilities. That summer we hired a cabinetmaker, and had the kitchen, closets, and all the furniture we needed built in his plant and installed in our new vacation home. Since then we have spent every summer in Italy in our apartment on Lago Maggiore.

In April 1999, we decided to build a totally new kitchen in the existing family room of our Saratoga home, as well as add on a larger family room, At the same time we built a small apartment, attached to the garage. It was intended to house Rose's mother Carmela, who had been living alone near down-town Saratoga since the death of her husband. Carmela never did occupy the apartment, and we used it to house students (mainly from poor countries) who had scholarships at Santa Clara University but needed a place to stay. I decided to help some of these students because I always remembered the help I originally received from Mrs. Bea, which made possible everything I had achieved in the U.S. We paid for the new expansion by refinancing the home and borrowing an amount large enough to cover the old mortgage and the new construction. The loan from Bank of America had now grown to over $300,000.

In the summer of 2000, while vacationing in Italy, Rose and I decided to purchase the apartment in Villa Sourour next door to ours, which had be-come available. The idea was to combine the two apartments into one. The combination, however, turned out to be too complex and costly. We decided to keep the two apartments separate and use the new acquisition to house our visiting friends and our children's families.

In 2001, we bought a small office building close to the university, in part-nership with three local real estate investors, two of whom were Santa Clara alumni. We paid $220,000, with a down payment of $20,000. The rest was financed through a local bank, and Rose and I had only a 10 percent share. The building had five small offices, occupied by four law firms and one ap-praiser, and we hired a property management firm to take charge. In 2005 we sold the building at four times the purchase price. We never realized a positive cash flow during the four and a half years we owned the building, but the increase in the value of the property more than made up for it. The purchase and sale of this building were our last real estate transactions. Buy-ing and selling real estate took time and effort. Rose helped greatly in taking care of the details, but we felt that it was much easier to deal with the stock market. A phone call was all it took to buy or sell whatever stock we wanted.

In the spring of 2004 we completed the last addition to our home. We transformed one of the original bedrooms into a hallway and a master bath-room, and added a new master bedroom. After this addition, only two walls remained from the house we bought in 1959. Moreover, all of our children had married and now reside in their own homes. Rose and I are living alone in a house with four bathrooms.

In the Saratoga garden, 1994

After the major technology bust in the early 2000s, venture capital investment and IPOs slowed to a crawl. Very few good opportunities developed
during the next several years. Sand Hill Financial's activity slowed down like
the rest. Moreover, many more VC firms, both small and large, had landed in
Silicon Valley during the boom years. A few of them went out of business, but
many remained and competed strongly for the little business available. The
new VC firms that emerged in Silicon Valley during the boom years brought
a major change in the way the VC business was done. Before the new arrivals,
VC firms would carefully analyze and evaluate the plans presented, quality
of the managers, adequacy of proposed funding, and merits of the product
or service being produced before making an investment. The start-ups were
the ones asking for funds. Many of the new generation of venture capitalists,
loaded with funds from banks, corporations, private equity firms, and rich investors, foreign and domestic, would seek out new start-ups and beg them to
take their money without much due diligence. By the year 2000 technology
investment had pushed the NASDAQ Stock Index over 5,000, and then turned
around for a major bust. Much venture capital was lost, and new IPOs were
greatly diminished. Silicon Valley experienced the losses and the pain.

During the first decade of the twenty-first century, as the technology bust worked its way out, a greater and more damaging bubble arose: subprime lending. Its burst caused great pain to millions of families who lost a large part of their savings. The burst also pushed the U.S. financial system close to total collapse, saved at the last moment by the U.S. Federal Reserve System and the U.S. Treasury. This led to the great recession of 2007 through 2009, which saw eight million jobs disappear. The burst of the housing bubble and wave of foreclosures that followed, along with the great recession, high un-employment, and a plunging stock market, killed most venture capital and IPO activities.

In 2009, as the economy and stock markets started to recover, and as a modest economic recovery continued in 2010 and the following years, ven-ture capital financing revived, concentrated in technology for alternative en-ergy, biotechnology, internet applications, and social internet. A number of successful IPOs have found their way to the stock market.

Since the technology stock bust, we have continued to buy and sell stocks, but have not been aggressive buyers or sellers. Moreover, during this period we have been giving a yearly amount of stocks to our children and grand-children. We also continue to give some of our stocks to various universities and charitable organizations.

Overall, Rose and I have done quite well buying and selling stocks. I made most of the decisions, and Rose did most of the bookkeeping. However, I do not have any great buying and selling strategies to offer to readers of this story. I follow a few basic guidelines. First, I buy stocks for the long run. I buy shares of companies in growing industries, and I keep the portfolio well diversified. Second, I add stocks to our portfolio every time severe market corrections occur, even though not necessarily at the lowest prices. Severe market corrections create good opportunities to buy stocks. For example, on January 2, 2008, with $50,000 an investor could have purchased about a thousand shares of American Express. In March 2009, with the same $50,000, an investor could have purchased a thousand shares of American Express, a thousand shares of Macy's, a thousand shares of Alcoa, a thousand shares of Bank of America, a thousand shares of Las Vegas Sands, and still have some money left over. It was clear to me that investing $50,000 or $100,000 in the stock market at the end of March 2009 would have brought a good return, after a few years. Such severe stock market breaks come quite often, each bringing good buying opportunities. Third, if a stock in our portfolio has not performed as expected but the prospects for the company continue to be good, I double up at the lower price; then after the required thirty days, I sell the shares purchased at the higher price, and use the loss to reduce that year's taxable capital gains. However, if a stock we own does not perform as expected after a year or longer, I sell it and take the loss if any. I always try to keep the stocks that have done well, and sell those that have not. I reason that if a stock is doing well, it means the company that the stock represents is also doing well. Psychologically, it is easier to do the opposite, and sell stocks that have done well, but I have always tried to avoid that trap. During years of large capital gains, even if not from stocks, I have found it very easy to eliminate losses from our stock portfolio in order to reduce our tax bill. Following those simple guidelines, and with a dose of good luck, throughout the years our stock portfolio has provided us with those extra things that have made our lives easier, richer, and happier

If any reader of this life story is interested in investing in the stock market, I suggest he or she first read Prof. Hirsh Shefrin's *Beyond Greed and Fear*, and Prof. Meir Statman's *What Investors Really Want*. After reading these books from two of the most talented finance professors anywhere, if he or she still wants to build a stock portfolio and experience the thrills and disappointments that come with the ups and downs of the market, following the guidelines above may help.

Looking Back

I started my journey as the son of a poor sharecropper, growing up in a large family, in a farmhouse without water and electricity, in a town that could offer only a third-grade education. However, with the help of a horse named Nino, I succeeded in escaping the sharecropper trap. With a lot of luck, strong determination, great help, and the prayers of my little brothers in heaven, I was able to complete my elementary and secondary education, obtain a visa to the U.S., complete a bachelor's degree in business, a master's degree in accounting, and a Ph.D. in economics. To get there, I worked as a quasi-cowboy, a kitchen helper, a pizza maker, and a restaurant chef, among other jobs. After obtaining my Ph.D., I became a university professor, U.S. citizen, economic consultant, speaker, and stock market and real estate investor.

According to official statistics, I am now among the top 1 percent of wealthy Americans. I started in the bottom 1 percent in Italy, and I have arrived at the top 1 percent in the U.S. It was a hard journey, but it was a good and adventurous one, much of it unplanned, and part of it unimaginable. In this respect, I am reminded of the words of John Stewart Mill, who wrote, "Next to birth, the chief cause of success in life is accident [luck] and opportunity." (J. S. Mill, *On Liberty and Other Writings*).

My experience in the U.S. turned out quite differently from what I expected at the age of twenty-four when I embarked on the *Vulcania* at the port city of Genova and landed in New York. God only knows how I became a university professor. At that time America was the most admired country in the world. Its people were generous and compassionate. They let me in to share their bounty and freedom. Today, the U.S.A., in spite of all the social, economic and cultural changes it has endured, is still a country full of opportunity and of people with great skill and imagination—people who are still willing to share their land with the world's rich and poor.

Mario and Rose with children and grandchildren, 2006

America did not fail me. I could have failed her. I could have given up on America many times. The struggle to get a visa, the time in Ellis Island, the unexpected cowboy job, the kitchen-boy job, and the terrible first day of the pizza job were all disappointments, but I did not give up. I saw many people struggle as I did. I also saw many of them doing well, some very well. They all worked, some harder than others. For the most part, however, their fortunes were earned. The money did not grow on trees, as some people in the old country came to believe.

Texas at that time may not have been truly representative of the rest of the U.S., but it was good for me to have landed there. It forced me to learn English on a fast track. No one spoke Italian there. It taught me that it was all up to me if I wanted to succeed. It made me see clearly that to remain in the U.S. I needed to complete my bachelor's degree. My master's degree opened the way to my Ph.D., which in turn opened the door to a university teaching position—the profession I finally desired to enter, and the profession I continue to enjoy.

One thing that Rose and I learned from our parents and brought with us to the U.S. was parsimony (frugality). After receiving tenure from the university and after a few profitable investments, our living standards improved. We lived well, but we never went overboard in spending. We always bought economical cars when we could have afforded fancier ones. We always flew economy class when we could have afforded the more expensive seats, and booked modest hotels instead of higher-priced ones. For some thirty-five years I commuted to work with a university colleague and good friend, Prof. John Whalen, who lived nearby. The car we used for commuting was always one we purchased together. We looked at the advertising section of the local newspaper, selected one of the cheapest cars advertised there, went to the dealer, and purchased the car without trying it out or even opening the hood. We paid for it, half each, using our credit cards. We shared the cost of gasoline, repairs, and taxes. We kept a car for five or six years, then turned it in to the dealer and picked up a new one of the same type.

Today, as I finish writing these memories, I fully believe that I have been very lucky. I have been married for fifty-seven years to the most supportive, hard-working, and loving wife I could ever have dreamed of. I am surrounded by three children, their spouses, and seven grandchildren, all of whom are helpful and caring, and doing well. I live with Rose in a spacious Saratoga home. The large yard has become my gymnasium. During my free time, I spade, rake, plant, prune, pick fruit and vegetables, and make a small amount of wine. Rose takes care of the roses, azaleas, camellias, rhododendrons, and other flowering plants.

Today I am writing from our summer home in Italy on beautiful Lago Maggiore. As I write, I am sitting in front of our large living room window overlooking the lake. At every pause, I admire the water that slowly and steadily flows toward the Ticino River, and from there continues on through small forests, cultivated fields, and cities large and small, benefitting them all, before disappearing in the vastness of the sea. I admire the small sailboats that silently pass by. I look at the children in canoes whose happy voices reach my window. I admire the green hills and the tall mountains that magnificently frame the lake. I write, and at the same time I immerse myself in such beautiful natural creation.

As I am getting close to the end of my journey, I feel that I have had a beautiful life. I feel happy about my journey, and about my story. I just hope that my grandchildren, and any other children, in reading this account of my life will find the way to become good, hardworking, loving, and compassionate people. I wrote this story for them.

COLOPHON

This book was designed and composed by Matt Kelsey. The typeface is Dante, designed by Giovanni Mardersteig in 1954 for the Officina Bodoni in Verona, Italy. The book was printed, sewn, and bound by Thomson-Shore in Dexter, Michigan, on paper with 30% post-consumer recycled content. The jacket photos were digitally printed by JP Graphics in Santa Clara, California. The front cover and flaps were printed by letterpress by Matt Kelsey at Camino Press in Saratoga, California.